P9-BHZ-517

ENTREPRENEURIAL FINANCE

ENTREPRENEURIAL FINANCE

FINANCE AND BUSINESS STRATEGIES FOR THE SERIOUS ENTREPRENEUR

THIRD EDITION

STEVEN ROGERS

WITH ROZA MAKONNEN

New York Chicago San Francisco Athens London
Madrid Mexico City Milan New Delhi
Singapore Sydney Toronto

3 4 5 6 7 8 9 0 DOC/DOC 1 2 0 9 8 7 6 5

ISBN 978-0-07-182539-9
MHID 0-07-182539-8

e-ISBN 978-0-07-182406-4
e-MHID 0-07-182406-5

This publication is designed to provide accurate and authoritative information in regard to the subject matter covered. It is sold with the understanding that neither the author nor the publisher is engaged in rendering legal, accounting, securities trading, or other professional services. If legal advice or other expert assistance is required, the services of a competent professional person should be sought.

—*From a Declaration of Principles Jointly Adopted by a Committee of the American Bar Association and a Committee of Publishers and Associations*

McGraw-Hill Education books are available at special quantity discounts to use as premiums and sales promotions or for use in corporate training programs. To contact a representative, please visit the Contact Us pages at www.mhprofessional.com.

Library of Congress Cataloging-in-Publication Data

Rogers, Steven.

[Entrepreneur's guide to finance and business]

Entrepreneurial finance : finance and business strategies for the serious entrepreneur / by Steve Rogers and Roza Makonnen. —Third edition.

pages em

ISBN 978-0-07-182539-9 (alk. paper)— ISBN 0-07-182539-8 (alk. paper) 1. Business enterprises—Finance. 2. Business planning. 3. Entrepreneurship. I. Makonnen, Roza. II. Title.

HG4026.R65 2014

658.15—dc23

2013048971

This book is dedicated to my two beautiful, brilliant, and selfless daughters, Akilah Naeem and Ariel Nailah!

Contents

Preface

To this day, one of the sights that is most pleasing to me is a room full of people who are earnestly learning entrepreneurial finance. For 18 years, it has been my great pleasure to educate and inspire more than 10,000 people of all types and in a variety of settings. In addition to the thousands of degree-seeking MBA students in Executive MBA and full- and part-time programs, I have taught more than a thousand students from the National Minority Business Supplier Program, the National Football League, the National Basketball League, the Urban League of Chicago, and the Network for Teaching Entrepreneurship, and given countless 3-hour sessions inside of other professors' programs. Recently I taught a session on entrepreneurship at the United Nations (UN), and I have also taught Executive MBAs in China, Germany, Hong Kong, Toronto, Miami, Boston, and New York. Soon I will be going to India and the Philippines, and hopefully after that to Brazil, Nigeria, and other nations on the continents of Africa, South America, Asia, and Europe. I hope to teach entrepreneurial finance students on every continent in the world several times within the next 3 years.

I can tell you that what I enjoy the most in my courses is bringing a few of my former students to my classroom as guest speakers to discuss their entrepreneurial journey. They share what students like to hear as "the rest of the story" from the case study that was just discussed in class. One of my favorite guest speakers is former student Doug Cook. He is the protagonist in the case study I wrote titled "Acquiring a Business." When Doug began as an MBA student, he had no interest in entrepreneurship. That quickly changed once he became a student. Two years after graduating, he purchased the first of 3 multimillion-dollar companies, in which he grew revenues more than 400% in 5 years!

I love the case study method of teaching entrepreneurial finance. I learned it as a student at the Harvard Business School and practiced it as a case study writer for a year after graduating. Professor Bill Sahlman, my professor, who created the entrepreneurial finance course more than 25 years ago, was the best at using the case study method. When I put together my course on entrepreneurial finance, each of the 10 weeks involves a case study discussion. The situation-based learning that occurs in case study discussions provides a close approximation to the decision making that takes place in entrepreneurial settings.

Students read the case in advance, prepare their analysis, and come to class ready for the discussion. I keep a list of all the students, saying which of them I have yet to cold-call and which of them I have already cold-called. So during each of the class sessions, whether it is week 1, week 8, or the last class, I know whom I have yet to cold-call. And my students like this method. I've never had a teacher evaluation that stated, "I wish Rogers did not cold-call us in class." During the discussion, without fail, especially in the first week or two of the course, I will ask a student, "What's your answer, Mr. MBA?" In reply, he will exclaim confidently, with his analysis, "It depends," and will start giving his explanation of the merits of deciding either way. Before his next breath, I stop him with a loud, thundering roar: "Depends is a brand of diaper; it is not an answer to an important decision in entrepreneurial finance." You can feel the hearts of all the students sink as their dependable explanation is removed from their arsenal. Well, this makes sense, right? How many employees want to hear their leader say, "It depends"? My entrepreneurial finance students must have the financial acumen and internal fortitude to make a decision, even though they do not have all the information. You must learn how to act in the face of uncertainty, and my students get that experience.

I found that one skill that every entrepreneur needs to have is the ability to calculate net present value (NPV) by hand on a calculator. Many people think I am old-fashioned, but I will tell you that despite all those fancy courses in finance that MBAs take, they always can master it by practicing it again and again. And for students who are new to finance, understanding how to calculate a ratio or NPV by hand gives them a new skill for life.

If there is one trait that I have always enjoyed seeing in my students, it is their ability to respond to the exhortation that I always give them: "To be a successful entrepreneur, you *must* know finance, and every one of you is capable of learning finance. It is my job to teach it to you!" After the course is over, countless students e-mail me to say how much the course made a difference in their life choices, such as to pursue acquiring a company, taking a job with an entrepreneurial firm, starting a new venture with a family member, or starting a tech venture. Every one of these e-mails is a treasure to me; it makes all the preparation worth it. Each e-mail is unique and wonderful to read; keep them coming!

Now let me also mention that I get to have another role, in addition to being a professor of entrepreneurial finance, and that is the position of academic director of the Initiative for a Competitive Inner City (ICIC) program. ICIC is a nonprofit organization that focuses on helping businesses located in the urban areas of America grow and prosper. In these programs, I bring in professors of other entrepreneurship subjects such as salesmanship, new venture planning, bank lending, venture capital, franchising, and the like. When I create a course for one of my favorite organizations, like the Young Presidents' Organization, the National Minority Supplier Development Council, the NFL, or any other group, I have the privilege of bringing in outstanding experts in these fields of finance and entrepreneurship. I have formed many friendships by working together for this cause: Derrick Collins, Greg White, Cheryl Mayberry-McKissack, Venita Fields, Al Sharp, Dean Donald P. Jacobs, Bill Sutter, Burt Cohen, Daniel Diermeier, Vicki Medvec, Keith Murnighan, and many others. Teaching alongside outstanding professionals is a great honor, privilege, and joy.

A few years into my teaching career, Bill Perez, at that time the CEO of S. C. Johnson Wax and Company, invited me to join the company's board of directors, on which I still serve happily to this day. Since then, I have had the privilege of serving on the boards of several large publicly traded and private corporations, as well as those of private equity funds, venture capital funds, and financial company investment committees. Sometimes people ask me why a professor of entrepreneurial finance sits on the boards of large companies. There are several reasons, but my favorite one is that I am given the opportunity to represent my students. One story really brings this to life. At one meeting of the board of directors of a publicly traded company, all the board members were present to make several decisions about the acquisition of another company. The investment banking firm, to which we were paying an extraordinary amount of money, brought in several of its people to present their recommendation on the valuation of the target company. The managing director put up a polished slide presentation and spreadsheet analysis as he smoothly walked us through the discussion. At one point, it appeared to me that he was telling us what was on the slide, but he had not done the analysis himself. I could not take such an approach lightly, and I finally exclaimed, "Hey, isn't there someone on your team in the back of the room who was a student of mine? Get him up here. I want to hear his recommendation." Sure enough, the vice president of the investment banking firm had been a former student of mine, and I put him in a seat at the table to walk us all through his recommendation, which we accepted. I could trust my former student's willingness to give an answer despite not knowing what the outcome would be. I was a proud professor that day.

I write this book, this story of opportunities, because I have been blessed with so many of my own. It's said that a good entrepreneur always sees sun in the clouds and a glass half full. My beautiful daughters, Akilah and Ariel, laugh at me when I tell them that I have gone through life always believing that when I walk through a door, the light will shine on me, no matter who else is in the room. Like every good entrepreneur, I believe in myself, but I also have enough humility to know that one does not go from the welfare rolls on Chicago's South Side to owning three successful companies, sitting on the boards of several Fortune 500 companies (S. C. Johnson, SuperValu, AMCORE Financial, and Harris Associates, a $60 billion mutual fund), and teaching at the finest business schools in America without a healthy supply of luck—and an abundance of caring people.

The first entrepreneur I ever met was a woman named Ollie Mae Rogers—the oldest daughter in a family of 10 kids, and the only one of them who never graduated from high school, let alone college. Fiercely independent, she left home at the age of 17 and got married. The marriage, I believe, was simply an excuse to leave home. Leaving home meant that she got her independence, and if she was nothing else, Ollie Mae, my mother, was a fireball of independence. When my older brother, my two sisters, and I buried her a few years ago, the eulogy fell to me. I described my mother as a Renaissance woman filled with paradoxes. She was a tough and gutsy woman whose extensive vocabulary flowed eloquently although she had barely finished the tenth grade.

I like to think of my mother as an eccentric "mom-and-pop" entrepreneur. Growing up, we were like the old *Sanford and Son* television series—selling used furniture at the weekend flea markets on Maxwell Street on Chicago's South Side. Nearly every Saturday and Sunday morning, my older brother, John (my personal hero), and I were up at 4 a.m. loading my mother's beat-up jalopy of a station wagon until we could fit no more "merchandise" on the seats, in the trunk, and on the roof. When I talk to prospective entrepreneurs, I tell them to go sell something at a flea market. You need to really live, breathe, and feel the rejection of hustling for "sells."

When I think back on it now, I realize that my mother just loved the art of the deal, and this, among other things, became part of my being. It was common for my mother to leave our space at the market and go shopping, leaving the operations to my brother and me—the savvy and sophisticated 5-year-old business maverick. That is how I learned to sell, negotiate, and schmooze a customer. I started my first little business venture in that very same market: a shoeshine stand. People would stroll by, and I'd lure them in with the oh-so-memorable pitch line: "Shine your shoes, comb your hair, and make you feel like a millionaire."

As far back as I can remember, I always held a job. When we weren't working the flea markets, my brother and I found other jobs; from helping the local milkman make his deliveries to working as a stock boy at the neighborhood grocery store, we did what we needed to do. By the time I reached high school, I was plucked out of the Chicago public schools by a nonprofit organization called A Better Chance, a private national program that identifies academically gifted minority kids from low-income communities and sends them to schools where their potential can be realized. (I now serve on the organization's board of directors.) I was sent to Radnor High School in Wayne, Pennsylvania. I played on the football team, and when the season was over, I worked as a janitor's assistant to send some money home to my mother.

My mother started running a small used-furniture storefront, and when I came home for the summer breaks, she would stop working and turn the operation over to me. So by the age of 15, I had to manage a few employees, open and close the business, negotiate with our customers, and run the daily operations. My mother, unbeknownst to her, was nurturing a budding entrepreneur. She truly is the reason that my brother, my sisters, and I have all gravitated to leadership positions in our professional lives. My brother is a supervisor of probation officers; my older sister, Deniece, owns her own delivery business; and my younger sister, Laura, is manager of a McDonald's restaurant.

I went on to attend Williams College (I am a former trustee), where, for the first time, the money I made was all mine. I must have had every job on the darn campus at some point. Williams is a liberal arts school, and at that time there were no finance courses or any other business classes to be found there. I majored in history. During my senior year at Williams, I took an accounting class at nearby North Adams State College. After graduating from Williams, I worked for Cummins Engine Company. At Cummins, I worked as a purchasing agent for a start-up venture in Rocky Mount, North Carolina, called Consolidated Diesel Company (CDC). At CDC, I was responsible for developing a new supplier organization, and it was there that I got my first taste of finance. It was a position that put me smack-dab in the middle of the expense line item "cost of goods sold" because I was ultimately responsible for buying several engine components. The greatest benefit of this experience was the negotiating skills that I continued to develop.

After 4 years, I left and was accepted at Harvard Business School (I am a former member of the HBS Visiting Committee), where I received my first formal education in finance. That was the main reason that I attended business school: I knew that I wanted to be an entrepreneur, and I also knew that if I was going to be successful, I needed to understand finance. My introductory finance class was taught by Professor Bill Sahlman. When I told him about my meager background in the subject, he told me to relax, that any novice can understand the subject with a little common sense. Though he never told me this, I quickly realized that the subject was made easier by having an outstanding professor like Sahlman, who could teach a user-friendly finance course that combined academic theory and real practices into a powerful lesson.

While I was at Harvard, I recognized what many entrepreneurs find out the hard way: being a successful entrepreneur is not easy. I knew about the failure rate, and I was never really interested in starting a company from scratch. I wanted to buy an existing business. It's funny when I think back on all the jobs that I had as a kid. My older brother had always had the same job first, so even back then, I was taking over an existing enterprise. I decided that going the franchise route was the smartest thing for me to do, and I applied for the franchisee program at McDonald's. My plan was to eventually buy a large number of the stores and become a fast-food mogul. Out of 30,000 applicants for the franchisee program that year, McDonald's accepted 50, and I was one of them.

The program required future franchisees to work 15 to 20 hours a week (for free, of course) over a 2-year period. I actually did my fast-food tour of duty with the McDonald's right around the corner from Harvard. So during my second year at Harvard Business School, my classmates would come in and see this hulking second-year MBA student, decked out in the official McDonald's pants and shirt, dropping their fries into the grease and cleaning the stalls of the bathroom. Of course they were thinking, "What the hell are you doing?" But I learned a valuable lesson over the years: you're making an investment in yourself, and why should you care what someone else thinks? I believe this is an important lesson for everyone. There's a certain level of humility that all entrepreneurs must have. You want to talk about risks? Taking risks is not just about taking risks with your money; it is about risking your reputation by being willing to be the janitor. If you don't have that mindset and you can't handle that, then entrepreneurship is not for you.

After graduating from HBS, I still had a year to go with the McDonald's ownership program. In order to earn money, I accepted a consulting job with Bain & Company. During the week, I would fly all over the United States on my consulting assignments, and on the weekends, I would return to the Soldiers Field Avenue McDonald's in Boston and put in the hours required.

Once I had completed the program and it was time for me to buy my own McDonald's, I could not come to an agreement with the corporation on a price for the store that it wanted to sell. We went around and around, and finally I decided that maybe franchising was not for me after all. Like my mother, I am not very good at taking orders, living my life in a template designed by someone else, and doing what someone else believes I should do. My experience with McDonald's was phenomenal, and I have nothing but respect for the company, but it was time for me to purchase my own business.

Eventually, after working with a business broker, I settled on purchasing a manufacturing business. Before I sold the company and left for my dream career of teaching, I had purchased an additional manufacturing firm and a retail business. Being your own boss and running your own business is both an exhilarating and a frightening prospect for most people. This is a club for hard workers. If you want an 8-to-5 job, do not join. This is a club whose members flourish on chaos, uncertainty, and ambiguity. These are people who thrive on solving problems.

It is my pleasure to provide this third edition of *Entrepreneurial Finance*, which has been updated and revised. I have received feedback from many students and fellow professors on the practical explanation of finance in this book, which has been retained. A new chapter on crowdfunding has been added to address this potentially powerful approach to financing a wide variety of entrepreneurial pursuits, not just in technology companies, but in the arts, the sciences, biotechnology, and community development. Some of the examples have been updated, especially the information that is relevant to the times we live in since the Great Recession of 2008–2009.

Another change is that I wrote the first 2 editions as a professor at Kellogg, where I taught for 17 years. I am writing this third edition as a new faculty member at my beloved alma mater, Harvard Business School, where I have been a professor for 2 years. It is an absolute joy to be back home!

I remain a strong believer in the idea that starting or acquiring a business during challenging economic times makes just as much or more sense than doing so during boom times. There are several examples of success stories like FedEx and Microsoft, which were started during recessions. Today and the near future still have their challenges, but the well-equipped student can navigate these challenges and succeed.

A year after purchasing my first business, I vividly remember returning from an early appointment and driving beside Lake Michigan on Lake Shore Drive. It was a gorgeous warm and sunny day, and I pulled off the road and got out of my car. There was no boss I had to call and no need to conjure up a reason for not returning to work. There was no manager to ask for an extended lunch break. I removed my socks and shoes, put my toes in the sand, and stayed there at the beach for the rest of the afternoon. Being an entrepreneur never felt so good.

Entrepreneurship is about getting your hands dirty *and* putting your toes in the sand. This book aims to help you get there. As Irving Berlin once advised a young songwriter by the name of George Gershwin, "Why the hell do you want to work for somebody else? Work for yourself!"

—Steven S. Rogers

Acknowledgments

I greatly appreciate the help with this book that I received from numerous people, including my former student and coauthor, Roza Makonnen. I also owe a major debt of gratitude to former students who helped me with the second edition: Thane Gauthier, Paul Smith, and David Wildermuth. Lastly, thanks go to my good friend, former employee, and student Scott T. Whitaker, who deserves most of the credit for assisting me with this third edition. Scott is a great friend who has worked with me for the past decade. He is a brilliant young man, and it has been my privilege to have him as a trusted friend.

ENTREPRENEURIAL FINANCE

1

The Entrepreneurial Spectrum

INTRODUCTION

While there are many sources of capital, there are basically 2 ways to finance a business: the capital can be invested in the form of debt or in the form of equity. In this book, we will discuss both forms of investment capital. However, be it debt or equity, the most important determinant of whether the capital will be provided is the entrepreneur and his management team. As venture capitalist Richard Kracum of Wind Point Partners said, "During the course of 70 investments we have made in many different kinds of situations over a 16-year period, we have observed that the quality of the CEO is the top factor in the success of the investment. We believe that the CEO represents approximately 80% of the variance of outcome of the transaction."

The importance of the entrepreneur can be further supported by a statement from Leslie Davis, former vice president at South Shore Bank in Chicago, who said, "The most important thing we consider when reviewing a loan application is the entrepreneur. Can we trust him to do what he said he would do in his business plan?" Banks, just like venture capitalists, bet on the jockey. Now, the horse (the business) can't be some run-down creature that's knocking on the door of the glue factory, but ultimately, financial backers have to trust the

TABLE 1-1 **Investor Ratings of Entrepreneurs**

Rating	Experience
A	Entrepreneurship and industry
B	Entrepreneurship or industry
C	No entrepreneurship or industry

management team. What are investors primarily looking for in entrepreneurs? Ideally, investors prefer people who have both entrepreneurial and specific industry experience.

As Table 1-1 shows, investors grade entrepreneurs as either A, B, or C. They believe that the best entrepreneurs to invest in are the A entrepreneurs, people who have experience as an owner or even an employee of an entrepreneurial firm, and also experience in the industry that the company will compete in.

The second most desirable investment candidates are the B entrepreneurs, who have experience either in entrepreneurship or in the industry, but not both.

The last category of people is the least attractive to investors. People who fall into this category should try to eliminate at least one of the shortcomings prior to seeking capital. As one investor said, "There is nothing worse than a young person with no experience. The combination is absolutely deadly." There is nothing a young person can do about her age except wait for time to pass, but experience can be gained by working for an entrepreneur and/or working in the desired industry.

THE ENTREPRENEURIAL SPECTRUM

When most people think of the term *entrepreneur*, they envision someone who starts a company from scratch. This is a major misconception. As the entrepreneurial spectrum in Figure 1-1 shows, the tent of entrepreneurship is broader and more inclusive. It includes not only those who start companies from scratch (i.e., start-up entrepreneurs), but also those people who acquire an established company through inheritance or a buyout (i.e., acquirers). The entrepreneurship tent also includes franchisors and franchisees. Finally, it also includes intrapreneurs, or corporate entrepreneurs. These are people who are gainfully employed

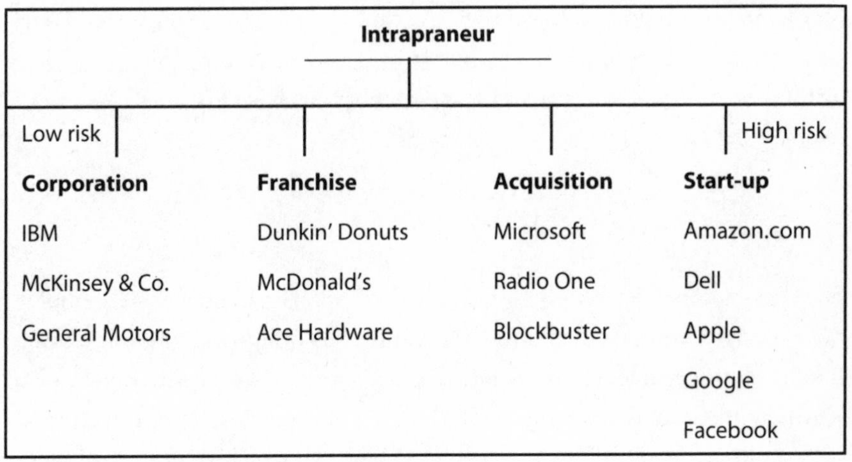

Figure 1-1 **The Entrepreneurial Spectrum**

at a Fortune 500 company and are proactively engaged in entrepreneurial activities in that setting. Chapter 11 is devoted to the topic of intrapreneurship. But be it via acquisition or start-up, each entrepreneurial process involves differing levels of business risk, as highlighted in Figure 1-1.

Corporations

While the major Fortune 500 corporations, such as IBM, are not entrepreneurial ventures, IBM and others are included on the spectrum simply as a business point of reference. Until the early 1980s, IBM epitomized corporate America: a huge, bureaucratic, and conservative multibillion-dollar company where employees were practically guaranteed lifetime employment. Although IBM became less conservative under the leadership of Louis Gerstner, the company's first non-IBM-trained CEO, it has always represented the antithesis of entrepreneurship, with its "Hail to IBM" corporate anthem, white shirts, dark suits, and policies forbidding smoking and drinking on the job and strongly discouraging them off the job.[1] In addition to the IBM profile, another great example of the antithesis of entrepreneurship was a statement made by a good friend, Lyle Logan, an executive at Northern Trust Corporation, a Fortune 500 company, who proudly said, "Steve, I have never attempted to pass myself off as an entrepreneur. I do not have a single entrepreneurial bone in my body. I am very happy as a corporate executive." As can be seen, the business risk associated with an established company like IBM is low. Such companies have a long history of profitable success and, more important, have extremely large cash reserves on hand.

Franchises

Franchising accounts for 40% of all retail sales in the United States, employs more than 8.1 million people and for roughly $769 billion in economic output.[2] Like a big, sturdy tree that continues to grow branches, a well-run franchise can spawn hundreds of entrepreneurs. The founder of a franchise—the franchisor—is a start-up entrepreneur, such as Bill Rosenberg, who founded Dunkin' Donuts in 1950 and now has approximately 10,500 stores in 30 countries.[3] These guys sell enough donuts in a year to circle the globe . . . twice! Rosenberg's franchisees (more than 7,000 in the United States alone[4]), who own and operate individual franchises, are also entrepreneurs. They take risks, operate their businesses expecting to gain a profit, and, like other entrepreneurs, can have cash flow problems. The country's first franchisees were a network of salesmen who in the 1850s paid the Singer Sewing Machine Company for the right to sell the newly patented machine in different regions of the country. The franchise system ultimately became popular, and franchisees began operating in the auto, oil, and food industries. Today, it's estimated that a new franchise outlet opens somewhere in the United States every 8 minutes.[5]

Franchisees are business owners who put their capital at risk and can go out of business if they do not generate enough profits to remain solvent.[6] By one estimate, there are more than 747,000 individual franchise business units in America,[7] of which 10,000 are home-based. The average initial investment in a franchise, not including real estate, is between $350,000 and $400,000.[8] Additional data from the International Franchise Association and the U.S. Department of Commerce, given in Table 1-2, show that the number of franchised establishments continually and rapidly grew from 1970 to a peak of 774,000 in 2008; however, the number of establishments dropped by 38,000 between 2008 and 2011 during the difficult economic times. Notably, the change in the number of establishments has turned positive, and there were as many in existence in 2012 as there had been in 2009;[9] this is a favorable trend.

TABLE 1-2 **Growth in Franchises in the United States (Selected Years)**

Year	Number of Franchises	Annual Revenues of Franchises (Billions of Dollars)
1970	396,000	120
1980	442,000	336
1990	533,000	716
2008	774,000	696
2009	747,000	674
2010	740,000	699
2011	736,000	733
2012	747,000	769

Source: U.S. Department of Commerce (1970–1990); International Franchise Association/IHS Global Insight Report (2008–2012).

Because a franchise is typically a turnkey operation, its business risk is significantly lower than that of a start-up. The success rate of franchisees is between 80 and 97%, according to research by Arthur Andersen and Co., which found that only 3% of franchises had gone out of business 5 years after starting their business. Another study undertaken by Arthur Andersen found that of all franchises opened between 1987 and 1997, 85% were still operated by their original owner, 11% had new owners, and 4% had closed. The International Franchise Association reports that 70% of franchisors charge an initial fee of $40,000 or less.[10]

Max Cooper is one of the largest McDonald's franchisees in North America, with 45 restaurants in Alabama. He stated his reasoning for becoming a franchisee entrepreneur as follows:

> You buy into a franchise because it's successful. The basics have been developed and you're buying the reputation. As with any company, to be a success in franchising, you have to have that burning desire. If you don't have it, don't do it. It isn't easy.[11]

Acquisitions

An acquirer is an entrepreneur who inherits or buys an existing business. This list includes Howard Schultz, who acquired Starbucks Coffee in 1987 for approximately $4 million when it had only 6 stores. Today, more than 40 million customers a week line up for their cafe mochas, cappuccinos, and caramel macchiatos in 18,000 Starbucks locations in 60 countries. Annual revenues top $13.3 billion.[12]

The list of successful acquirers also includes folks like Jim McCann, who purchased the almost bankrupt 1-800-Flowers.com, Inc. in 1983, turned it around, grew annual revenues to $782 million by 2006,[13] and restored those revenues to $716 million in 2012, after tough economic times.[14] Another successful entrepreneur who falls into this category is Cathy Hughes, who over the past 32 years has purchased 71 radio stations and divested 17. With these 54 stations plus Internet and programming assets, in 2012 Radio One (NYSE: ROIA) generated $425 million in annual revenues.[15]

One of the most prominent entrepreneurs who falls into this category is Wayne Huizenga, *Inc.* magazine's 1996 Entrepreneur of the Year and Ernst & Young's 2005 World Entrepreneur of the Year. His reputation as a great entrepreneur comes partially from the fact that he is one of the few people in the United States to have ever owned 3 multibillion-dollar businesses. Like Richard Dreyfuss's character in the movie *Down and Out in Beverly Hills*, a millionaire who owned a clothes hanger–manufacturing company, Wayne Huizenga is living proof that an entrepreneur does not have to be in a glamorous industry to be successful. His success came from buying businesses in the low- or no-tech, unglamorous industries of garbage, burglar alarms, videos, sports, hotels, and used cars.

Huizenga has never started a business from scratch. His strategy has been to dominate an industry by buying as many of the companies in the industry as he could as quickly as possible and consolidating them. This strategy is known as the "roll-up," "platform," or "poof" strategy—starting and growing a company through industry consolidation. (While the term *roll-up* is self-explanatory, the other 2 terms may need brief explanations. The term *platform* comes from the act of buying a large company in an industry to serve as the platform for adding other companies. The term *poof* comes from the idea that as an acquirer, one day the entrepreneur has no businesses and the next, "poof"—like magic—she purchases a company and is in business. Then "poof" again, and the company grows exponentially via additional acquisitions.) As Jim Blosser, one of Huizenga's executives, noted, "Wayne doesn't like start-ups. Let someone else do the R&D. He'd prefer to pay a little more for a concept that has demonstrated some success and may just need help in capital and management."[16]

Huizenga's entrepreneurial career began in 1961 when he purchased his first company, Southern Sanitation Company, in Florida. The company's assets were a garbage truck and a $500-a-month truck route, which he worked personally, rising at 2:30 a.m. every day. This company ultimately became the multibillion-dollar Waste Management Inc., which Huizenga had grown nationally through aggressive acquisitions. In one 9-month period, Waste Management bought 100 smaller companies across the country. In 10 years, the company grew from $5 million a year to annual profits of $106.5 million on nearly $1 billion in revenues. In 4 more years, revenue doubled again.[17]

Huizenga then exited this business and went into the video rental business by purchasing the entire Blockbuster Video franchise for $32 million in 1984, after having been unable to purchase the Blockbuster franchise for the state of Florida because the state's territorial rights had already been sold to other entrepreneurs before Huizenga made his offer. When he acquired Blockbuster Video, it had 8 corporate and 11 franchise stores nationally. The franchisor was generating $7 million annually through direct rentals from the 8 stores, plus franchise fees and royalties from the 11 franchised stores.[18] Under Huizenga, who didn't even own a VCR at the time, Blockbuster flourished. For the next 7 years, through internal growth and acquisitions, Blockbuster averaged a new store opening every 17 hours, resulting in its becoming larger than its next 550 competitors combined. Over this period of time, the price of its stock increased 4,100%; someone who had invested $25,000 in Blockbuster stock in 1984 would have found that 7 years later, that investment would be worth $1.1 million, and an investment of $1 million in 1984 would have turned into $41 million during this time period. In January 1994, Huizenga sold Blockbuster Video, which had grown to 4,300 stores in 23 countries, to Viacom for $8.5 billion.

Huizenga pursued the same roll-up strategy in the auto business by rapidly buying as many dealerships as he possibly could and bundling them together under the AutoNation brand. By 2001, AutoNation was the largest automobile retailer in the United States, a title that it still holds in 2013. By the way, if you ever find yourself behind the wheel of a National or Alamo rental car, you're also driving one of Huizenga's vehicles—both companies are among his holdings. What Huizenga eventually hopes to do is to have an entire life cycle for a car. In other words, he buys cars from the manufacturer, sells some of them as new, leases or rents the balance, and later sells the rented cars as used.

Huizenga also owns or previously owned practically every professional sports franchise in Florida, including the National Football League's Miami Dolphins, the National Hockey League's Florida Panthers, and Major League Baseball's Florida Marlins. He never owned the National Basketball League's Miami Heat; his cousin did.

Now, here's your bonus points question—the one I always ask my MBA students. What's the common theme among all of Huizenga's various businesses—videos, waste, sports, and automobiles? Each one of them involves the rental of products, generating significant, predictable, and, perhaps most important, recurring revenues. The video business rents the same video over and over again, and the car rental business rents the same car a multitude of times. In waste management, he rented the trash containers. But what's being rented in the sports business? He rents the seats in the stadiums and arenas that he owns. Other businesses that are in the seat rental business are airlines, movie theaters, public transportation, and universities!

Another example of an acquirer is Bill Gates, the founder of Microsoft. The company's initial success came from an operating system called MS-DOS, which was originally owned by a company called Seattle Computer Products. In 1980, IBM was looking for an operating system. After hearing about Bill Gates, who had dropped out of Harvard to start Microsoft in 1975 with his friend Paul Allen, the IBM representatives went to Albuquerque, New Mexico, where Gates and Allen were, to see if Gates could provide them with the operating system they needed. At the time, Microsoft's product was a version of the programming language BASIC for the Altair 8800, arguably the world's first personal computer. BASIC had been invented in 1964 by John Kenney and Thomas Kurtz.[19] As he did not have an operating system, Gates recommended that IBM contact another company called Digital Research. Gary Kildall, the owner of Digital Research, was absent when the IBM representatives visited, and his staff refused to sign a nondisclosure statement with IBM without his consent, so the representatives went back to Gates to see if he could recommend someone else. True opportunistic entrepreneur that he is, Gates told them that he had an operating system to provide to them and finalized a deal with IBM. Once he had done so, he went out and bought the operating system, Q-DOS, from Seattle Computer Products for $50,000 and customized it for IBM's first PC, which was introduced in August 1981. The rest is entrepreneurial history. So Bill Gates, one of the world's wealthiest people, with a personal net worth in excess of $67 billion,[20] achieved his initial entrepreneurial success as an acquirer and has continued on this path ever since. Despite its court battles, Microsoft continues to grow, investing billions of dollars to acquire 66 technologies and companies since 1994.[21] In June 2012, Microsoft paid $1.2 billion in cash for Yammer, an enterprise social network system,[22] and in May 2011, it invested $8.5 billion in cash for the ubiquitous online service Skype, a global digital connection platform for voice and visual communications. There is still plenty of "dry powder," too, since Microsoft recorded $77.0 billion in cash on its books by its fiscal year end of June 2013.[23]

Start-Ups

Creating a company from nothing other than an idea for a product or service is the most difficult and risky way to be a successful entrepreneur. Two great examples of start-up entrepreneurs are Steve Wozniak, a college dropout, and Steve Jobs of Apple Computer. As an engineer at Hewlett-Packard, Wozniak approached the company with an idea for a small personal computer. The company did not take him seriously and rejected his idea; this decision turned out to be one of the greatest intrapreneurial blunders in history. With $1,300 of his own money, Wozniak and his friend Steve Jobs launched Apple Computer from his parents' garage.

The Apple Computer start-up is a great example of a start-up that was successful because of the revolutionary technological innovation created by the technology genius Wozniak. Other entrepreneurial firms that were successful as a result of technological innovations include Amazon.com, founded by Jeff Bezos; Google, with Larry Page and Sergey Brin; and Facebook, with Mark Zuckerberg.

Entrepreneurial start-ups have not been limited to technology companies. In 1993, Kate Spade quit her job as the accessories editor for *Mademoiselle* and, with her husband, Andy, started her own women's handbag company called Kate Spade, Inc. Her bags, a combination of whimsy and function, have scored big returns on the initial $35,000 investment from Andy's 401(k). In 1999, sales had reached $50 million. Neiman Marcus purchased a 56% stake in February 1999 for $33.6 million.[24] In 2006, revenues surged to $84 million when the company was acquired as a wholly-owned subsidiary of Fifth & Pacific Companies, Inc. (NYSE:FNP). As of 2013, Kate Spade LLC revenues in the United States and China were a combined $44.9 million.[25]

Finally, there are also numerous successful start-ups that began from an idea other than the entrepreneur's. For example, Mario and Cheryl Tricoci are the owners of a $40 million international day spa company headquartered in Chicago called Mario Tricoci's. In 1986, after returning from a vacation at a premier spa outside the United States, they noticed that there were virtually no day spas in the country, only those with weeklong stay requirements. Therefore, they started their day spa company, based on the ideas and styles that they had seen during their international travels.[26]

ENTREPRENEURIAL FINANCE

In a recent survey of business owners, the functional area they cited as being the one in which they had the weakest skill was the area of financial management—accounting, bookkeeping, the raising of capital, and the daily management of cash flow. Interestingly, these business owners also indicated that they spent most of their time on finance-related activities. Unfortunately, the findings of this survey are an accurate portrayal of most entrepreneurs—they are comfortable with the day-to-day operation of their businesses and with the marketing and sales of their products or services, but they are very uncomfortable with the financial management of their companies. Entrepreneurs cannot afford this discomfort. They must realize that financial management is not as difficult as it is made out to be. It must be used and embraced because it is one of the key factors for entrepreneurial success.

Prospective and existing "high-growth" entrepreneurs who currently are not financial managers will appreciate this book. Its objective is to be a user-friendly guide that will provide entrepreneurs with an understanding of the fundamentals of financial management and analysis that will enable them to better manage the financial resources of their business and create economic value. Entrepreneurial finance is distinct from corporate finance; it is more integrative, including the analysis of qualitative issues such as marketing, sales, personnel management, and strategic planning. The questions that will be answered will include:

- What financial tools can be used to manage the cash flow of the business efficiently?
- Why is valuation important?
- What is the value of the company?
- Finally, how, where, and when can financial resources be acquired to finance the business?

2

Financial Statements

INTRODUCTION

One of the most important competencies of an entrepreneur is understanding the financial statements of her own enterprise. Therefore, the discussion in this chapter is intended as an overview of the main relevant issues concerning key financial statements. The objective is to teach the purpose of the different statements, their components, and their significance to entrepreneurs who are not financial managers. This is the final step toward making financial statement analysis, which will be the focus of the next chapter, simple and user-friendly.

Financial statements are important because they provide valuable information that is typically used by business managers and investors. However, it is not necessary for the entrepreneur to be able to personally develop financial statements.

Financial Statements and Pro Formas

Projecting the future is challenging, but it must be done. Debt and equity investors know that financial projections that go out 3 to 5 years into the future are at best guesstimates—they have to be, as no one can predict the future (unless, of course, guaranteed future contracts have been signed). Potential investors are looking for projections that are grounded in defensible logic. When asked how financiers know when pro formas are correct, a venture capitalist responded, "We don't know. In all likelihood, they will be ultimately wrong. In a start-up, it is rare for pro formas to ever match reality. We are looking for logical, defensible reasoning behind the numbers versus B.S.—'Blue Sky'—projections simply pulled out of the air."

In this chapter, we will focus on 3 financial statements: the income statement, the balance sheet, and the statement of cash flows. Each of these statements, in one way or another, describes a company's financial health. For example, the income statement describes a company's profitability. It is a measurement of the company's financial performance over time. Is the company making or losing money? On the other hand, the balance sheet describes the financial condition of a company at a particular time. Does it own more than it owes? Can it remain in business?

THE INCOME STATEMENT

The income statement, also known as the profit and loss (P&L) statement, is a scoreboard for a business and is usually prepared in accordance with generally accepted accounting principles (GAAP). It records the flow of resources over time by stating the financial condition of a business over the course of a period, usually a month, quarter, or year. It shows the revenues (i.e., sales) achieved by a company during that particular period and the expenses (i.e., costs) associated with generating these revenues. That is the reason why the income statement, in addition to being known as the P&L statement, is also referred to as the statement of revenues and expenses.

The difference between a company's total revenues and its total expenses is its net income. When the revenues are greater than the costs, the company has earned a profit. When the costs are greater than the revenues, the company has incurred a loss.

The income statement is used to calculate a company's cash flow, which is also known as EBITDA: earnings (i.e., net income or profit) before interest expense (i.e., the cost of debt), taxes (i.e., the payments to the government based on a company's profit), depreciation (i.e., noncash expenditures for the decline in value of tangible assets), and amortization (i.e., noncash expenditures for the decline in value of intangible assets such as patents or goodwill). To determine a company's EBITDA for any period—i.e., the cash being generated by the company after paying all the expenses directly related to its operations, and therefore the cash available to pay for nonoperational expenses such as taxes and principal and interest payments on debt—one must utilize the income statement. A sample income statement is provided in Figure 2-1.

The income statement is divided into 2 sections: "Revenues," a measure of the resources generated from the sales of products and services, and "Expenses," a measure of the costs associated with the selling of these products or services. The accounting equation to remember is Equation 2-1.

Net Income

$$\text{Revenues} - \text{expenses} = \text{net income} \tag{2-1}$$

Revenues	$8,000
Expenses	
Cost of goods sold	$2,000
Gross profit	**$6,000**
Operating expenses	
Wages	$1,000
Rent	300
Selling expense	400
Depreciation	500
Amortization	300
Total operating expense	$2,500
Operating profit or profit before interest and taxes	**$3,500**
Interest expense	200
Profit before taxes	**$3,300**
Income tax expense	$1,320
Net income	**$1,980**

Figure 2-1 **Bruce Company Income Statement, Year Ended 12/31/2012**

Using the information contained in Figure 2-1, we can calculate EBITDA at the end of the year for the Bruce Company, as shown in Figure 2-2. As you can see, we added back "noncash" expenses, or those for which no cash is actually disbursed, such as depreciation and amortization, to determine the company's true cash position—EBITDA.

Let us define and analyze each revenue and expense item on the typical income statement.

Revenues

- Receipts from the sale of products and services
- Returns on investments, such as interest earned on a company's marketable securities, including stocks and bonds
- Franchising fees paid by franchisees
- Rental property income

Expenses

- Cost of goods sold
- Operating expenses
- Financing expenses
- Tax expenses

Net income	$1,980
+ Interest expense	200
+ Taxes	1,320
+ Depreciation	500
+ Amortization	300
EBITDA	**$4,300**

Figure 2-2 **Sample EBITDA Calculation**

Cost of Goods Sold

The cost of goods sold (known as the COGS) or the cost of services rendered is the cost of the raw materials and direct labor required to produce the product or service that generated the revenue. The COGS does *not* include any overhead, such as utilities or management costs. The difference between revenues and the COGS is gross profit, also known as gross margin. The proper way to calculate the gross profit is simply to subtract the COGS, as defined earlier, from the revenues produced by the sale of the company's goods or services. Other income, such as interest earned on investments, should not be included.

The reason for this is that in the world of finance, internal comparisons of a company's year-to-year performance, and also external comparisons of a company's performance to that of another company or an entire industry, are quite common. These kinds of comparisons are called *internal and external benchmarking*. Therefore, in order to make "apples-to-apples" comparisons that are not skewed by, for example, Company A's revenues being stronger than Company B's because the former is getting higher interest payments on its investments, only the revenues from operations are used. To determine gross profit from total revenues, regardless of the source, would be to ignore the obvious definition of the COGS, which is the cost of *only* the goods that are sold to generate revenues.

Operating Expenses

Operating expenses, also known as selling, general, and administrative expenses (SG&A), are all of the other tangible and intangible (e.g., depreciation and amortization) expenses required to carry on the day-to-day activities of a company. Included in this category are fixed costs (i.e., those costs that do not vary with the volume of business), such as insurance, rent, and management salaries, and variable costs (i.e., the costs that vary depending upon the volume produced), such as utilities (e.g., electricity and water) and invoice documents. For example, in the Bruce income statement in Figure 2-1, the rent is $300 per year—an amount that remains the same whether 200 or 2,000 widgets per year were produced.

Another simple way to think about fixed versus variable costs is to determine the expenses that would be affected by, for example, closing the company for a month. The rent would still be due to the landlord, and interest payments on bank loans would still be due to the bank. These are the fixed costs. On the other hand, since the company is closed and is not producing or shipping anything for a month, there would be no need to buy invoice documents, and the utility bills would decrease dramatically, since electricity and water were not being used.

Excluded from this category are interest expenses, which are not operating expenses, but rather financing expenses. Therefore, revenues minus the sum of the COGS and operating expenses equals operating income, or EBIT (earnings before interest and taxes). The operating income is then used to make any interest payments on debt. The balance is called earnings before taxes (EBT), and these funds are then used to pay taxes on the company's EBT figure.

As stated earlier, "intangible, noncash" expenses—expenses that do not require actual cash disbursements, such as depreciation and amortization—are also included in the operating expenses category. Under GAAP, every company is allowed to "write off" (i.e., expense) a portion of its tangible assets each year over the life of the asset. The theory behind this practice is that the value of all assets typically depreciates over time as a result of natural deterioration and regular use. Therefore, the depreciation of an asset is a cost to the company because the value of the asset is declining. As we will see in the discussion of the balance sheet later in this chapter, the depreciated value of the asset is recognized on the balance sheet, and the amount the asset depreciates each year is presented on the income statement.

The amount to be depreciated each year is determined by the accounting method that the company selects to recognize depreciation. The most common methods are straight-line (in which an equal percentage of the asset's cost minus salvage value is recognized each year for a predetermined number of useful years) and accelerated (i.e., double-declining-balance or sum-of-the-years'-digits, which recognize a larger portion of the depreciation in the early years).

The method used to calculate depreciation can have a significant impact on the timing of reported income. Using the straight-line depreciation method rather than one of the 2 accelerated methods, double-declining-balance or sum-of-the-years'-digits, will result in a higher net income in the early periods and lower net income in the later years of an asset's estimated useful life. Also, the change in net income from one period to the next is greater under the double-declining-balance method than it is under the sum-of-the-years'-digits method. This makes the former method the most extreme form of depreciation. Finally, the 2 accelerated methods produce low levels of net income in the early periods that increase rapidly over the asset's life.[1]

While depreciation is the expensing of tangible assets, amortization is the expensing of intangible assets. Intangible assets include such items as goodwill (i.e., the surplus paid over an asset's book value), franchise rights, patents, trademarks, exploration rights, copyrights, and noncompete agreements. These items must be amortized, generally in equal annual amounts, over 15 years.

Other Expenses

Found on the income statement, financing expenses are basically the interest payments made on loans to the business. And finally, tax expenses are the taxes due on the company's profits. There are also other taxes that a company incurs, including unemployment and real estate taxes, but these fall into the operating expenses category.

If a company has a negative profit before taxes—in other words, a loss—then corporate taxes are not due to the government. In fact, not only will taxes not be due, but the company's losses can also be used to reduce tax obligations on future positive profits. This is called a *tax-loss carryforward*, where a company's previous losses can be carried forward against future profits. Interestingly, a company with a history of annual losses can be more valuable to a prospective buyer than a company that regularly has a breakeven or profitable financial history. Since tax-loss carryforwards are transferable from seller to buyer, they are attractive to a prospective buyer because they are assets for companies that are trying to shield future profits.

At the end of the year, if a company's net income after taxes is positive, it is retained in the form of retained earnings, reflected on the next year's beginning balance sheet, or distributed to investors as dividends, as shown in Equation 2-2.

Retained Earnings and Shareholders' Dividends

Revenues – expenses = net income
→ Retained earnings and shareholders' dividends (2-2)

Before we end the discussion of the income statement, it is imperative that we clear up a few terms that are commonly used interchangeably. These include:

- Revenues and sales
- Margins, profits, earnings, and income

The 3 different kinds of margins: profits, earnings, and income—in the order of their appearance on the income statement—are as follows:

- *Gross*. The difference between revenues and COGS.
- *Operating*. Revenues – (COGS + operating expenses).
- *Net*. The difference between revenues and *all* of the company's costs.

Cash Versus Accrual Accounting

A final point to be made about the income statement is that it can be affected by the accounting method selected by the entrepreneur. The options for the entrepreneur are cash or accrual accounting. Typically, a company will select the accounting method that provides the greatest immediate tax benefit. It must also be noted that a company can, during its lifetime, change from one method to another only once, and this change must be approved by the Internal Revenue Service (IRS). The IRS usually approves a requested switch from cash to accrual accounting, but it usually rejects a request to change from accrual to cash accounting. What is the main difference between cash and accrual accounting? Simply stated, it is the time at which a company recognizes its revenues and expenses. Table 2-1 clearly shows the difference.

The accrual accounting method gives the reader of the income statement a richer and more complete depiction of the business's financial condition, since all revenues generated by the business and all expenses incurred are included, regardless of whether actual cash has been received or disbursed. Because this

TABLE 2-1 Cash Versus Accrual Accounting

Accounting Method	Revenues Recognized	Expenses Recognized
Cash	When actual cash is received from the customer	When actual cash is paid to the supplier
Accrual	When the product is shipped and the invoice is mailed	When the invoice is received from the supplier

method recognizes items immediately, many business owners try to use it to their advantage. For example, just before the end of the year, many owners will increase their inventories dramatically. The result is an increase in expenses and therefore a reduction in profits and taxes.

For publicly owned companies, where the markets reward revenue and profit growth with an increasing stock price, many owners prefer to use the accrual method because it helps them achieve the aforementioned increases. Unlike many privately owned companies, which seek to minimize taxes by reducing their reported EBT, public companies seek to show the highest possible EBT, as well as revenue growth. Given this objective, it is not unheard of for a company's owner to get too aggressive and sometimes even act unethically with regard to growth.

For example, Premiere Laser Systems, Inc. a spin-off from Pfizer, won FDA approval for a new laser device that promised to make drilling cavities painless. The publicly owned company, trading on the Nasdaq stock exchange, shipped and recognized revenues on $2.5 million in products to Henry Schein, Inc., the powerhouse distributor in the dental business, in December 1997. The only problem was that Henry Schein claimed that it had never ordered the products, refused to pay, and alleged that the products had been shipped to it so that Premiere could show current and future stockholders an increase in revenues. Obviously, the supplier used the accrual method, which allowed it to recognize the revenue immediately upon shipment. Had its accounting method been cash, the revenue would have never been recognized because the recipient company refused to pay.[2] Premiere settled a number of class action suits; it also cooperated with a securities investigation and replaced its CEO. The company eventually filed for Chapter 11 bankruptcy in March 2000.[3]

Another "fishy numbers" case involved Sunbeam Corporation, which conceded that while under the leadership of Al Dunlap, known as "Chainsaw Al," its "1997 financial statements, audited by Arthur Andersen LLP, might not be accurate and should not be relied upon."[4] Sunbeam filed for Chapter 11 bankruptcy protection in 2001 after 3 years of trying to turn around its fortunes. The company was saddled with a debt load of $2.6 billion.[5]

Private-practice physicians usually operate some of the most profitable small businesses in the country. Typically, doctors use the cash accounting method, which gives the reader a more limited picture of the company's financial condition. Physicians and others who use this method do so primarily because their revenues come from notoriously slow payers, such as insurance companies and the government, also known as third-party payers. Therefore, instead of recognizing this unpaid revenue and paying taxes immediately on the profits that it helps to generate, they use the cash method to delay revenue recognition until the cash is actually received, thereby reducing the company's profit before taxes and consequently the taxes paid. Using this method does not result in tax avoidance or elimination, however; it simply delays tax payments into future years.

Not all companies are allowed to use the cash method, including the following:

- Companies with average annual revenues of $10 million or more
- Companies where inventories are a heavy part of their business, such as auto dealerships and grocery wholesalers

Let's look at Figure 2-3, which shows an end-of-the-year income statement using both methods. The company has sold and invoiced $1 million worth of merchandise and has received payment for $600,000. The merchandise cost was $500,000, an amount for which the company has been billed. The company has paid its suppliers $400,000.

As is obvious from this simple example, the accounting method that a company uses can affect not only the taxes owed, but also the 3 profit categories mentioned earlier. All 3 would be lower as a percentage of revenues under the cash method than under the accrual method. Therefore, it is imperative that

	Cash Method	Accrual Method
Revenues	$600,000	$1,000,000
Cost	$400,000	$500,000
Profit before taxes	$200,000	$500,000
Taxes (50% rate)	$100,000	$250,000
Profit after taxes	$100,000	$250,000

Figure 2-3 **Cash versus Accrual Accounting Example**

when comparing income statement items against those of other companies, the comparison be made with the statements of companies using the same accounting method.

As mentioned earlier, a company can change its accounting method with the approval of the IRS. To see the impact of these changes, examine Figure 2-4.

Why would someone in a business with receivables want to switch from the cash method to the accrual accounting method when the result can be an increase in taxes? There could be several legitimate business reasons, including the following:

- For better comparison purposes, the company may want to use the same accounting method used by its competitors.
- The entrepreneur may be preparing the company to go public or to be sold. The accrual method would show the company to be bigger and more profitable than it would appear using the cash method.

	Cash Business with No Receivables	Business with Receivables
Cash to accrual	• Revenues remain the same.	• Revenues increase.
	• Expenses increase.	• Expenses increase.
	• Profit before taxes decreases.	• Profit before taxes increases.
	• Taxes decrease.	• Taxes increase.
	• Net income decreases.	• Net income increases.
Accrual to cash	• Revenues remain the same.	• Revenues decrease.
	• Expenses decrease.	• Expenses decrease.
	• Profit before taxes increases.	• Profit before taxes decreases.
	• Taxes increase.	• Taxes decrease.
	• Net income increases.	• Net income decreases.

Figure 2-4 **Comparison of Changes in Accounting Methods**

Before ending the discussion on accounting methods, it should be pointed out that in December 1999, the IRS issued several rules regarding this topic. Specifically, the IRS ruled, "if you produce, purchase, or sell merchandise in your business, you must keep an inventory and use the accrual method for purchases and sales of merchandise," with the exception that taxpayers with 3 years' average annual gross income under $1 million or small businesses with 3 years' average annual gross income less than $10 million can choose the cash method.[6]

THE BALANCE SHEET

An example of a balance sheet is shown in Figure 2-5.

The information contained on the balance sheet is also often presented in the format shown in Figure 2-6. The balance sheet is a financial snapshot of a company's assets, liabilities, and stockholders' equity at a particular time. Bankers have historically relied on the analysis of ratios of various assets and liabilities on the balance sheet to determine a company's creditworthiness and solvency position.

On the balance sheet, a company's assets are separated into current and long-term categories. Current assets are those items that can be converted into cash within one year, including a company's cash balance, the dollar amount due to the company from customers (i.e., accounts receivable), inventory, marketable securities, and prepaid expenses.

Long-term assets, tangible and intangible, are the remaining assets. They are recorded at their original cost, not their present market value, minus the accumulated depreciation from each year's depreciation expense, which is found on the income statement. The assets that fall into this category include buildings, land, equipment, furnaces, automobiles, trucks, and lighting fixtures.

As stated earlier in this chapter, all long-term assets, except land, can be depreciated over time. This is permissible under GAAP despite the fact that some assets, in fact, appreciate over time. An example is real estate, which usually tends to appreciate over time, although the balance sheet does not reflect this fact. Therefore, it is commonly known that the balance sheet often undervalues a company's assets, especially when real estate is owned. This fact was highlighted in the mid-1980s during the leveraged-buyout, hostile-takeover craze. Corporate

Assets	
Current assets	
Cash	$300
Accounts receivable	300
Less: Uncollectibles	(10)
Inventory	600
Total current assets	**$1,190**
Property, plant, and equipment	
Property	$5,000
Buildings	4,000
Less: Accumulated depreciation	(1,000)
Equipment	3,000
Less: Accumulated depreciation	(1,000)
Total property, plant, and equipment	**$10,000**
Other assets	
Automobiles	$4,500
Patents	1,000
Total other assets	**$5,500**
Total assets	**$16,690**
Liabilities and shareholders' equity	
Current liabilities	
Accounts payable	$500
Wages	700
Short-term debt	900
Total current liabilities	**$2,100**
Long-term liabilities	
Bank loans	$4,000
Mortgages	5,000
Total long-term liabilities	**$7,000**
Shareholders' equity	
Contributed capital	$5,000
Retained earnings	2,590
Total shareholders' equity	**$7,590**
Total liabilities and shareholders' equity	**$16,690**

Figure 2-5 **Bruce Company Balance Sheet, Year End 12/31/12**

- Long-term
- Tangible
- Intangible

Liabilities

- Current
- Long-term

Equity

- Stock—common, preferred, etc.
- Retained earnings

Figure 2-6 Balance Sheet Information

raiders, as the hostile-takeover artists were known, would forcibly buy a company at an exorbitant price because they believed that the company had "hidden value" in excess of what the financial statements showed. One of the primary items they were concerned with was the real estate that the company owned, which was recorded on the balance sheet at cost minus accumulated depreciation. The raiders would take over the company, financing the purchase primarily with debt. Then they would sell the real estate at market prices, using the proceeds to reduce their debt obligations, and lease the property from the new owners.

The other components of the balance sheet are the liabilities and shareholders' (stockholders') equity sections. A company's liabilities consist of the amounts that the company owes to its creditors, secured and unsecured. The liabilities section of the balance sheet, like the assets section, is divided into current and long-term categories. Current liabilities are those that must be paid within 12 months. Included in this category is the current portion of any principal payments due on loans for which the company is responsible—remember, the current interest payments on the loan are on the income statement—and accounts payable, which is very simply money owed to suppliers. Long-term liabilities are all of the company's other obligations. For example, if the company owns real estate and has a mortgage, the total balance due on that mortgage minus the current portion would be reflected in the long-term liabilities category.

Stockholders' equity is the difference between total assets and total liabilities. It is the net worth of the company, including the stock issued by the company and the accumulated earnings that the company has retained each year. Remember, the retained earnings are an accumulation of the profits from the income statement. Therefore, the company's net worth is not necessarily the company's value or what it would sell for. A company with a negative net worth, where total liabilities exceed total assets, may sell for quite a bit of money without any problems. As we will see in Chapter 5, a company's net worth typically has no bearing on its valuation. A few important equations to remember are shown in Equation 2-3.

Shareholders' Equity

Total assets – total liabilities = shareholders' equity

Net worth = total assets – total liabilities

Therefore

Net worth = shareholders' equity (2-3)

Finally, the items on the balance sheet are also used to compute a company's working capital and working capital needs. Net working capital is simply a measure of the company's ability to pay its bills—in other words, the company's short-term financial strength. A company's net working capital is measured as shown in Equation 2-4.

Net Working Capital

Net working capital = current assets – current liabilities (2-4)

The fact that 2 companies have the exact same level of working capital does not mean that they have equal short-term financial strength. Look, for example, at Figure 2-7. While both companies have the same amount of working capital, a banker would prefer to lend to Cheers Company because Cheers has greater

	Hill Company	Cheers Company
Current assets	$1,000,000	$600,000
Current liabilities	500,000	100,000
Working capital	$500,000	$500,000

Figure 2-7 **Working Capital Comparison**

financial strength. Specifically, for every dollar that Cheers owes, it has $6 in potentially liquid assets, whereas Hill Company has only $2 in assets for every dollar owed.

Now look at the example in Figure 2-8. It shows that a company with greater working capital than another is again not necessarily stronger. With a 10-to-1 asset-to-liability ratio, Jardine is obviously financially stronger than Webb, which has a 2-to-1 ratio, despite the fact that Webb has more working capital.

The entrepreneur must recognize that potential investors use the company's working capital situation to determine whether they will provide financing. In addition, loan covenants may establish a working capital level that the company must always maintain or risk technical loan default, resulting in the entire loan being called for immediate payment.

The balance sheet assumes greater importance for manufacturing companies than for service companies, primarily because the former tend to have tangible assets, such as machinery and real estate, whereas the latter tend to have people as their primary assets.

THE STATEMENT OF CASH FLOWS

The statement of cash flows uses information from the 2 other financial statements, the balance sheet (B/S) and the income statement (I/S), to develop a statement that explains changes in cash flows resulting from operations, investing, and financing activities. Figure 2-9 provides an example of a cash flow statement.

	Jardine Company	**Webb Company**
Current assets	$10,000,000	$20,000,000
Current liabilities	1,000,000	10,000,000
Working capital	$9,000,000	$10,000,000

Figure 2-8 **Working Capital Comparison**

Cash flow from operations	
Net income	$400,000
Noncash expenditures	
Depreciation	110,000
Amortization	95,000
Net working capital	10,000
Cash available for investing and financing activities	**$615,000**
Cash flow from investing activities	
Equipment purchases	($140,000)
Automobile purchases	(50,000)
Sale of old equipment	70,000
Cash available for investing activities	**$495,000**
Cash flow from financing activities	
Dividends paid	($30,000)
Mortgage payments	(100,000)
Loan payments	(200,000)
Repurchase of company stock	(65,000)
Net cash flow	**$100,000**

Figure 2-9 **Richardson Company Cash Flow Statement, Year Ended 12/31/12**

The relationship between the sources and uses of cash is shown in Equation 2-5.

Cash Flow

Cash sources – cash uses = net cash flow
→ Fund operations and return to investors (2-5)

Cash Flow Ledgers and Planners

The cash flow ledger, regardless of accounting issues such as the cash versus the accrual method or noncash expenses such as depreciation, provides a summary of the increases (inflows) and decreases (outflows) in actual cash over a period of time. It provides important information primarily to the entrepreneur, but also possibly to investors and creditors (such as banks), about the balance of the cash account, enabling them to assess a company's ability to meet its debt payments when they come due. A famous (but unnamed) economist once said, "Cash flow is more important than your mother"—well, maybe it is not *more* important, but it is essential because it is the lifeline of any business. Cash flow is different from profit and more important, as we will see later in this chapter.

The cash flow at the end of a period (e.g., a month) is calculated as shown in Figure 2-10, and Figure 2-11 provides an example of a monthly cash flow ledger. It indicates, on a transaction basis, all the cash received and disbursed during a month long period. As shown, the cash balance at the end of the month is equal to the total cash received less the total cash disbursed for the month.

The successful entrepreneurs are those who know their company's actual cash position on any given day. Therefore, unlike the comparatively few times that they need to reread the income statement and balance sheet, it is recommended that entrepreneurs, especially the inexperienced and those in the early stages of their ventures, review the cash flow ledger at least weekly.

Figure 2-12 provides a weekly cash flow projection summary, which every new and inexperienced entrepreneur should prepare immediately upon opening for business and each month thereafter. It indicates the anticipated cash inflows during the month and the cash payments to be made. In the figure, the anticipated cash inflows for the month (59) are less than the expected cash outflows for the month (60); therefore, the cash balance for the month will be negative 1.

The projection in Figure 2-12 was prepared at the end of September for the following month. It anticipates the cash inflows during the month and the cash payments to be made. The "Cash in" section includes expected payments

	Cash on hand at the beginning of the month
plus	Monthly cash received from customer payments and other sources
equals	Total cash
minus	Monthly cash disbursements for fixed and variable costs
equals	**Cash available at the end of the month**

Figure 2-10 **Sample Cash Flow Calculation**

Date	Explanation	To/From	Received	Disbursed	Balance
6/30/12					$1,000
7/1/12	Silkscreen start-up supplies	Ace Arts		$ 250	750
7/2/12	Bought 4 doz. T-shirts	Joe		240	510
7/6/12	Monthly registration fee	Flea market		100	410
7/6/12	Business cards	Print shop		20	390
7/6/12	Flyers	Print shop		10	380
7/7/12	Sold 4 doz. @ $12	Flea market	$ 576		956
7/10/12	Bought 5 doz. T-shirts	Joe		300	656
7/14/12	Sold 4 doz. @ $12, 1 doz. @ $10	Flea market	696		1,352
7/16/12	Bought 5 doz. T-shirts	Joe		300	1,122
7/16/12	Silkscreen ink	Print shop		50	1,002
7/16/12	Flyers	Print shop		10	992
7/21/12	Sold 3 doz. @ $12 (rained)	Flea market	432		1,424
7/25/12	Bought 2 doz. T-shirts	Joe		120	1,304
7/26/12	Sold 4 doz. @ $12	Flea market	576		1,880
Totals			**$2,280**	**$1,400**	**$1,880**

Source: Adapted from Steve Mariotti, *The Young Entrepreneur's Guide to Starting and Running a Business* (New York: Times Business, 1996).

Figure 2-11 **Oscar's Business Ledger**

from specific customers based on the terms of the invoices and the aging of the corresponding receivables. The terms were net 30, which means that the payment was due 30 days following the invoice date. However, the entrepreneur who completed this projection did not simply project October 29 because that was 30 days after invoicing. To do so would be too theoretical and, quite frankly, naïve on the entrepreneur's part. Instead, he used common sense and factored in the extra 7 days that Customer 1 typically takes before paying her bills. Thus, the product was invoiced on September 22, and the entrepreneur is forecasting the actual receipt of payment on October 29. This section also includes the cash payments expected each week throughout the month. These are expected to be actual cash payments that customers make when they pick up their merchandise. In these cases, the entrepreneur is not supplying any credit to the customer.

By doing this kind of projection each month, the entrepreneur can schedule his payments to suppliers to match his expected cash receipts. This planner

Week of	Oct. 1	Oct. 8	Oct. 15	Oct. 22	Oct. 29	Oct.'s Total Cash Received
(Cash in)						
1. Beginning cash	10					10
2. Receivables						
Customer 1					5	5
Customer 2		3	3	3		9
Customer 3		8				8
Customer 4			12			12
3. Cash payments	5	3	1	1	5	15
	15	**14**	**16**	**4**	**10**	**59**
(Cash out)						
1. Payroll	3	3	3	3	3	15
2. Loan payments			6			6
3. Rent	5					5
4. Insurance						
Property	2					2
Health	3					3
5. Vendor payments						
Vendor 1	1	2	3	4	4	14
Vendor 2	1		3			4
Vendor 3		2	6			8
Vendor 4	1		2			3
	16	**7**	**23**	**7**	**7**	**60**

Source: Teri Lammers, "The Weekly Cash-Flow Planner," *Inc.*, June 1992, p. 99

Figure 2-12 **Sample Weekly Cash Flow Projections**

allows him to be proactive, as all entrepreneurs should be, with regard to the money that he owes to his suppliers. It enables him to let specific vendors know in advance that his payment will probably be late. The cash flow ledger and planner are simple and very useful tools that the entrepreneur should use to manage cash flow successfully.

DEVELOPMENT OF PRO FORMAS

Entrepreneurs should develop pro forma financial statements for all new entrepreneurial opportunities, including either start-ups or existing companies that are being purchased. Any pro forma should have figures for at least 3 years and 3 scenarios—a best-case, a worst-case, and a most-likely-case scenario. If only one scenario is provided, then the automatic assumption is that it is the best case because most people always put their best, not their worst, foot forward. A company's historical performance drives the financial projections for that company's future, unless there is other information that indicates that past performance is not a good indicator of future performance.

For example, if a new contract has been signed with a new customer, then this could be used to adjust the financial projections. Otherwise, historical numbers must be used.

For instance, Livent Inc. created major musicals such as *Joseph and the Amazing Technicolor Dreamcoat* and *Ragtime*. In 1998, the company added Chicago's Oriental Theatre to the 3 other company-owned theaters in New York, Toronto, and Vancouver. Livent's pro formas for the newly renovated Oriental Theatre were allegedly based on its success with *Joseph*, which it had staged 2 years earlier at the Chicago theater and in similar venues throughout the country. Livent's projections were as follows:

Oriental Theatre

- 80% capacity
- 52 weeks per year
- $40 million annual gross revenues

Before the end of 1998, Livent Inc. experienced major financial difficulties and filed for Chapter 11 bankruptcy. In bankruptcy court, an attorney for the city of Chicago, which filed a condemnation case, challenged the legitimacy of the pro formas. He argued that the $40 million annual projected gross revenues was out of line with reality and intentionally fraudulent, given the fact that "in a recent year, a similar theater located in downtown Chicago and similar in size, reported an annual gross of just $20,455,000"![7]

When there are no historical data, financial projections for a start-up company can be determined in one of the following ways:

- Conduct an industry analysis and select a company within the same industry that can be used as a comparable. Where possible, review the sales figures for this company to determine its sales history from Year 1 as well as its sales growth in the past few years. Extrapolate from these figures and use the data to determine sales growth for your company. Cost figures may be determined from cost data obtained through research on, e.g., a publicly owned company in the same industry.
- If you have already secured sales commitments, use these commitments to calculate the worst-case scenario. Use larger amounts to calculate the best-case and most-likely-case scenarios.
- If the product or service is completely new, market research can be undertaken to determine the overall market demand for this new product or service. Identify the size of the market and assume that the company will get a specific percentage of the total market, depending on the total number of competitors. Also, identify the potential customers and estimate the number of units that can be sold to each. It is critical that, whenever possible, this market research be based on both secondary research (third-party market reports and/or articles from credible sources) and primary research (direct conversations with and/or surveys of potential customers in the targeted segment). This ensures that the projections are based on reliable, defensible information sources and are not just "back of the envelope" guesses.
- Alternatively, you can use specific figures for your projections, based on your own assumptions or expectations. It is important that you state what these assumptions are and justify why you believe them to be realistic.

An important issue for a start-up company to consider is to make sure that all the necessary equipment financing needs are included.

Before closing this section on pro forma development, a major warning must be given. It is important that the worst-case-scenario pro formas show that the cash flow can service the company's debt. Otherwise, procuring financing, particularly debt financing, may prove to be virtually impossible. This does not mean that the pro formas should be developed by working backward and "plugging" numbers. For example, if the principal payments on debt obligations are $7,000 per month, it would be wrong to forecast the monthly revenue size, gross margins, and so on such that at least $7,000 in after-tax cash flow would be generated to service this obligation.

Pro formas should be developed from the top down, forecasting defensible revenues, legitimate variable costs, including labor and materials; and market-rate fixed costs such as rent. If, after developing the pro formas in this manner, it is clear that the debt cannot be serviced, the action that needs to be taken is not to plug numbers, but rather to:

- Reduce the amount of the debt.
- Lower the interest rates on the debt.
- Extend the terms of the loan.

All of these actions are designed to free up cash flow to service short-term debt.

Even if the entrepreneur is successful in raising capital using pro formas filled with plugged numbers, she will ultimately experience difficulties when the company's performance proves to be lower than the projections and the cash flow is not sufficient to meet the debt obligations. Finally, experienced business investors, such as bankers and venture capitalists, can easily detect pro formas filled with plugged numbers because the projections are typically at a level showing that all the company's debt can be serviced, with maybe a little cash left over. Therefore, do not plug numbers. A pro forma development case study for Clark Company is included at the end of Chapter 3.

CHECKLIST OF FINANCIAL INFORMATION

To enable investors to better understand the information presented in the pro formas, it is best to provide a summary of financial data and then present the detailed financial tables. Data should include:

- Historical financial statements (i.e., for 3 to 5 years):
    - Cash flow statement

- Income statement
- Balance sheet

- Pro formas (i.e., for 3 to 5 years). Financial projections (as described previously) should be provided under 3 scenarios—best, worst, and most-likely cases—where each scenario is based upon a different set of assumptions. For example, the worst-case scenario may assume no growth from Year 1 to Year 2, the best-case scenario may assume 5% growth, and the most-likely-case scenario may assume a 2% growth rate. A summary of the assumptions should also be provided.
- Detailed description of banking relationships for business accounts and payroll.
- The terms and rates of loans and their amortization period.
- The proposed financing plan, including:
  - The amount being requested.
    - Sources and uses of funds. [*Note:* This information is important for several reasons. First, financiers need to know how their funds are going to be used. Second, identifying other investors who are willing to provide you with resources (sources) will encourage potential investors to make a similar commitment—people find it easier to invest once they know that others have already done so. Third, value-added investors may be able to help you find alternative ways of getting resources.]
  - Payback and collateral.
    - Proposed strategy for the liquidation of investors' positions.
- Financing plan for the immediate term, short term, and long term.
- Working capital needs.
- Line of credit.
- Cash flow from operations—outside investors, sell debt, or IPO.

3

Financial Statement Analysis

INTRODUCTION

Sadly, it is common to hear entrepreneurs say, "I do not know anything about finance, because I was never good with numbers. Therefore, I focus on my product and let someone else worry about the numbers." Someone with such an attitude can never achieve successful high-growth entrepreneurship. Financial statement analysis is not brain surgery! Everyone can understand it. In fact, no matter how distasteful or uncomfortable it might be to the high-growth entrepreneur, he must learn and use financial statement analysis. Finance is like medicine. No one likes it because it usually tastes awful, but everyone knows that it is good for you.

PROACTIVE ANALYSIS

Entrepreneurs must engage in proactive analysis of their financial statements in order to better manage their company and influence the business decisions of the company's managers, as well as attract capital from investors and creditors.[1]

Financial statements must be used as tangible management tools, not simply as reporting documents. While the entrepreneur does not need to be able to develop these statements herself—that job is done by the CFO—she must be able to completely understand every line item. The entrepreneur who cannot do this will have a much more difficult time growing the company and raising capital. For example, one of the fundamentals of finance says that accounts receivable (A/R) and inventory should not grow at an annual rate faster than revenue growth. If they do, it is a sign that the company's working capital is being depleted because the accounts receivable and inventory represent a drag on a company's cash.

A case in point: The management team at Lucent Technologies failed to do a proactive analysis of this relationship. The result? The stock price declined 30% shortly after the company reported its 1999 financial results. The results showed that compared with the previous year, revenues had grown an impressive 20%. Unfortunately, A/R and inventory had grown 41% and 54%, respectively!

Another problem for entrepreneurs who do not analyze their financial statements proactively is that these entrepreneurs also risk being taken advantage of or exploited. There are numerous accounts of companies losing money because employees were stealing products and cash. In many instances, the theft was not recognized immediately because the owners had excluded themselves from all financial statement analysis. Not surprisingly, many of the thieves are bookkeepers, accountants, accounts receivable and payable clerks, and CFOs. All of the aforementioned are positions that are intimately involved in the company's financials.

Automated Equipment Inc. is a family-run manufacturing business in Niles, Illinois. The company's bookkeeper was a friendly 33-year-old woman who was inflating payouts to vendors, then altering the names on the checks and depositing them in accounts that were under her control. It took the company 4 years to discover the embezzlement, and by then the woman had stolen nearly $610,000, leaving the company in near financial ruin. Among other things, the bookkeeper had purchased a Cadillac sport-utility vehicle, expensive clothing, and fine meats. Oh, and she also put a $30,000 addition on her home. The theft forced the company to lay off 4 of its 11 employees, including the owner's wife and a 27-year worker. By the way, the bookkeeper had a separate federal student loan conviction from her *previous* job.

Bette Wildermuth, a longtime business broker in Richmond, Virginia, has 25 years' worth of stories of business owners getting surprised by the people they trust. Often, she's the one who catches the shenanigans when she's poring over their financials at the time of a sale. "I was asked by the owner of a fabrication company to come talk about the possibility of selling his company. He specifically asked me to come on a Wednesday afternoon because his bookkeeper would not be there. You see, he didn't want to cause her any worry over a possible job loss. After all, she'd been with his company for 15 years." Wildermuth was left alone with the books and records to try to determine a valuation. After about two hours, she said, the owner returned and proudly asked, "Did you notice that our sales are up and we're continuing to make a profit?" Wildermuth had noticed this and congratulated him. "I also told him that an astute buyer would notice that and more, and that both of us would have the same question. 'Bob,' I asked, 'Why are you paying your home mortgage from the business account?' He told me that that was impossible because his mortgage had been paid off years ago." It turned out that the sweet, Norman Rockwellesque woman who had handled his finances for 15 years was robbing him blind. She was also paying her personal Visa card from the company books. "When I told him what was going on," Wildermuth remembers, "he looked like he had been punched in the stomach."

Another great example to highlight this point is the story of Rae Puccini, who, by the time she was 55 years old, had been convicted 8 times over 2 decades for stealing money from her employers. In July 2000, while facing another conviction for the same crime, she committed suicide. Her final crime was using her position as the office manager to steal $800,000 from her employer, Edelman, Combs & Latturner (ECL), a prominent Chicago-based law firm that had hired her in 1996. The lawsuit against her stated:

> She forged signatures, cut herself "bonus" checks and transferred money from her bosses' bank account. She used the firm's American Express credit card to pay for a Caribbean cruise and a vacation at the Grand Hotel on Mackinac Island, Michigan. She also used the credit card to pay for a Mexico vacation with her boyfriend as well as groceries, flowers, furniture and liquor. Her 2000 Buick LeSabre was paid for by a $35,000 bonus that she paid herself. Her most expensive gift to herself was the $200,000 house that she purchased in the suburbs, using a $42,000 check that she cut from the firm.[2]

How did she pull off this incredible crime? First, she created a fake résumé to hide her prison record. Second, she earned her employers' trust easily. Third, she worked long hours to create an impression that she was very dedicated to the firm. As an attorney at another law firm, from which she also stole money, stated, "She ostensibly was very loyal and trusted. She came in early and stayed late."[3] The final reason was that no one in the law firm was involved in the supervision and analysis of its financials. She was practically given carte blanche, without any checks and balances. She was finally caught when the ECL partners asked her to show documentation explaining how the company's cash had been spent. When she hedged, the partners looked through her work area and found incriminating evidence.[4]

Approximately one month before her death, Puccini went to a funeral home, selected flowers, and paid for her body to be cremated. She donated many of her clothes to Goodwill and set up a postfuneral dinner at a Greek restaurant. Her final act was to type a confessional letter that included the statement, "No one knew what I was doing with the finances of ECL."[5] She was absolutely correct.

When an entrepreneur is involved in his company's finances, such sordid stories regarding losses of cash to theft can be practically eliminated because the entrepreneur's knowledge and participation serve as a deterrent.

To utilize the financial statements as management tools, the entrepreneur must have them prepared more than once a year. Having monthly financial statements developed by an outside accounting firm can be expensive. In addition, monthly statements, by definition, are short-term-focused, and analysis of them may encourage entrepreneurs to micromanage and overreact. The ideal is to produce quarterly statements, which should be completed, and be in the entrepreneur's hand for analysis, no later than 30 days following the close of a quarter.

In this chapter, we will learn that the data contained in financial statements can be analyzed to tell an interesting and compelling story about the financial condition of a business. Included in the financial statement analysis discussion will be a case study. We will examine the income statement of the Clark Company to determine what is taking place with its operations, despite the fact that we know nothing about the industry or the company's products or services. Using information provided in this statement, we will then prepare financial projections (i.e., pro formas) for the next year based on key assumptions.

Total revenues	$8,000	100.00%
COGS	2,000	25.00%
Gross margins	**$6,000**	**75.00%**
Operating expenses		
Wages	$1,000	12.50%
Rent	300	3.75%
Selling expenses	400	5.00%
Depreciation	500	6.25%
Amortization	300	3.75%
Total operating expense	**$2,500**	**31.25%**
Operating profit	**$3,500**	**43.75%**
Interest expense	200	2.50%
Profit before taxes	**$3,300**	**41.25%**
Income tax expenses	1,320	16.50%
Net income	**$1,980**	**24.75%**

Figure 3-1 **Income Statement Analysis**

INCOME STATEMENT ANALYSIS

In terms of financial analysis, all items, including expenses and the three types of margins—gross, operating, and net—mentioned in Chapter 2, are analyzed in terms of percentage of revenues. As Figure 3-1 shows, the cost of goods sold (COGS) percent plus the gross profit percent should equal 100%. The COGS percent plus the total operating expense percent plus the interest expense percent plus the tax expense percent plus the net income percent should also equal 100%.

RATIO ANALYSIS

A ratio analysis, using 2 or more financial statement numbers, may be undertaken for several reasons. Entrepreneurs, along with bankers, creditors, and stockholders, typically use ratio analysis to objectively appraise the financial condition of a company and to identify its vulnerabilities and strengths. As we will discuss later, ratio analysis is probably the most important financial tool that the entrepreneur can use to proactively operate a company. Therefore, the entrepreneur should review the various ratios that we discuss in this section at least quarterly, along with the three key financial reports: income statement, balance sheet, and cash flow statement. There are 6 key ratio categories:

- Profitability ratios
- Liquidity ratios
- Leverage (capital structure) ratios
- Operating ratios
- Cash ratios
- Valuation ratios

Table 3-1 provides a description of selected financial ratios and the formulas used to calculate them.

TABLE 3-1 Financial Accounting Ratios

Ratio	Description	Formula
Profitability ratios	**Measure earning potential.**	
Gross margin percentage	Measures the gross profit margin that the company is achieving on sales—that is, the profit after COGS is deducted from revenues.	(Sales – COGS)/sales
Return on equity	Measures the return on invested capital. Shows how hard management is making the equity in the business work.	Net income/ stockholders' equity
Net operating income return	Measures income generated from operations without regard to the company's financing and taxes.	[Sales - expenses (excluding interest)]/ sales

TABLE 3-1 ***Continued.***

Ratio	Description	Formula
Net profit margin	Measures the net profit margin that the company is achieving on sales.	Net profit/sales
Liquidity ratios	**Measure a company's ability to meet its short-term payments.**	
Current ratio	Measures whether current bills can be paid. A 2-to-1 ratio minimum should be targeted.	Current assets/current liabilities
Quick ratio (acid-test ratio)	Measures liquidity. Assesses whether current bills can be paid without selling inventory or other illiquid current assets. A 1-to-1 ratio minimum should be targeted.	(Current assets – inventory and other illiquid assets)/current liabilities
Leverage ratios	**Evaluate a company's capital structure and long-term potential solvency.**	
Debt/equity ratio	Measures the degree to which the company has leveraged itself. Ideally, the ratio should be as low as possible, giving the company greater flexibility to borrow.	Total liabilities/ stockholders' equity
Operating ratios	**Focus on the use of assets and the performance of management.**	
Days payable	Measures the speed at which the company is paying its bills. Ideally, a company should wait to pay the bills as long as possible without negatively affecting product service or shipments from suppliers.	Accounts payable/ (COGS/365)
Collection ratio ("days receivable")	Measures the quality of the accounts receivable. It shows the average number of days it takes to collect receivables. The ideal situation is to get paid as quickly as possible.	Accounts receivable/ (revenues/365)

TABLE 3-1 ***Continued.***

Ratio	Description	Formula
Inventory turns	Measures the number of times inventory is sold and replenished during a given time period. It measures the speed at which inventory is turned into sales.	COGS/average inventory outstanding
Days inventory carried	Measures the average amount of daily inventory being carried.	Inventory/(COGS/365)
Cash flow ratios	**Measure a company's cash position.**	
Cash flow cycle	Measures the number of days it takes to convert inventory and receivables into cash.	(Receivables + inventory)/COGS
Cash flow debt coverage ratio	Measures whether a company can meet its debt service requirements. A 1.25-to-1 ratio minimum should be targeted.	EBITDA/(interest + principal due on debt)
Valuation ratios	**Measure returns to investors.**	
Price/earnings (P/E) ratio	Measures the price that investors are willing to pay for a company's stock for each dollar of the company's earnings. For example, a P/E ratio of 8 means that investors are willing to pay $8 for every dollar of a company's earnings.	Price of stock/ earnings per share

A company's ratios should not be examined without a proper context, meaning, do not disregard the effect of sequential periods of time (for example, successive quarters or years). Looking at a single period renders the ratios virtually meaningless. The greatest benefit of historical and present-day ratios derived from two analytical measurements—internal and external—is the ability to do annual internal comparisons. This type of analysis will show if there are any trends within a company across time. For example, a comparison can be made of selected income statement line items across a 2-year, 5-year, or 10-year period. This type of analysis will help to assess the soundness of a company's activities as well as identify important trends. Basically, it allows the entrepreneur to answer the question, is my internal performance better today than it was last year, 5 years ago, or 10 years ago? If the answer is yes, then the next question is, how did it get better? If the answer is no, then the next question is, why didn't it get better? Deeper analysis should be undertaken to determine not only why things are getting worse, but also what is making things better. If the entrepreneur knows and understands the detailed reasons why her ratios improved over time, then she can use that information for prescriptive elements of future strategic plans.

The entrepreneur should also do an external comparison of her company's ratios against those of the industry. This comparison should be against both the industry's averages and the best and worst performers within the industry. This will allow the entrepreneur to assess the company's operations, financial condition, and activities against comparable companies. (Table 3-2 shows a comparison of turnover ratios.) Successful entrepreneurs know that respecting and understanding the competition is a basic business requirement, and the first step to take toward that endeavor is to understand how you compare with the competition. Ratio analysis is one of the most objective ways to do such measurements.

Many banks provide business loans on the condition that the company maintains certain minimum ratios, such as debt/equity, net worth, and acid test.

TABLE 3-2 **Inventory Turnover Ratios**

Store	**Turnover**
Costco	12.6
Carrefour SA	10.0
Wal-Mart	8.3
Amazon.com	8.3
Target	6.5
Barnes & Noble	3.5
Industry Avg.	2.6

Source: S&P Capital IQ, 2013.

These conditions are usually included in the covenant section of the loan agreement, Not maintaining the minimum ratios puts the company technically in default on the loan. Other investors, such as venture capitalists, may use ratio attainment as "milestones" for determining whether and when they will invest more capital. For example, they may tell the entrepreneur that his next round of financing will occur when the company achieves 50% gross margin in each of 4 consecutive quarters.

In addition to performing historical and present ratio analyses internally and externally, the entrepreneur should also use ratios to drive the future of the business. For example, the entrepreneur's strategic plans may include growing revenues while decreasing inventory. Therefore, the days of inventory carried must be reduced while the inventory turnover ratio is increased to some targeted number. Simply stating these objectives is not enough, however. After determining the respective targeted numbers, a strategic plan must be developed and implemented to actually reduce the amount of inventory carried and to ship new inventory that is received by customers quickly.

Such a relationship between the two ratios would look as shown in Table 3-3.

As you can see in the table, the amount of average daily inventory being carried decreases from 43 days' worth of inventory to 28 over a projected 5-year period. Now, if the entrepreneur's goal is also to increase revenues over this same period of time, then she must turn the smaller volume of daily inventory each year more frequently. And, as the table shows, that is in fact what the entrepreneur forecasts: to increase the inventory turns from 8 times a year to 14. The just-in-time inventory model, pioneered and perfected by Toyota Corporation, works only if a company's vendors and partners are highly synchronized.

Events outside the company's control can also cause big problems. In the aftermath of the earthquake, tsunami, nuclear alert, and power outages in

TABLE 3-3 **Inventory Ratio Comparison Example**

	2008	2009	2010	2011	2012
Inventory turns	8	11	11	12	14
Days of inventory carried	43	34	33	30	28

northeastern Japan in March 2011, for nearly 2 months, Merck KGaA, a subsidiary of a German company, temporarily ceased manufacturing and exporting Xirallic, a product used by automotive companies around the world to make "pearl-effect" paints. At the time, this Japanese factory was the only location in the world that manufactured Xirallic for customers such as Ford, Nissan, Chrysler, GM, Toyota, and Volkswagen. Toyota lost one-third of its 200 colors, affecting 20% of its vehicle volume.[6] Each automaker was forced to stop ordering new vehicles in colors that required this paint additive until full production resumed in September of that year. Merck lost an estimated $73 million in sales during the 2-month halt, and only afterward began planning to develop a second plant in Germany as a backup location.

Another proactive way to use ratios is for the entrepreneur to set short-term, medium-term, and long-term objectives with regard to internal and external ratios. For example, the short-term plan, covering the next 12 months, is to get the days receivables ratio back down to the best level in the company's 10-year history. The medium-term (i.e., 24 months) plan may be to get the company's days receivable down to at least the industry average. Finally, the long-term (i.e., 36 months) plan may be to make the company's days receivable the lowest in the industry, making it the market leader. Thus, ratios have immense value to the entrepreneur as analytical and proactive management tools. And successful entrepreneurs regularly compare their performance against historical highs, lows, and trends, as well as against the industry.

What are good and bad ratios? Well, it depends on which ratios are being examined and, more important, the specific industry. Regarding the first point, good days receivable are determined by a company's invoice terms. The standard invoice has the following terms: "2/10, net 30 days." This means that the payer can take a 2% discount if the invoice is paid within 10 days. After 10 days, the invoice's gross amount must be paid within the next 20 days. Thus, the customer is being given a total of 30 days following the date of the invoice to pay the bill. If the company does business under these terms, then days receivable of 45 days or greater are considered bad. The ideal target is to have days receivable no more than 5 days greater than the invoice.

The second factor that determines what are good and bad ratios is the industry (see Table 3-4 for good and bad key ratios for several industries). For

TABLE 3-4 **Key Ratios for Various Industries**

Industry	Ratio	Better	Worse
Software Publishing	Current ratio	2.2	0.8
	Inventory turns	n/a	n/a
	Days receivable	33.0	83.0
Grocery Stores	Current ratio	3.1	1.0
	Inventory turns	20.0	10.3
	Days receivable	0.0	3.0
Oil & Gas	Current ratio	3.0	0.7
Extraction	Inventory turns	n/a	n/a
	Days receivable	12.0	58.0
Plumbing & Heating	Current ratio	2.5	1.2
Contractors	Inventory turns	0.0	23.9
	Days receivable	27.0	74.0
Airlines	Current ratio	2.2	0.7
	Inventory turns	N/A	N/A
	Days receivable	2.0	29.0
Physicians Offices	Current ratio	2.9	1.1
	Inventory turns	n/a	n/a
	Days receivable	12.0	46.0
Chocolate Candy	Current ratio	4.4	1.4
Manufacturing	Inventory turns	7.8	3.6
	Days receivable	14.0	39.0

Source: Risk Management Association, Annual Statement Studies: Financial Ratio Benchmarks, 2013.

example, if we analyze 2 different technology industries, we will see distinctly different ideas of what are considered good operating margins. In the office equipment industry, the company with the strongest operating margin is Pitney Bowes at 15.2%.[7] That is significantly lower than that of GlaxoSmithKline, the pharmaceutical industry leader, which had an operating margin of 28%![8] As stated earlier, everything is relative. Both of these companies have significantly better operating margins than Amazon.com, whose operating margin was 1.1% in 2012.[9]

Typically, the financial ratios of successful firms are never lower than the industry average. For example, companies in the commercial airline industry carry, on average, 11 days of inventory. Alaska Air carries half that amount, or 5.5 days of inventory.[10]

There are some instances where it is perfectly acceptable for a company's ratios to be worse than the industry average. This occurs when the below-average ratios are part of the company's strategic plan. For example, inventory turns and days inventory carried that are slower and greater, respectively, than the industry average may not be signs of negative performance. It could be that the company's strategic plan requires it to carry levels of inventory greater than the industry average; as a result, inventory turns would be slower. For example, if a company promises overnight delivery, while its competitors ship in 14 days, that company's inventory carried will be higher and its turns will be slower. Ideally, the gross margins should be higher than the industry's because the company should be able to charge a premium for the faster deliveries. Given this fact, it is essential that the entrepreneur perform a comparison of industry averages when writing the business plan, when developing the projections, and, most important, before submitting the plan to prospective investors.

An example of a company that ran with higher expenses than its competitors was Commonwealth Worldwide Chauffeured Transportation. Dawson Rutter, the company's founder and CEO, dropped out of three universities before starting the company. Over a 4-year period, Commonwealth grew its business from 40 customers to 4,000 and increased its revenues over 248%. Rutter had the philosophy of "building the church for Easter Sunday." He clarified, "We create infrastructure in anticipation of revenue. That ensures delivery will be impeccable 100% of the time. We can always handle 105% of our absolute busiest day. Is that a more expensive way of doing it? You bet. But the fact is we don't lose customers, which means we can afford to pay that premium."[11]

How can entrepreneurs find out industry averages for private companies? Figure 3-2 lists periodicals and other resources that are commonly used to compare an existing company's performance with that of the industry, as well as to determine whether the pro formas in a business plan are in line with the performance of the industry being entered.

BREAKEVEN ANALYSIS

The analysis of financial statements should also be used to determine a company's breakeven (BE) point. Successful entrepreneurs know how many widgets, meals, or hours of service they have to sell, serve, or provide, respectively, before they can take any real cash out of the company. Equation 3-1 shows the equation for calculating a company's BE point.

Breakeven Point

Fixed expenses ÷ gross margin = total breakeven sales
Total breakeven sales ÷ unit price = number of units to sell (3-1)

Using the information for the Bruce Company contained in Figures 2-1 and 2-4, one can prepare a selected set of financial ratios and BE for the company. Table 3-5 shows the financial ratios, BE, and an explanation of the numbers.

Annual Statement Studies, Risk Management Association (formerly Robert Morris Associates)

Almanac of Business and Industrial Financial Ratios, Prentice Hall

Bizstats.com

Industry Norms and Key Business Ratios, Dun & Bradstreet

Risk Management Association eCompare2, online financial statement analysis tool

Value Line Investment Survey

Figure 3-2 **Industry Ratio Sources**

TABLE 3-5 **Selected Financial Accounting Ratios for the Bruce Company**

Ratio	Amount	Explanation
Gross margin percentage	75%	75 cents of every dollar of sales goes to gross profit, or the product's labor and material costs were 25 cents.
Return on equity	26%	The company is getting a return of 26% on the capital invested in the company.
Net profit margin	24.75%	More than 24 cents of every dollar of sales goes to the bottom line.
Current ratio	0.57	The ratio is less than 1, which indicates that the company can't meet its short-term financial obligations.
Quick ratio (acid-test ratio)	0.28	The ratio is less than 1, which means that the company can't pay its debt.
Debt/equity ratio	1.2	The company owes $1.20 of debt for every dollar of equity.
Collection ratio	13 days	It takes 13 days on average to collect receivables.
Inventory turns	3.33	Inventory turns 3.33 times.
Cash flow cycle	0.45 day	It would take less than a day to convert inventory to cash.
Breakeven point		BE = $700 ÷ 0.75 = $933

MEASURING GROWTH

When measuring the growth of a company, the entrepreneur should be sure to do it completely. Many people use compounded annual growth rate (CAGR) analysis when measuring and discussing growth. In addition to CAGR, another means of measurement is simple growth. Before going any further, let's discuss the two. In finance, both terms are typically used to discuss the rate of growth of money over a certain period of time.

Simple interest is the rate of growth relative to only the initial investment or original revenues. This base number is the present value (PV). Future value (FV) is the sum of the initial investment and the amount earned from the interest calculation. Thus, the simple interest rate or the rate of growth of a company with revenues of $3,885,000 in Year 1 and $4,584,300 in Year 2 is 18%, because $699,300, the difference between revenues in Years 1 and 2, is 18% of Year 1 revenues. Using the simple interest rate of 18%, Year 3's revenues would be $5,283,600. This was determined by simply adding $699,300, or 18% of the initial number, $3,885,000, to Year 2's revenue number. Therefore, an 18% simple growth rate would add $699,300 to the previous year's revenue each year to determine the level of revenues for the next year. In conclusion, the formula to determine the simple growth rate is the equation shown in Equation 3-2.

Simple Growth Rate

$$\text{Simple growth rate} = \frac{\text{dollars of growth}}{\text{initial investment} \times \text{time}} \tag{3-2}$$

Using Equation 3-2, let's input the numbers to answer the question, at what simple interest rate must $3,885,000 grow in 2 years to equal $5,283,600? Another way to look at this question is, if you received a 2-year loan of $3,885,000 at 18% simple interest, what would you owe in total principal and interest? The answer would be $5,283,600, as calculated in Figure 3-3.

Year 1 (present value)	= $3,885,000
Year 3 (future value)	= $5,283,600
Dollars of growth (or FV – PV)	= $1,398,600
Time	= 2 years

Figure 3-3 **Components of Dollar of Growth Calculation**

Year 2: $4,584,300 (i.e., $3,885,000 × 1.18)

Year 3: $5,409,474 (i.e., $4,584,300 × 1.18)

Figure 3-4 **CAGR Example**

The concept of compounding is commonly used by financial institutions such as banks with regard to both the money they lend and the deposits they receive. CAGR analysis—which is popular among professionals with graduate business school backgrounds, including consultants and commercial and investment bankers—simply shows the interest rate, compounded annually, that must be achieved to grow a company from revenues in Year 1 to revenues in a future year. That sounds similar to what we just said about simple interest. However, the word *compounded*, which is not included in the definition of simple interest, makes a huge difference. Compounding means that you earn interest not only on the initial investment (i.e., the PV), as was the case with simple growth, but also on the interest earned each year, or the actual dollars of growth. Therefore, unlike simple growth, the compounded rate of growth each year reflects the initial investment plus the earnings on reinvested earnings.

Let's use the same numbers as in the simple growth rate discussions to illustrate the concept of CAGR. A company with an 18% CAGR and Year 1 revenues of $3,885,000 will have the future revenues shown in Figure 3-4.

In comparing simple annual growth with compounded annual growth, the comparison in Table 3-6 clearly shows the latter to be more advantageous to investors or entrepreneurs who want rapid growth.

TABLE 3-6 **Simple and Compounded Annual Growth Comparison**

Revenues at 18% Rate	Simple Growth	Compounded Annually
Year 1	$3,885,000	$3,885,000
Year 2	$4,584,300	$4,584,300
Year 3	$5,283,600	$5,409,474
Year 4	$5,982,900	$6,383,179
Year 5	$6,682,200	$7,532,151

As you can see in Table 3-6, the first-year growth with compounding is the same as with simple growth because the base is the same. The shortcoming with using CAGR is that it looks at only 2 years, the beginning year and the ending year, completely ignoring the years in between. Therefore, when it is used alone, this popular growth measurement tells an incomplete story that can be misleading.

For example, 2 companies with Year 1 revenues of $3,885,000 and Year 5 revenues of $7,532,151, as shown in Table 3-7, will show the same 18% CAGR despite the fact that the revenues in Years 2, 3, and 4 looked very different.

The reason why both companies have the same CAGR is that both had the same revenues in Year 1 and Year 5. The formula for CAGR considers only these 2 data points. It ignores what happens in between because theoretically, based on the information given about Year 1 and Year 5 and based on how CAGR is calculated, CAGR means that in any given year throughout the 5-year period, the company's annual compounded growth in revenues was an even 18%. That is to say, the growth followed a linear progression. But as Table 3-7 shows, that is not always the case. Company 2's revenues declined in three consecutive years. So the major shortcoming of using CAGR is that it does not take into account the actual growth rates from year to year over the 5-year period. Therefore, a more complete analysis using CAGR must include the analysis of real annual growth rates to see if there are any trends.

Finally, if we want to determine the actual revenues in Year 5 (i.e., FV) of a company that had revenues of $3,885,000 in Year 1 (PV) and was growing at a compounded annual rate of 18%, the formula shown in Figure 3-5 could be used.

TABLE 3-7 **CAGR Comparison**

	Company 1	**Company 2**
Year 1	$3,885,000	$3,885,000
Year 2	$4,584,300	$3,000,000
Year 3	$5,409,474	$2,900,000
Year 4	$6,383,179	$2,700,000
Year 5	$7,532,151	$7,532,151

Future value = present value x (1 + Year 1 rate) x
(1 + Year 2 rate) x (1 + Year 3 rate) x (1 + Year 4 rate)

Future value = $3,885,000 x (1.18) x (1.18) x (1.18) x (1.18)

Future value = $3,885,000 x $(1.18)^4$

Future value = $7,532,151

Note: 1 is added to each year's interest rate to show that for every dollar invested, 18% will be returned.

Figure 3-5 **Sample Future Value Calculation**

CASE STUDY—CLARK COMPANY

Figure 3-6 presents an income statement for the Clark Company for 3 years. There is no information given regarding the company's industry, products, or services. This information is not needed. Numbers alone can tell a story, and every entrepreneur must get comfortable with being able to review financial statements, understand what is going on with the company, and recognize its strengths, weaknesses, and potential value. A successful entrepreneur must have the ability, willingness, and comfort to make decisions based on ambiguous, imperfect, or incomplete information. The analysis of Figure 3-6 gives you the opportunity to demonstrate this trait. As you will see, it is an itty-bitty, tiny business. Nevertheless, the analysis would be exactly the same if each line item were multiplied by $1 million. The point being made is that the analysis of a small company's financials is the same as that of a large company's. The only difference is the number of zeros to the left of the decimal points. An appropriate analogy can be made to swimming. If you can swim in 4 feet of water, you can also swim in 10 feet of water and deeper.

By examining the income statement, we will be able to better understand how management is handling the company's overall operations. Using financial ratio analysis, we will assess how well the company's resources are being managed. A good analysis will enable a potential buyer to assess, for example, whether the company is worth acquiring, based on its strengths and weaknesses, and to determine how much to pay for it.

	2010	2011	2012
Revenues	137,367	134,352	113,456
Returns and allowances			588
Cost of goods sold	42,925	38,032	40,858
Gross profits	**94,442**	**96,320**	**72,010**
Operating expenses			
Advertising	3,685	3,405	2,904
Bad debts	150	50	130
Automobile expense	1,432	460	732
Depreciation	1,670	1,670	835
Employee benefits programs			
Insurance	2,470	2,914	1,915
Interest			
Mortgage			
Other	153		2,373
Legal and professional services	1,821	1,493	
Office expense	10,424	8,218	8,965
Rent	14,900	20,720	13,360
Repairs and maintenance	1,293	2,025	
Supplies	305	180	195
Taxes and licenses	11,473	5,790	1,062
Travel	730	1,125	
Meals and entertainment	108	220	192
Utilities	2,474	2,945	2,427
Wages	5,722	11,349	12,214
Other			
Freight	1,216	1,645	874
Sales tax			7,842
Total expenses	**60,026**	**64,209**	**56,020**
Net profit or loss	**34,416**	**32,111**	**15,990**

* *Note*: The cash accounting method was used for 2010 and 2011. The accrual accounting method was used for 2012

Figure 3-6 **Clark Company Income Statement (Selected Years)**

When analyzing the numbers, it is important to (1) look at the numbers and compare them with historical performance or with a benchmark such as an industry average, to assess how the company is performing in that specific area, and (2) highlight any trends. The importance of trends as one looks at financial statements is that they are used to predict the future. One should always ask: Is there a trend in this line item? Is it an upward or a downward trend? What are the main reasons for this trend? What does the trend mean for the future?

The following assumptions should be made in the analysis of the Clark Company case:

- This company is a cash business; there are no receivables.
- It is owner-operated.
- The numbers provided are correct.

An analysis of every line item could be made, but our analysis will focus on three of the most important items: revenue, gross profit, and net profit.

Revenue Analysis

The analysis of a company's historical annual revenue includes answers to the following questions: What are the sales growth rates for the past few years? What is the trend in sales growth? Is it declining or increasing? Why are revenues increasing or decreasing? Not only should you be concerned about whether or not revenues are increasing, but you should also ask whether the increase is consistent with what is taking place in the industry. Sales increasing for a short period may not be good enough. You need to compare a company's sales growth with the rate at which you want it to grow. The absolute minimum amount that you want sales to grow, at an annual rate, is at the rate of inflation, which from 1914 through 2012 averaged approximately 3.35% per year.[12] For example, in the professional sports industry, since 2003, the average annual percentage increase in ticket prices for the 4 major sports leagues (i.e., the NBA, NFL, NHL, and MLB) has been 3.39%.[13] The revenue in the solar panel manufacturing industry from 2003 to 2012 rose 32.3%.[14]

Revenue for the Clark Company has been declining. Revenues declined by 2% between 2010 and 2011 and by 16% between 2011 and 2012. This downward trend is a cause for concern. Some of the reasons for the decline in revenues may be:

- Price increases resulting from higher costs.
- The owner is despondent, and either he is not managing his business properly or he simply is not present at the company.
- Increased competition, as a result of the high gross margins, could be putting pressure on prices. One way to keep prices high is to have a patent on a product, which allows the owner to set the price fairly high. This assumes, of course, that there is a demand for the product or service. When the patent expires, the business will inevitably face competition.
- The product could be becoming obsolete.
- An unanticipated event or an act of God, known in the legal profession as a "force majeure," could be one reason for the decline in revenue. For example, there could have been a tornado or a severe rainstorm, and the storage area where the entire inventory was kept could have been flooded, thereby damaging inventory and reducing the volume that was available for sale.
- There could have construction outside of the company's place of business that prevented easy access by customers.

Thus, there are, in some instances, legitimate reasons why revenue could be decreasing that have nothing to do with the soundness of the business or its management. When undertaking financial analysis, it is important to consider all likely scenarios.

While strong revenue growth is typically viewed positively, it can also be a sign of bad tidings. The fundamentals of finance associate excellent revenue increases with at least corresponding increases in the company's net income. The best example of this point is Microsoft. From 1990, when Microsoft introduced its Windows 3.0 operating system, to 1999, its revenues grew 17 times, from $1.18 billion to $19.8 billion. During the same time period, its net income grew an astounding 28 times, from $279 million to $7.79 billion! On a larger scale, the Fortune 500 demonstrated this concept in historic fashion between 2000 and 2006. Aided by strong productivity gains and a growing economy, the largest American companies grew earnings an astonishing 80% while revenue growth grew 38%. During this period, posttax profit margins hit 7.9%, a 27% increase over the already impressive 6.2% margins in 2000.[15]

But if revenues are growing because prices have been lowered, then that means that the company is probably growing at the expense of margins. Therefore, the growth may not, in fact, be profitable. For example, during the period from 1991 to 1997, Hewlett-Packard's revenue from personal computers increased dramatically to approximately $9 billion in annual revenues. Also during this period, its market share increased from 1 to 4%. In 1998, with the support of price cuts, sales increased 13%. Despite all this good news, HP's hardware business experienced a loss of in excess of $100 million.[16]

Another issue with regard to revenue growth that you should be aware of is that the growth may be occurring because competitors are conceding the market. Competitors may be leaving the market because the product will soon be obsolete; or perhaps they are leaving because the ever-increasing cost of doing business—things such as liability insurance—is driving them out of the market. Thus, it is just as important for the entrepreneur to know why she is experiencing excellent growth as it is to know the reasons for low or no growth. The successful entrepreneur knows that revenues should be grown strategically. It is well-managed growth that ultimately improves the profitability of the company.

Sometimes growing too fast can be just as damaging as not growing at all. A few problems that are common when rapid growth occurs are poor quality, late deliveries, an overworked labor force, cash shortages, and brand dilution. Unmanaged growth is usually not profitable. For example, Michael Dell, the founder of Dell Computers, which grew 87% per year for the first 8 years and 27% annually since 1992, said, "I've learned from experience that a company can grow too fast. You have to be careful about expanding too quickly because you won't have the experience or the infrastructure to succeed."[17] This comment was made after he experienced a $94 million charge against earnings in 1993 for, among other things, the failure of a line of poor-quality laptops.

The story of 180s, a sports apparel company, further demonstrates the dangers of growing too fast. At one point, the company was ranked number 32 on the prestigious Inc. 500 list of fastest-growing companies. The firm grew revenues from $1 million in 1999 to $50 million in 2004. However, by 2005,

180s was suffocating under too much debt and was taken over by a private equity firm. Lamenting the company's impending sale, Bernie Tenenbaum, a venture capitalist who had considered investing in 180s at one point, said, "I'd say they'd be lucky to get 10 cents on the dollar." Actually, he was optimistic—it turned out to be 8 cents on the dollar. Bill Besselman, a onetime partner with the co-owners of the firm, explains their failure: "In the end, they grew the top line, but they didn't manage the bottom line. They got sucked into the vortex."[18]

Even Starbucks, one of the greatest entrepreneurial stories of all time, at one point suffered from unmanageable growth that diluted its brand and caused it to fall behind Dunkin' Donuts in customer loyalty. Starbucks chairman Howard Schultz explained how growing too fast caused this problem: "Over the past ten years, in order to achieve the growth, development, and scale necessary to go from less than 1,000 stores to 13,000 stores and beyond, we have had to make a series of decisions that, in retrospect, have led to the watering down of the Starbucks experience, and, what some might call the commoditization of our brand."[19] In 2008, Starbucks took steps to correct this problem by announcing the closing of 600 underperforming stores across the United States.

The Largest Customer

Inherent in the growth issue is a key question: How large is the company's largest customer? Ideally, an entrepreneur's largest customer should account for no more than 10 to 15% of the company's total revenues. The reasoning is that a company should be able to lose its largest customer and still remain in business. Of course, the ideal is often not the reality. One survey of 300 manufacturers in the apparel and home goods industries showed that over half of these firms received more than 20% of their sales from their largest customer.[20] The goal should be to diversify your client base while maintaining the benefits of economies of scale. An example of a company that suffered as a result of not properly diversifying is Boston Communications Group, Inc. (BCGI). In 2004, Verizon Wireless, which represented approximately 20% of BCGI sales, decided to end the relationship between the two companies.[21] BCGI's shares, which had traded as high as $22 in 2003, dropped 50% in one year. The company was unable to recover. In 2006, it laid off 21% of its workforce and fired two of its top officials.

The company was finally purchased in 2007 by India-based Megasoft Ltd. for $3.60 per share, less than 20% of its 2003 value.[22]

Interestingly, many companies find that losing the customer that generates the largest amount of revenue actually improves the company's profitability, because the largest customers are rarely the most profitable. The reason is that customers who purchase large volumes are often invoiced at lower prices. For example, Morse Industries, a private lamp manufacturer, was ecstatic when it got Wal-Mart Stores, Inc. ("Wal-Mart"), the country's largest retailer, as a customer. The addition of Wal-Mart increased its revenue by more than 50% in 1 year. But after 1 year, the company decided to drop Wal-Mart as a customer. Why? The revenues of Morse Industries had grown enormously, but the gross, operating, and net margins had actually declined because the company charged Wal-Mart 25% less than it charged its other customers. Another reason for the decline was that Wal-Mart's orders were so large that Morse Industries' labor force could barely produce enough. The result was that orders placed by other consumers, who were not receiving a discount and therefore were generating higher margins, were being delayed or even canceled. Several of these long-term, excellent, paying customers quietly moved their business from Morse Industries to another supplier.

The founder of Morse solved the company's problem after he performed an analysis of his company's growth and found that it was not profitable. His analysis included using the matrix shown in Figure 3-7 to define each customer and the importance of that customer.

High volume Low margin	High volume Low margin
Low volume low margin	Low volume High margin

Source: Susan Greco, "Choose or Lose," *Inc.*, December 1998, p. 58.

Figure 3-7 **Customer Analysis Matrix**

He defined the categories as follows:

- *High volume/low margin.* Customers that provided revenues greater than $1 million per year, with gross margins of no more than 35%.
- *Low volume/low margin.* Customers that provided revenues of less than $1 million per year, with gross margins of no more than 35%.
- *Low volume/high margin.* Customers that provided revenues of less than $1 million per year, with gross margins in excess of 35%.
- *High volume/high margin.* Customers that provided revenues greater than $1 million per year, with gross margins in excess of 35%.

His initial response was simply to drop the customers in the low-volume/low-margin section. But on second thought, he decided to analyze the data even further to determine how profitable each customer was to the company by performing a contribution margin analysis on each customer.

Equation 3-3 shows the contribution margin formula.

Contribution Margin

Revenues – variable costs = contribution margin
→ Fixed costs and profits (3-2)

The contribution margin is the difference between revenues and all the variable costs (i.e., the costs that would not be incurred if this customer left) associated with a unit of product. Therefore, it is the profit available, after break-even, to contribute to the company's fixed costs and profits.

The contribution margin analysis is presented in Table 3-8. Clearly, as you can see from the table, the least profitable business was not the low-margin/low-volume business, but rather the high-volume/low-margin business. Therefore, Morse attempted to raise its prices to customers who fell into these two categories. Several of them refused to accept the price increase, including Wal-Mart, so he dropped them. His growth strategy for returning the company to profitability included attempting to grow the volume of the remaining customers, who fell into the high-volume/high-margin and low-volume/high-margin categories,

TABLE 3-8 **Customer Analysis Calculation**

	High Volume/ Low Margin/	Low Volume/ Low Margin	Low Volume/ High Margin	High Volume/ High Margin
Annual revenues	$12,000,000	$800,000	$900,000	$3,000,000
Variable costs	10,000,000	600,000	500,000	1,500,000
Contribution margin	$2,000,000	$200,000	$400,000	$1,500,000
Percentage	**17%**	**25%**	**44%**	**50%**

without decreasing prices. The second part of the strategy was the implementation of a policy that all new business had to have at least a 40% contribution margin. While his revenues in the immediate term went down, his net profits and cash flow increased dramatically. Ultimately, his revenues increased, as a result of his ability to maintain high quality standards and ship promptly. Most important, his profit dollars and percentages also increased.

The lesson: growth for the sake of growth, without regard to profitability, is both foolish and harmful and will inevitably lead to insolvency. Many businesses engage in such growth in the name of gaining market share. But evidence repeatedly shows that the companies with the strongest market share are rarely the most profitable. A study of more than 3,000 public companies showed that more than 70% of the time, firms with the greatest market share do not have the highest returns, as the examples in Figure 3-8 show. The study found that the key to success for smaller, more profitable competitors was their absolute vigilance in controlling costs and eliminating customers who returned low margins.

Two examples illustrate the danger of focusing on sales. In 2012, Toyota sold approximately 9.75 million vehicles worldwide and U.S. carmaker General Motors sold 9.29 million vehicles.[23] Toyota earned $14 billion in profit, while its American counterpart, GM, lost $31 billion.[24] How did this happen? GM obviously wasn't focusing on profits. In the world of video game consoles, the importance of profitability rather than market share was demonstrated in the

Category	High Market Share	Higher Returns
Discount stores	Wal-Mart	Family Dollar
Office furniture	Ricoh Company Ltd	Chyron Corp.
Pharmaceuticals	Johnson & Johnson	Alcon, Inc.

Figure 3-8 **High Market Share versus High Returns**

battle among Nintendo, Sony, and Microsoft. Sony's Playstation and Microsoft's Xbox consoles had dominated the market for years. In early 2006, however, Nintendo recorded close to a billion dollars in profit on its Wii console, while Sony's game division was barely profitable and Microsoft lost money on Xbox.[25] Neither of the three console-makers could withstand the economic slowdown, however, from 2007 to 2012, as sales declined consistently for each company. By 2012, Nintendo's operating profits weakened to negative $386 million on $6.7 billion in sales.[26]

Additional support for the case for looking at the bottom line comes from evidence from a survey completed by J. Scott Armstrong and Kesten C. Green that showed that companies that adopt what they call "competitor-oriented objectives" actually end up hurting their own profitability. To restate their point, the more a firm tries to beat its competitors, as opposed to maximize profits, the worse it will fare. A 2006 Harvard Business School study, "Manage for Profit, Not for Market Share,"[27] estimated that companies that let market share or sales volume guide their actions sacrifice 1 to 3% of their revenue. In hard numbers, a manager of a $5 billion business leaves between $50 and $150 million in his customers' and competitors' pockets every year by focusing on market share rather than on the bottom line.

GROSS MARGINS

One of the initial financial ratios that business financiers examine when reviewing the income statement is the gross margin. What is a good gross margin? Well, a "good" gross margin, like all the other items we will be analyzing, is relative and depends on the industry in which a company operates. In general, gross margins of 35% and above are considered to be very good. Table 3-9 provides comparative gross margins for different companies.

Gasoline stations generally have razor-thin gross margins, ranging between 9 and 11%.[27] Desktop and laptop hardware, which have become commoditized products, have gross margins that are also very slim, which makes it difficult for their makers to compete. The average price at which a retailer sells a computer is only about 10 to 15% higher than what it costs to produce it. However, some computer hardware manufacturers have been able to achieve gross margins that are higher than the industry average.

There are several industries in which companies make very decent gross margins. For example, Nike's average gross margin is about 43.6%, whereas

TABLE 3-9 **Comparative Gross Margin Percentages**

Company/Industry	Gross Margin, %
Amazon.com	24.75
Hewlett-Packard	23.2
Google	58.9
Nike	43.6
Starbucks (2000)	56.0
Starbucks (2007)	23.3
Starbucks (2012)	56.3
Starbucks—espresso	90.0
Starbucks—coffee	70.0
Kroger	20.6
eBay	70.0
Yahoo!	67.5
Salesforce.com	77.6
Microsoft	74.0

Source: Company financial statements for fiscal year end 2012 as compiled by Hoovers/Dun & Bradstreet Company; accessed August 2013.

Starbucks, as indicated in Table 3-9, applies toward its gross profit 70 cents of every dollar it makes selling coffee. Or more profoundly, as Table 3-9 also shows, a cup of Starbucks espresso, with a 90% gross margin, costs only 10% of its selling price![28] Starbucks' overall corporate gross margin had fallen to roughly 23% in 2007, which is less than half of what its margins had been just 7 years earlier, but rebounded to its historical level of above 56% by 2012. Much of the drop was attributed to the increasing percentage of food and other lower-margin products sold in Starbucks stores alongside the coffee cups. Microsoft still enjoys a gross margin of 74%.

Gross margins are also very high in other businesses, some of them illegal. University of Chicago economist Steven Levitt and Harvard sociologist Sudir Venkadisch undertook an analysis of the financial books of a drug gang—a very rare set of financial statements to analyze. Not surprisingly, they found that the gang was able to reap very high gross margins—approximately 80%— by selling crack cocaine.[29]

A venture capitalist once stated, "Gross margin is the entrepreneur's best friend. It can absorb all manner of adversity with two exceptions, philanthropy or pricing stupidity. Actually, in this case the two are synonymous."[30] Good gross margins provide a novice entrepreneur with breathing space, allowing her a chance to make costly mistakes and still be potentially profitable. On the other hand, in a low-gross-margin business—such as grocery stores, for example—management mistakes and waste, as well as theft and pilferage, must be minimized, because the margins are too thin to be able to absorb these costs. A low-gross-margin business must also have volume, whereas a high-gross-margin business may be able to sacrifice unit volume sales because its ultimate profit comes from the high margins. The ideal business, like eBay, dominates its industry in terms of units of volume, while at the same time maintaining high gross margins. This is a rarity. High-gross-margin industries inevitably attract competitors who compete on price, thereby reducing gross margins throughout the industry.

For example, independent retailers of books used to enjoy gross margins in excess of 35%. Those attractive gross margins were the primary reason that Amazon.com entered the market and now dominates it. In fact, 25 years ago, independent retailers sold 60% of all book titles. Since 1991, the independents' share of the book market has declined from 32% to 10%. The big competitors increased because of the attractiveness of the gross margins.[31]

I always tell my MBA students, "If you leave here, start your own business, and are lucky enough to have good gross margins, for God's sake, don't brag about it." If someone asks you, "How's business?" your standard reply should be a simple shrug of the shoulders and a polite response of, "Not bad; could always be better."

Gross margins are a factor that the entrepreneur should focus on very heavily, both in the business plan and in operations. Good, healthy gross margins do not usually happen by chance. They may happen by chance for the "mom-and-pop" entrepreneur who runs a business haphazardly. Because the strategy is to sell whatever it can sell at whatever cost, the mom-and-pop enterprise expects to absorb the costs and take whatever falls to the bottom line.

A high-growth entrepreneur, in contrast, is one who manages with a plan in mind. This entrepreneur expects to grow the company at a certain rate and plans to have a certain level of gross margins. A high-growth entrepreneur is one who wants to have a company for the purpose of wealth creation and therefore is an absolute bulldog when it comes to managing gross margins. The question that logically follows is, how can gross margins be increased?

Cut Labor and/or Material Costs

The following are ways to reduce labor costs:

- Train the workforce to increase productivity.
- Reduce the labor force and have fewer employees work more efficiently. Cisco, the global leader in networking equipment, reduced its 66,000-strong workforce by 4,000 in late 2013, at the same time it reported a quarterly profit of $2.3 billion, which was 18% higher than the $1.9 billion in profit generated in the same quarter of the prior year.
- Reduce employee absenteeism (employees who do not show up for work without notice), which results in increased labor costs because of the need for expensive temp or overtime pay. In the call center industry, for example, average per day absenteeism is 6%; outsourced

call centers face 10% per day absenteeism rates, while in-house telecommunications firms experience only 4.8%.[32]

- Make the workforce more productive by upgrading technology. For example, McDonald's franchisees reduced labor costs through automation, to the point where 1 person can now do what it used to take 4 people to do in terms of cooking and food preparation.
- Increase volume. The cost per item produced or cost per service rendered should go down as the volume goes up. Labor costs should go down as employees gain more experience. People learn more and therefore should become more efficient, even if this is not done through the introduction of new technology.
- Find a cheaper labor force. Companies can move their operations to a different region of the country or abroad, where labor is cheaper. For example, Nike manufactures all its products outside the United States in low-labor-cost countries such as China and Thailand, where unskilled labor can cost as little as $0.67 per hour, or 3% of the average hourly compensation cost for production workers in the United States for the same year. Even skilled labor can be significantly cheaper outside the United States. Draft Dynamix, the leading fantasy sports draft software company, used software programmers in India to build its first product. The programmers cost approximately $20 per hour for work that costs as much as $75 per hour in the United States. Over the course of a year, outsourcing the work to India saved Draft Dynamix in excess of $90,000. The CEO of Draft Dynamix, Ted Kasten, provided perspective on overseas labor: "I would caution that it isn't a one-for-one savings. Working with overseas software consultants and programmers requires more time per task than a U.S. based programmer due to time differences and distance." "Still," he explained, "we wouldn't have made it without these programmers. The cash we saved from these labor costs enabled us to survive long enough to start generating revenue." Draft Dynamix was ultimately able to license its product to CBS Sportline and ESPN.com, two of the leading fantasy sports websites on the Internet, and secured another round of angel financing.

- Provide employees with stock options, restricted stock units, or other incentive programs in lieu of higher salaries.
- Reduce employee benefit costs. Employer health insurance premiums have risen 81% since 2000. In fact, a survey of small businesses conducted by the National Federation of Independent Business and Wells Fargo showed that the cost of health insurance was the number 1 concern of small-business owners. The world of health insurance is ever changing, but options such as health savings accounts, health reimbursement arrangements and government-sponsored benefits included in the Affordable Care Act offer mechanisms enabling employers to control costs.[33]
- Continually turn over the workforce, reducing the number of higher-paid unskilled workers. For example, fast-food restaurants expect and want a certain amount of annual turnover in their unskilled employees because newer workers cost less.
- Implement good management skills. One of the easiest ways to reduce labor costs is simply for entrepreneurs to manage their employees. They need to follow the good old way of managing people, which means stating expectations, giving employees the necessary tools, and holding them accountable for their performance.

The following are ways to reduce material costs:

- Obtain competitive bids from suppliers, which may allow for the purchase of materials at lower cost.
- Buy in higher volumes to get volume discounts. The problem here is the inventory carrying cost. Ideally, one does not want to increase inventory. Therefore, the entrepreneur should make commitments to its suppliers to buy a certain volume within a specified period of time. Such a commitment should result in price-volume discounts. The commitment versus buy strategy allows entrepreneurs to keep inventories low, costs down, and cash available for other investments or uses.
- Outsource part of the production. Someone else may be able to produce a piece of a product or render a specific part of a service at a lower cost.

- Use a substitute material that can be purchased at a lower cost in the production process. Ideally, you want to keep the quality of the product the same, but there is a possibility that you can actually get a substitute material that may be less expensive.
- Manage waste, pilferage, and obsolescence. Materials that have been stolen, thrown away, or destroyed, or that are just sitting around because of obsolescence, negatively affect material costs.
- Do quality control checks throughout the various stages of the manufacturing process before additional value is added. This is in contrast to the traditional way of checking quality only at the end of the process. Waste and rework costs are always greater when you use the process of checking quality at the end.
- Let the most experienced and trained people perform the most detail-oriented or labor-intensive work—for example, cutting all patterns—because they should be able to get more cuts per square yard than an inexperienced person. For example:

	Worker 1	**Worker 2**
Material cost per yard	$10	$10
Units cut per yard	4	2
Cost per unit	$2.50	$5

Thus, the cost per unit for Worker 1 is lower because there is less material wasted.

Raise the Price

Raising the price of the product or service will enable the entrepreneur to increase gross margins, assuming, of course, that costs do not increase proportionately. While a great deal is made in the press of the various factors that can allow a company to have pricing power, the best way to increase profitability through price increases is by differentiating and creating value for which the consumer will pay. Linear Technology Corporation, a $1.3 billion semiconductor company based in Milpitas, California, is a prime example of creating pricing power through differentiation. In contrast to industry heavyweights like Intel, which focus on bigger clients with huge demand for commodity-like chips, Linear has chosen to operate on the periphery and sell to smaller clients with needs that Linear can service better than the competition. The result? Linear's chips are priced a third more than its rivals', and the company made a 45% net profit margin in FY2012, besting the tech industry's best-known profit powerhouses, Microsoft Corp. and Google Inc., which earned 23% and 21%, respectively.[34]

Amazingly, there have been companies that, for a short time, were successful in challenging the importance of business fundamentals with regard to gross margins. For the most part, this was true in the e-commerce industry during the dot-com boom, where most companies were primarily focused on growing revenues, even when it was at the expense of gross margins. For example, buy .com formerly sold merchandise, including CDs, books, videos, software, and computer equipment, at cost and, shockingly, sometimes even below cost. The company guaranteed that it had the lowest prices available on the Internet. The result was zero and sometimes negative gross margins! Despite these facts, buy .com, which was founded in 1996, had 1998 revenues of $111 million and a public market valuation in excess of $400 million.[35]

But reality set in, and by September 2001, the vultures were circling with stockholder class action lawsuits. In just over a year, buy.com's stock price had dropped from its opening-day price of just over $30 a share to about $0.08 per share. Its stock was delisted from the Nasdaq on August 14, 2001. Infamous cases of this kind—where managers "fumble the fundamentals"—play out every day in far more subtle ways in every business sector. When entrepreneurs ignore the fundamentals of finance or simply trust someone else to stand guard, they invite trouble to the table.

Before we close this section on gross margin, let us analyze the Clark Company. What are the gross margins for the Clark Company? They are as follows:

- 2010: 70%
- 2011: 72%
- 2012: 64%

The company has excellent gross margins—in excess of 60% for all 3 years. However, one sees an 8 percentage point decline in gross margins in 2012, indicating that something has changed.

What are some of the possible reasons for a decline in gross margins?

- There may have been a change in the product mix being sold. A higher percentage of lower-margin items may have been sold.
- The cost of supplies may have gone up.
- The company may have changed its accounting system from a cash system to an accrual system (as, in fact, it did). This change in accounting system does not change the timing of cash receipts; and since this is a cash business, and therefore the company does not have receivables, the change in the system will not affect the timing of when revenues are recognized. However, the change in the accounting system forces the company to recognize costs earlier. The result of this change is potentially lower gross margins because costs are being recognized earlier, and therefore lower net profit as well.
- The company may be buying from different suppliers at higher costs and/or selling to different customers.

An examination of the income statement shows that 2012 was the first year in which products were returned. Also, and more important, as the note at the bottom of the statement shows, there was a change in the accounting method, from cash to accrual. As we just stated, the change does not affect revenues, because this is a cash business, but it does have a negative effect on all 3 margins because more expenses are being recognized. Therefore, as a result of the change, we are not comparing "apples to apples" with the prior year.

NET MARGINS

What are acceptable net margins? We've determined that the Clark Company has outstanding gross margins. But how do its net margins compare? In general, net margins of 5% or better are considered very good. According to Hussman Funds, since 1955, the average profit margins of the 500 largest U.S. companies have ranged between 5.5% and 7.5%. In 2012, the S&P 500 Index of U.S. companies generated a posttax profit margin of 8.4%.[36] The top 10 companies in the S&P Index in terms of net margin are shown in Table 3-10.

Privately owned companies want to minimize taxes, and therefore they reduce operating income, which in turn reduces their net income. The point being made is that for these companies, net income is usually a manipulated number that understates the company's true financial performance. A few exceptions might be companies that are preparing to go public or be sold. These companies may want to look as financially strong as possible.

In contrast, a publicly owned company aggressively seeks positive net margins, as high as possible, because the net margin affects the stock price. As one money manager remarked, "There is a greater tendency among companies to pull out the stops to generate the kind of positive earnings that Wall Street demands."[37]

The greatest example of this kind of chicanery was the case of Enron, the onetime darling of Wall Street. Through off-balance-sheet transactions, Enron

TABLE 3-10 Net Margins of Top 10 S&P 500 Companies

Company	Net Margin, % (CY2012)
Yahoo! Inc.	79.1
Regeneron Pharmaceuticals, Inc.	54.4
Public Storage	50.2
HCP, Inc.	43.8
Intercontinental Exchange, Inc.	40.5
Avalonbay Communities Inc.	40.0
Equity Residential	39.6
MasterCard Incorporated	37.3
SLM Corporation	37.2
Verisign, Inc.	36.6

Source: S&P Capital IQ; accessed August 28, 2013.

masked hundreds of millions of dollars of losses in its effort to continually beat analysts' estimates. The house of cards eventually crumbled, and 1 year after ranking number 7 on the Fortune 500, Enron filed for bankruptcy. The carnage was severe, with more than 5,600 employees losing their jobs, and in many cases their life savings. More than 20,000 creditors were left holding $63 billion in debt, and tens of billions in shareholder value was lost.[38,39]

Government regulation has targeted this kind of fraudulent behavior, and it has had an impact. A 2002 survey indicated that 59% of CFOs disclosed more information in financial statements than they had previously done, and 57% said that they planned to disclose more information in the next 12 months.[40] Moreover, the Sarbanes-Oxley reform act targeted this kind of abuse and changed the way in which corporate boardrooms and audit firms operate. However, this problem will never completely go away. Therefore, when analyzing the financial statements of a privately or publicly owned company, beware. Things—especially net income—may be significantly different from what the statements show.

The problem with looking just at net income for a public or a private company is that income does not pay the bills. Cash flow pays the bills. Net income typically understates the company's cash flow because it includes noncash expenses such as depreciation and amortization. In addition, expenditures that have nothing to do with the operation of the company may also be included, thereby lowering the company's net income. It is common for owners of private companies to run certain personal expenditures through their income statement because they view this as one of the perks of ownership. Therefore, one must realize that net income can be, and usually is, a manipulated number. For example, the late Leona Helmsley, owner of several upscale hotels in New York while she was alive, made improvements to her personal home and charged them against her company, thereby reducing the taxes owed. She was convicted of tax evasion as a result and served time in prison. One of the smoking guns used to convict her was an employee who quoted her as saying, "Only poor people pay taxes."

The reality that net income can be a manipulated number is best illustrated by a controversy regarding the 1995 movie *Forrest Gump*. The movie has grossed more than $600 million worldwide, making it one of the highest-grossing movies in history. A fellow who agreed to take a percentage of the movie's net income as his compensation wrote the story. Believe it or not, this movie never reported a positive net income, and thus the writer was due nothing. The issue was in dispute for a number of years before being resolved, finally opening the door for the long-awaited sequel to the original blockbuster. What's the entrepreneurial moral of the story? As an investor, never agree to take a percentage of the net income because you cannot control the expenses, be they real or make-believe.

Conversely, if you are the entrepreneur, always try to compensate investors based on net income, never on revenues. Basing compensation on revenues has gotten many entrepreneurs in financial trouble, because giving someone a percentage of revenues ("off the top") ignores whether a company has a positive cash flow.

The final problem that must be highlighted, with regard to putting too much importance on net earnings, is that the net earnings figure does not tell you where the earnings came from. Did they come from strong company operations or from financial instruments? A fundamentally sound company derives most of its earnings from operations, specifically from product sales or services rendered, not from interest earned on invested capital. The primary reliance upon interest earned would force the company to be in the money management business.

Before we close this section, let us analyze the net income of the Clark Company. The net margins for the Clark Company are 25, 24, and 14% for 2010, 2011, and 2012, respectively. This would indicate that the company's net margins are outstanding. The trend, however, is downward, with the caveat that the final year was negatively affected by the change in accounting method previously discussed.

OTHER ISSUES TO CONSIDER

Is the Owner Managing the Business Full Time?

When evaluating the income statement of the Clark Company, one can find evidence that the owner may not be at the place of business on a full-time basis. First, there is an increase in wages, which may represent the hiring of a new employee to run the business because the owner is taking more time off. An examination of a company's financial statements requires a thorough analysis of the wages section. It is important to ask: Who are the employees?

Do these employees actually exist? In some cities like Chicago, dead men have been known to vote in elections, and they also appear on city payrolls. During the due diligence, if the name of an employee is provided, you should look to see whether the last name of the employee matches that of the owner. It would also be wise to follow up with the question, "How many employees are relatives, and what are their specific tasks and responsibilities?" Wages may have increased because a relative of the owner has been added to the payroll and is being paid an exorbitant wage for doing nothing or for doing something as simple as opening and locking up the company every day.

Figure 3-9 presents financial projections for 2013 for the Clark Company, based on historical information.

How can you be sure that the numbers are correct? In all likelihood, they will not be. It is rare that the actual numbers meet the projections. Pro forma development is simply educated guessing.

Revenues

Historically, if we look at the Clark Company pro forma income statement shown in Figure 3-9, the best case is a decrease in revenue of 2%; the worst case is a decrease of 16%. And the most-likely-case scenario is taken as an average of these two extremes—a decrease of 9%. This is a reasonable, logical argument for preparing the projections for sales revenue.

Gross Margins

With regard to gross margins, there were no clear trends during the 3 years of data that were provided. Gross margins increased between 2010 and 2011 and then declined between 2011 and 2012. The best-case gross margin would be 72%, the worst-case gross margin would be 64%, and the most-likely-case scenario would be an average of the two—68%. Again, there is very logical reasoning behind the development of these projections, which is what financiers hope to find.

	Best Case	Worst Case	Most Likely Case
Income			
Gross sales	111,187	95,303	103,245
Returns and allowances			
Cost of goods sold	31,132	35,262	33,555
Gross profits	80,055	60,041	69,690
Expenses			
Advertising	3,336	2,859	3,097
Bad debts	111	95	103
Automobile expense	1,112	953	1,032
Depreciation	835	835	835
Employee benefits programs			
Insurance	2,224	1,906	2,065
Interest			
Mortgage			
Other			
Professional services			
Office expense	9,200	9,200	9,200
Other business property	13,400	13,400	13,400
Repairs and maintenance			
Supplies	226	226	226
Taxes and licenses	1,112	953	1,032
Travel			
Meals and entertainment	173	173	173
Utilities	2,600	2,600	2,600
Wages	12,200	12,200	12,200
Other			
Freight	1,245	1,245	1,245
Sales tax	7,783	6,671	7,227
Total expenses	55,556	53,317	54,437
Net profit or loss	**24,499**	**6,724**	**15,253**

Figure 3-9 **Clark Company Pro Forma Income Statement for 2013**

4

Cash Flow Management

INTRODUCTION

Nothing is as important to a business as positive cash flow. As I often tell my students, "For any business, depending on the entrepreneur's gender, positive cash flow is King or Queen!" Without cash, an entrepreneur will not be able to buy inventory or equipment, make payroll, pay bills and utilities, or repay debt. Cash is necessary not only to keep a business going, but also to grow the business. Seth Godin, who is renowned for his digital marketing insights, founded Yoyodyne, an online direct-marketing company that he later sold to Yahoo! for $30 million. As an entrepreneur who bootstrapped his business for the first few years, he notes that happiness for a business owner boils down to one simple thing: positive cash flow.[1] Companies that cannot achieve positive cash flow are essentially involuntary not-for-profit organizations that eventually become insolvent. Negative cash flow leads most high-flying digital companies to become duds.

TYPES OF CASH FLOW

On the financial statements, a business's cash flow is its EBITDA, which is an acronym for earnings before interest, taxes, depreciation, and amortization.

EBITDA is the cash available to service debt (i.e., make principal and interest payments), pay taxes, buy capital equipment, and return profits to shareholders after paying all of acompany's operating expenses. A company's EBITDA is calculated as shown in Equation 4-1.

EBITDA

Net earnings
+ interest
+ taxes
+ depreciation
+ amortization
= EBITDA (4-1)

Note that a company's true cash position includes the adding back of depreciation and amortization. While these two items are expensed on an income statement, they are noncash expenditures, as was explained in Chapter 2. Their usefulness is to reduce taxable profits on an income statement, which increases the company's cash flow. This practice of adding back depreciation and amortization explains why a company with negative net earnings on its income statement can still have a positive cash flow.

While EBITDA (also known as cash flow from operations, or CFO) is important for the entrepreneur to understand, he must also understand that this is simply a cash flow calculation used for cash flow statement purposes. It illustrates what the company's cash flow should ideally be. Unfortunately for entrepreneurs, the ideal and the actual are often miles apart. It is common to hear entrepreneurs say, "On paper, my cash flow numbers show the company to be rich and making plenty of money, but in reality, we are cash-poor and starving." The reason this comment is so often made is that money owed to the company has not been paid. For example, the company could have had such an extraordinary amount of growth in revenues in one month that all of the actual cash had to be used to finance that growth by paying overtime to employees and paying for the raw materials used to make the product. About 90% of the month's products were shipped on the last day of the month, and the terms are net 30. Such a scenario describes a situation in which, on the income statement for that month, the cash flow looks strong, but the reality is that the cash will not actually arrive until at least 30 days later. This "paper-rich, cash-poor" situation resulted from taking advantage of the opportunity to increase profitable revenues.

A paper-rich, cash-poor situation is related to poor cash flow management when money from customers is past due. To succeed, the entrepreneur must be an absolutely vigilant bulldog about maximizing the actual day-to-day cash flow of the business.

Ensuring that a company has adequate cash on hand to fund its operations and pay off its obligations is essential. It is important to put a system in place that enables the entrepreneur to properly monitor and manage both expected cash receipts (i.e., cash inflows) and payables (i.e., cash outflows). The lack of an efficient cash flow management system can have severe negative consequences for a company's bottom line. For example, for service companies, whose expenses are heavily front-loaded into labor costs, profits diminish with every additional week that it takes to get fees paid. For manufacturers, this problem is even more severe, since they often have to spend proportionately large amounts of money up front on materials, production, and inventory, and they have long lag times between cash outflows and the receipt of money from customers. How does the delay in cash receipts diminish profits?

The importance of managing a company's cash needs accurately is highlighted by the following example. The Gartner Group is a high-tech consulting firm that generated $1.62 billion in revenues in 2012. While cofounder Manuel Fernandez and his partners (including the firm's namesake, Gideon Gartner) were raising capital for the company, they decided to limit the capital they raised to $30 million, even though they could have raised twice as much. They placed this limit because they wanted to restrict the amount of equity they would have to give up. However, they did not anticipate the problems that they would face as they tried to develop a new product for their company, nor did they adequately assess their cash needs during this crucial period.

One problem that arose was that the manufacturer of a component for the company's hardware product went out of business. Given that, at the time, this was the only company that was equipped to manufacture the component, Gartner had to delay the production of its hardware until a second manufacturer could be found. Once this manufacturer was identified, Gartner had to spend several months redesigning the component so that the new manufacturer could produce it. In the meantime, the company had been paying its fixed costs, so it ran out of money and filed for Chapter 11. The lesson that Fernandez learned, the hard way, is that it is essential to focus on cash flow. As he notes, "We were obsessed with revenues and profits and trying to hold on to the equity," rather than on cash flow.[2] Looking at cash flow every day is a practice that few entrepreneurs have, particularly when they are starting their companies.

There are endless examples of entrepreneurs who neglect to pursue prudent cash flow management. During good economic times, when a company is growing fast, it is easy to overlook cash flow controls, sometimes without suffering immediate negative consequences. But during challenging downturns in the economy, inattentive entrepreneurs may face a cash crunch. As a CPA once told me, "The best thing about volatile economic conditions is that they remind managers to refocus their attention on the basics." In fact, during a cash flow crunch, fast growth usually exacerbates the problems because companies are spending cash on inventory, supplies, and additional payroll—often at an accelerated rate because of the fast growth—while waiting long periods to collect receivables.

A case in point is Douglas Roberson, president of Atlantic Network Systems, a data and voice systems integrator, whose company's revenues quadrupled from $100,000 in its first year to $460,000 in the next. During this growth period, the members of his staff did not concern themselves with cash flow because sales were growing at such a phenomenal rate. "I actually believed that the more money companies owed us, the better shape we were in," Roberson confessed.[3] It was not until his company went through an extended period in which it was unable to collect its receivables that he realized the importance of managing cash. The company had to use all its existing lines of credit to keep its operations going while waiting for bills to be paid. It was a real-life lesson. He, like most entrepreneurs, learned that managing cash flow was different from just accumulating sales. As he noted, "If you don't do serious projections about how much cash you'll need to handle sales—and how long it will take to collect on invoices—you can wind up out of business, no matter how fast you're growing."[4]

CASH FLOW FORECASTS

Preparing a cash flow forecast allows an entrepreneur to determine an enterprise's financing needs. If an entrepreneur finds that the business has a forecasted cash shortage as a result of rapid growth, then it might be necessary to raise external money to meet the company's financial needs. A good cash flow forecast will allow the entrepreneur to determine the exact amount of cash needed and also when it is needed.

In general, there are several reasons why businesses raise outside capital. First, seasonal needs, such as holiday sales, may require the purchase of additional materials and the payment of additional production expenses to meet this temporary increase in demand. Second, more capital may be needed to finance long-term sales growth. As a company's sales grow, more inventory must be purchased, and additional workers will be needed. All these activities will require additional cash, which may not be on hand. A good cash flow forecast will allow an entrepreneur to forecast financing needs for these activities. Third, an entrepreneur may have to purchase expensive capital equipment or make expensive repairs to existing equipment.

Entrepreneurs must know that projected cash flow determines the amount of capital a company needs in the future. The following steps should be taken to make that determination:

- Prepare a 36-month or 60-month cash flow forecast in a spreadsheet, based on 12 months of historical financial results (or as many months as are available).
- To make the projection, use CFO plus debt obligations (i.e., interest and principal payments), which is called net cash flow, and add a row to calculate cumulative monthly net cash flow.
- Find the largest cumulative negative cash flow number—this is the amount of capital required.

To better illustrate these steps, let's look at the 5-year net cash flow numbers for the Johnson Company, shown in Table 4-1. With the information in Table 4-1, the Johnson Company can easily determine its capital needs by completing the chart in Table 4-2.

By plugging in the numbers from the cash flow projection, the Johnson Company would determine that $260 is needed because that is the largest cumulative number over the projected time frame.

TABLE 4-1 **Projected Net Cash Flow Calculation**

Year	Projected Net Cash Flow
1	−100
2	−90
3	−70
4	85
5	100

The obvious question now is, when should you get the cash? There are two schools of thought on the answer to this question. The first is that you should get only what you need from year to year, or a "series of funding." The second is that you should get the maximum that you will need at once. Both have advantages and disadvantages, as shown here.

Series of Funding

Pros

- It keeps the entrepreneur disciplined and minimizes wasting money.
- The entrepreneur is paying only for current expenses.
- The new series of capital comes in at a higher valuation, thereby allowing less equity to be surrendered.

Cons

- There is no certainly that more capital will be available in the future.
- Resources must be allocated to securing additional funding.

TABLE 4-2 **Cumulative Net Cash Flow Calculation**

	Year 1	Year 2	Year 3	Year 4	Year 5
Projected NCF	−100	−90	−70	85	100
Cumulative projected NCF	−100	−190	−260	−175	−75

All Funding at One Time

Pros

- There is no need to allocate resources to raising future funding.
- It avoids the risk of capital not being available in the future.

Cons

- Forecasts may be wrong. For example, incoming cash flows may occur earlier than Year 4, so that less up-front capital is required. If this should happen, in the case of an equity capital investment, too much equity is surrendered, or in the case of a debt capital investment, interest on unnecessary capital will be paid.
- Receiving too much capital at one time spoils the inexperienced entrepreneur and could lead to unnecessary waste of the capital.
- Invested capital comes in at a lower valuation.

CASH FLOW MANAGEMENT

Cash flow management can be as simple as preserving future cash by not spending as much today. For example, in order to deal with seasonal sales, a company may choose not to spend as much in October if December—when October's bills come due—is traditionally a poor sales month and won't generate enough receipts to cover those bills.[5] Cash flow management can also involve making somewhat complicated decisions about delaying payments to a supplier in order to use cash resources to temporarily increase production. Or it can involve making decisions about borrowing or using factoring companies to generate cash quickly to meet short-term cash shortages.

The relationship between the sources and uses of cash is shown in Equation 4-2.

Sources and Uses of Cash

Sources of cash – uses of cash = net cash flow

→ Fund capital expenditures and return to investors (4-2)

Sources of Cash or Cash Inflows

- Accounts receivable
- Cash payments
- Other income (i.e., income from investments)
- Borrowing

Uses of Cash or Cash Outflows

- Payroll
- Utilities—heat, electricity, telephone, and so on
- Loan payments—interest plus principal
- Rent
- Insurance—health, property, and so on
- Taxes

Key Cash Flow Goals

The goal of good cash management is obvious: to have enough cash on hand when you need it. The major goal of prudent cash flow management is to ensure that there is enough cash on hand to meet the demands for cash at any given time. This is done by getting cash not only from operations (i.e., managing cash inflows, including accounts receivable) and disciplined spending (i.e., managing accounts payable), but also through the use of external capital (i.e., borrowing). While this may appear to be a simple concept, in reality, it is a process that even the most experienced financial officers and executives find difficult to carry out successfully.

The trick to handling cash flow is in the timing—as an entrepreneur, you want your customers to pay as soon as possible (if possible in advance), while you pay your suppliers and vendors as late as possible without jeopardizing your relationship with them or your credit standing. The idea is that money that is collected in receivables today, and that does not have to go out as payables, is, in fact, an important source of internally generated working capital.

While it may not be the most fun thing to do, it is important for an entrepreneur to spend time (at least an hour a day) working on cash flow. It is without a doubt one of the most crucial things an entrepreneur can do for a business. This exercise forces an entrepreneur to think about what he is doing in terms of cold, hard cash.

Cash Flow Ledgers and Projections

The cash flow ledger provides important information about the balance of the cash account, enabling the entrepreneur to assess the company's ability to fund its operations and also meet debt payments as they come due. It indicates, on a transaction basis, all cash received and disbursed during a month's period. Successful entrepreneurs are those who know their company's actual cash position on any given day. Therefore, it is recommended that entrepreneurs, especially those who are inexperienced or those who are in the early stages of their ventures, review their cash flow ledger at least weekly.

In addition to the ledger, a weekly cash flow projection summary, as discussed in Chapter 2, should be prepared when opening a business and every month thereafter. This projection indicates the anticipated cash inflows during the month along with the cash payments to be made. By doing this kind of projection each month, the entrepreneur can schedule payments to suppliers to match expected cash receipts. This allows the entrepreneur to be proactive with regard to the money owed to suppliers and enables her to let specific vendors know in advance that a payment will probably be late. The cash flow ledger and projections are simple and very useful tools that should be used to manage cash flow successfully. It is important to be consistent and work through each line item so that forecasts can be as accurate as possible.

To prepare cash flow forecasts, the entrepreneur should first look at historical cash flow, if this information is available. Construct monthly historical cash flows for at least the past year—if possible, for the past few years. It will be easier to forecast many items, such as utility bills, if what has been spent in the past is known.

Using these historical figures, prepare forecasts for the weekly cash flows for a month at a time. First, determine the cash inflows for each month—usually cash sales and accounts receivable. Then determine the cash outflows—utilities, payroll and other employee-related expenses, inventory, equipment purchases, and so on. Compare inflows with outflows to determine the company's net cash position.

The cash flow forecast allows an entrepreneur to track actual performance against forecasts and plans. Each month, an entrepreneur should compare the forecast with the actual results and calculate the variance between the actual amount incurred and the forecast line by line. Then calculate the percentage variance (i.e., the actual minus the forecast divided by the forecast). Focus on the areas where overspending occurred, looking at the dollar amount and the percentage over the budget. Where the difference is significant, determine whether the expenditure was justified, and, if it was not, how to reduce it. By doing this every month, an entrepreneur will find that he can control expenses much more effectively.

ACCOUNTS RECEIVABLE

The major area of vulnerability for many entrepreneurs is accounts receivable. On any given day, it is estimated that 5 million businesses are behind on their bills.[6] As stated earlier, many entrepreneurs, particularly in the early or fast-growth stages of their business, focus more on generating sales than they do on collecting receivables. While this is never a good idea, it is worse during slow economic times, when more customers take longer to pay their bills—usually the result is a cash crunch for a company.

This problem is not unique to American entrepreneurs. In Australia, a survey conducted by Dun & Bradstreet and Roy Morgan Research showed that the majority of small and medium-sized enterprises no longer expect to be paid on time. As for the old standard 30-day payment period, only 30% of these firms expect their customers to pay them within that time. In the United Kingdom, 67% of small businesses indicated that late payment from other businesses was a cause of cash flow difficulties.[7] Every year, Pepperdine University surveys small-business owners. The survey is designed to give an overview of current issues and problems facing these business owners, as well as a brief look at their expectations for the coming year. In 2013, in , small-business owners were asked about their priorities. For example, in the coming year, would they put more of an emphasis on increasing sales? What about collecting debt? The answers given are shown in Table 4-3,[8] and they suggest that collecting debt is not a primary concern.

TABLE 4-3 **Business Owner Priorities**

	Sales Existing Products	Sales New Products	Control Costs (incl. Labor)	Raising Financing	Finding Talented People	Other
Increase emphasis	50%	21%	9%	8%	7%	4%

Source: Capital Markets Report 2014 by Pepperdine Private Capital Markets Project.

In a similar study, the National Federation of Independent Business (NFIB) conducts a survey every 5 or 6 years to establish the priorities of small businesses. The results of the most recent survey are enlightening: cash flow wasn't even a top 10 concern. In fact, it was number 13![9]

Alan Burkhard, president of The Placers, Inc., a Wilmington, Delaware–based temporary placement and permanent job search firm, initially did not recognize the importance of having good financial controls for accounts receivable. He notes, "I always told myself that accounts receivable didn't create sales, so they weren't worth paying attention to."[10] He held this belief until a time when, although his company was generating record sales, he was having difficulty running his company because of cash problems. The root of the problem: an inefficient accounts receivable system.

"None of our customers paid us in any kind of timely fashion. And 60–70% of our delinquent accounts were actually owed by our regular customers. Every single week we had to pay salaries and payroll taxes for every temp we placed on a job. But it was taking us 60 or 90 days or longer to collect our bills from the companies that were hiring those temps."[11] By allowing its customers to take so long to pay, The Placers was actually giving them an interest-free loan to cover their own payroll costs.

Unfortunately, it is quite common for entrepreneurs to complain about their need for more working capital when in fact the company already has the money in accounts receivable. When you are an entrepreneur, you had better be an absolutely vigilant bulldog (as noted at the beginning of this chapter) when it comes to collecting your receivables. This is the lifeblood of the business—collecting your receivables as quickly as possible. Candidly, when I first owned my business, I was a bit of a wimp. I was afraid that if I called my customers and said something, well, they would no longer do business with me. I learned very quickly that if you do not say something, you are not going to be sitting around for very long saying, "Where's my money?" Instead, you're going to be saying, "Where's my business?" The money simply needs to be collected by whatever means necessary. As one entrepreneur stated, "I get on the phone and beg."[12]

Accounts Receivable Systems

A good accounts receivable collection system is proactive. It also allows the entrepreneur to do business with customers who may not have a credit history, or even those who have a bad credit history. The major components of an effective system include these steps:

- Before you go into business, perform an analysis of the industry's payment practices. Is this an industry characterized by historically slow-paying customers, such as the government or health insurance companies? If an industry is characterized by slow-paying customers, this does not necessarily mean that you should not enter it; it simply means that you should be even more diligent about developing and maintaining a disciplined system.
- Have all new customers complete a credit report before you provide any services or products. The report should be simple but thorough and should contain the following information:
  - The age of the company
  - The owner(s) of the company
  - Whether the company has ever declared Chapter 7 or 11 bankruptcy and whether the owner has ever declared Chapter 13
  - The current name of the company and any previous names
  - The maximum credit level desired
  - The telephone numbers and the fax numbers and/or addresses of three supplier references, along with the length and terms of the relationship with these suppliers

  - The name of the company's primary bank, its account number(s), and a contact number for the bank officer responsible for managing the company's accounts
  - Whether or not the company agrees to pay invoices according to your terms
- Consider the following options if a potential customer does not have a credit history or has a bad one:
  - At the time of order receipt, require an up-front payment equal to the cost of goods sold for the order, with the balance due at the time of shipment. This ensures that your costs are covered if the customer cancels the order after production has begun.
  - Obtain a 100% payment before work on the order can begin.
  - Require a 100% payment before or at the time of delivery (COD).
  - Request a 33% payment at order receipt and 33% at the time of shipment, with the balance due 30 days later.
- Contact all references immediately and inquire about their credit experience with the prospective customer. Questions should include:
  - How many years have they had this customer?
  - What is the maximum amount of credit they have provided this customer? Have there been any increases or decreases in the credit limit? If so, why?
  - What are their invoice terms?
  - Does the customer typically pay within 10, 30, 60, or 90 days?
  - Have they ever received any checks from this customer, and have any of them bounced?
  - Do they recommend this company as a good customer?
  - Have they had any problems doing business with this company?

If all the references are satisfactory, inform your customers that their orders will be processed immediately. Also remind customers of the company's invoice terms and ask if they have any problems adhering to them. Specifically, ask customers how they normally pay their bills. The reason behind this question is that some companies have their own system for paying bills, regardless of the supplier's invoice terms.

Successful entrepreneurs know how their key customers pay their bills. For example:

- Some customers pay their bills once a month, typically on the thirtieth or thirty-first. For the company to be paid on the thirtieth, the merchandise must be received by the tenth; if it is not, the payment will be made on the thirtieth of the next month.
- Some customers pay 30 days after receipt of the goods or services. Therefore, the supplier is penalized if the shipment is delayed by the carrier.
- Some customers pay 30 days after products that were damaged during delivery have been replaced.

It is also important to ask customers for the name of the accounts payable clerk who will be responsible for paying invoices. When I operated my business, you'd better believe that I knew every accounts payable clerk at every one of my customers. I knew their names, their kids' names, the flowers they liked. Heck, their employers must have wondered why we were so cozy. You know why? Any edge I could gain in getting my bills paid earlier was well worth a few timely cards, a few nice words, and flowers on a birthday.

Other important key steps toward the effective management of accounts receivable include the following:

- All invoices should be mailed on the same day that the product is shipped or the services rendered. Do not hold invoices until the next day or the end of the week, and do not wait and send invoices once a month. Such a practice will certainly delay payment.
- Make sure that the invoice highlights the payment terms in bold capital letters or in a different color from the rest of the invoice. The terms should be printed at the top of the page of the invoice. The most common invoice terms are "2/10, net 30." This means that if the customer pays within 10 days of the invoice date, she is allowed a

2% discount. Otherwise, the entire invoice amount is due within 30 days of the invoice date.

- Manage the collection of accounts receivable. It is naïve to expect all customers to pay in a timely fashion. In the business of collecting receivables, the squeaky wheel does in fact get the oil.
- The entrepreneur should have a weekly receivables aging report showing the customer accounts that are outstanding for 30 days or more.
- For invoices that have not been paid seven days after the due date, automatic action of some kind should be taken.
- Excellent payment history is no longer than 10 days more than the invoice terms. If the terms are net 30 and payment occurs in 50 days, then no future orders should be sent before receipt of some kind of payment, as mentioned earlier.

Collecting accounts receivable can be an intimidating experience, especially for the inexperienced entrepreneur. In many instances, the new entrepreneur is afraid to implement a system similar to the one discussed here because of the fear of losing revenue if the customer gets offended. Such a concern is foolish and naïve. It is also a good idea to have someone other than you send the strong letters and make the tough phone calls. At my company, a woman named Angela—our CFO—was our resident pit bull. We had a system in place where our terms were net 30, and if we weren't paid by the thirty-fifth day, an automatic reminder went out to the customer—a neon green sheet of paper in a neon green envelope. It said, "Just a reminder if you've forgotten us." If we hadn't been paid 5 days after that, another notice—this one hot pink—went out. I had one customer call me to say, "Steve, every time I open one of these doggone notices, I get blinded by the sheets of paper. Why don't you stop sending them to me?" I replied, "Listen, I just own the company. Angela runs everything out there. Now the way that I can get Angela to stop is for you to simply pay on time. It's a simple solution."

But everyone has his own system, and occasionally the entrepreneur needs to show a little "tough love." I love the story that Bette Wildermuth, a business broker in Richmond, Virginia, tells about one of her clients. "This gentleman owns an excavation company. He always does excellent work, meets the developers' time schedule, and makes sure his crews clean up after themselves. Usually he gets paid within 10 days of completing the job. But every once in a while, a developer really drags things out. The excavator's solution: he puts on his muddiest contractor boots and goes to the developer's fancy office with the nice oriental rugs. When he arrives, he announces in a very loud voice that he has come to pick up the overdue check and plans to sit in the lobby until it's ready. Needless to say, this does tend to speed up the process."

For the entrepreneur who just doesn't have the stomach for collections, one option is to get "credit insurance," where the insurer pays the claim within 60 days and then assumes the responsibility for collection. Baltimore, Maryland–based Euler Hermes (formerly known as American Credit Indemnity Company), the world's largest issuer of trade-related credit insurance, charges 1% of the sales insured and will insure only receivables from customers who historically have paid within 30 days.[13]

Remember, good customers typically expect to pay their bills within 5 to 10 days after the due date unless they have a special payables system, as was mentioned earlier. Even those customers plan to pay, but according to their system. A bad customer is one who is very cavalier about paying bills. These types of customers will pay only when they are forced to do so, even when they have the money. Ultimately, the experienced entrepreneur sees that these are not profitable customers and does not mind losing them.

When such a decision has been made, extreme action should be taken within 60 days, such as hiring a lawyer, at a cost of approximately $2,000, to get a "writ of attachment" against the delinquent customer's corporate bank account. This action generally gets the customer's immediate attention for settling the delinquency.[14]

Before leaving the subject of an accounts receivable system, here are a few don'ts:

- Don't be rude to customers. Don't threaten them.
- Don't assume that a slow-paying customer is a thief or a bum. It may be that the customer has fallen on temporary tough economic times.
- Don't take legal action against a customer until the bill is at least 45 days past due and you have personally spoken to the customer and tried to get payment.

- Don't pay independent sales representatives until you receive payment from the customer. Some sales representatives do not care if a customer is a known delinquent payer. Taking an order from such a customer may not bother the salesperson, since he is not the one who is investing in raw materials. Therefore, discourage such action with a policy that specifies that sales representatives will not receive their full commission if payment is received more than a certain number of days late. For example, if the payment is 15 days late, the commission is reduced by 15%.

To check on the quality of accounts receivable, several ratios can be used. The first step in checking the quality is to determine what the company's collection ratio, or "days receivable" or "accounts receivable turnover," is. This ratio measures the quality of a company's accounts receivable. It shows the average number of days it takes to collect accounts receivable. To look at it another way, this ratio indicates the number of days, on average, that it takes a business to convert its receivables to cash. Equation 4-3 shows the equation to calculate days receivable.

Days Receivable

Days receivable = outstanding receivables/annual sales/365 days (4-3)

The same formula can be restated as Equation 4-4.

Days Receivable

Days receivable = outstanding receivables/average daily sales (4-4)

In this case, average daily sales can be calculated using Equation 4-5.

Average Daily Sales

Average daily sales = annual sales/365 days (4-5)

The goal is to get the customers to pay as soon as possible. Therefore, a low days receivable number is desirable. At a minimum, a company's days receivable should be equal to the industry's average. Also, it should not exceed the company's days payable ratio, because if it does, this indicates that bills are being paid faster than payments are being received.

$5 million in sales/365 days = $13,699 (average daily sales)
$800,000 in receivables/$13,699 = 58.4 days

Figure 4-1 Receivables Turnover Ratio Calculation

For example, a company with $5 million in annual revenues and $800,000 in accounts receivable has an accounts receivable turnover ratio of 58.4 days, calculated as shown in Figure 4-1.

This number would indicate that, on average, it takes the company approximately 58 days to convert receivables into cash. Is this good or bad? Well, most important, it depends on the invoice terms. If the terms are 30 days, this is bad even if the industry average is higher. This says that customers are paying almost 1 month later than they should. That is money that could be reinvested and could generate returns if the company received it closer to the invoice terms.

Companies usually do not understand the importance of collecting their accounts receivable quickly and consistently. Entrepreneurs usually focus their resources on boosting sales, rather than on faster collection of receivables, because the benefits of higher sales are easier to quantify. Entrepreneurs sometimes ignore the costs of inefficient collection systems because they do not really understand the effects of these inefficiencies on the company's bottom line. However, it is easy to quantify the benefits of faster collection of accounts receivable in terms of dollars saved. Faster collection means that the company will not have to use external financing for current payables. Equation 4-6 is the formula for calculating dollars saved as a result of faster collection of accounts receivable.

Dollars Saved

$$\text{Dollars saved} = (\text{gross annual sales} \times \text{annual interest rate}) \times \text{days saved}/365 \text{ days} \qquad (4\text{-}6)$$

In calculating dollars saved, use the most recent complete year's sales figures unless the company is growing rapidly and has a good projection for the

($4,000,000 × 8.75) × 5 days/365 days = $4,795 in savings

Figure 4-2 **Accounts Receivable Collection Savings**

current year. For the annual interest rate, include the cost of debt capital. To find the days saved, subtract the company's improved days sales outstanding (DSO) from its original DSO. The equation for DSO is shown in Equation 4-7.

Days Sales Outstanding[15]

$$\text{Days sales outstanding} = \frac{\text{average accounts receivable balance over past 3 months} \times 90 \text{ days}}{\text{total sales over past 3 months}} \quad (4\text{-}7)$$

For example, suppose a $4 million company, borrowing at the prime rate of 6.75% plus 2 points (i.e., 2%), improves its days sales outstanding by 5 days. The total amount of dollars the company saves by improving its collection of accounts receivable is shown in Figure 4-2.

ACCOUNTS PAYABLE

The ideal situation is to collect all your receivables quickly while paying your outstanding bills as late as possible without jeopardizing the service you get from your suppliers. However, delaying payables is not always necessarily a good thing. If you have cash on hand or can borrow at low rates, should you take discounts? Yes. As Jay Goltz, the author of *The Street Smart Entrepreneur*, explains:

> Suppose your supplier terms are 2, 10 net 30—2% discount if you pay in 10 days; the entire balance is due in 30 days. You don't take a discount and pay in 40 days instead of 30. Basically, you have borrowed from your vendor for 30 days, which is essentially one-twelfth of a year. The loan cost equals 2% (i.e., the 10-day discount) of the invoice annualized, which is 24%. If every month you lose a 2% discount, it is like paying 24% over the course of a year.[16]

COGS/365 days = average daily costs
Accounts payable/average daily costs = number of days it takes to pay

Figure 4-3 **Accounts Payable Turnover Ratio Calculation**

To determine whether or not the company's accounts payable are what they should be, analyze the accounts payable turnover ratio and compare it with the industry average. This ratio measures the average number of days it takes the company to pay its bills. The ratio can be calculated as shown in Figure 4-3.

Management of Accounts Payable

To improve the accounts payable days, the entrepreneur can take the following actions recommended by several professionals:

- Negotiate better payment terms, such as net 45 or net 60, instead of net 30.
- Time payments according to their due dates, such as 30 days following the receipt of material, rather than on some artificial schedule.
- Plan cash flow realities. For example, to avoid big cash outflows, some companies pay their employees' payroll biweekly and then pay their outstanding bills during the other two weeks of the month.
- Avoid interest penalty charges. If you have to stretch out your own payables because of temporary cash flow problems, make sure you are not late with those bills that incur additional interest charges.
- Communicate with your suppliers. If you establish a good working relationship with a supplier and make regular payments, you can usually avoid paying late charges by contacting the owner in advance if you expect to make a late payment or if you need to request a payment extension.
- Set scheduling goals. Try to establish a final date by which all payables are to be paid. While it is unrealistic to assume that you will always be

on schedule, it is important to keep the accounts payable as close to the scheduled goal date as possible.

- Be organized. Keep a paper trail, and keep close track of details, especially of the aging of bills. Invest in a good accounts payable system.
- Look for warning signs, including low cash levels, that could result in future problems paying vendors and suppliers. Reevaluate your collection controls to ensure that you are collecting cash as soon as possible.
- Prioritize. You can't devote the same amount of time to all payables. Organize your payables based on some type of priority rating. For example, fixed expenses such as rent may be paid first, utilities second, and then other bills.
- Identify problems early. Verify the accuracy of the information on invoices from suppliers.
- Provide supervision from the top.
- Have specialists monitor the accounts payable daily.
- Try to stretch your accounts payable as much as possible without hurting your relationships with vendors and without damaging your credit status.

THE CASH GAP

You now own a business. Whether it's a manufacturing, retail, or service firm, you soon discover a simple truth: first you pay for the goods or services, and then eventually someone else—your customer—pays you. The period between the payment of cash and the receipt of cash is called the *cash gap* or *cash conversion cycle*. How long do your goods sit in inventory? How many days is it before you have to pay your suppliers? Finally, how many days does it take your customers to pay you? The answers to those three questions are plugged into the cash gap formula, shown in Equation 4-8.

Cash Gap Calculation

$$\begin{array}{ll} & \text{Inventory days} \\ + & \text{days receivable} \\ - & \text{days payable} \\ \hline = & \text{cash gap} \end{array} \qquad (4\text{-}8)$$

That interval between the payment of cash and the receipt of cash must be financed. The longer the time, the more interest a company must pay on capital borrowed from a lender, thereby using working capital. The wise way to reduce the need for working capital is to decrease the gap. The entrepreneur's goal must be to continually shorten the gap, because for each day that it is decreased, the daily interest cost saved goes entirely and directly to pretax profits.

Let's explore this concept in more detail, using an example and illustrations. We can make the following assumptions for the Varnadoe Company:

- Days inventory carried[a]: 40.5
- Days payable[a]: 40
- Days receivable[a]: 35
- Annual revenues: $50 million
- Gross profit[a]: 30%
- Cost of debt: 6%

Therefore, the cash gap can be calculated as shown in Figure 4-4.

To determine the savings from reducing the cash gap by one day, the calculation shown in Figure 4-5 should be made.

As you can see from the figure, for every day that the cash gap is reduced, the savings of $5,753 will go directly to profits before taxes, thereby increasing the Varnadoe Company's cash flow. Using the Varnadoe Company's information, Figure 4-5 illustrates the cash gap concept.

	Inventory days	40.5
+	days receivable	35.0
–	days payable	40.0
=	cash gap	35.5 days

Figure 4-4 **Cash Gap Calculation**

[a] The formulas for these ratios can be found in Chapter 3.

Determine the company's daily revenues:
$50 million ÷ 365 = $136,986

Determine the cost of goods sold:
1.00 – 0.30 (gross profit) = 0.70

Determine the COGS for one day of revenue:
0.70 (COGS) × $136,986 (daily revenue) = $95,890

The cash gap:
35.5 days

Determine how much Varnadoe Company needs to borrow to cover 35.5 days of COGS:
35.5 × $95,890 (COGS for 1 day's revenue) = $3,404,109

Determine the interest expense to be paid on the borrowed money:
$3,404,109 × 0.06 (cost of debt) = $204,246

Determine the savings from reducing the cash gap by 1 day:
$204,246 ÷ 35.5 (cash gap) = $5,753

Figure 4-5 **Cash Gap Reduction Calculation**

There are only three ways in which a company can reduce its cash gap: (1) increase the number of days it takes to pay for inventory, (2) decrease the number of days it takes to collect receivables, or (3) increase the inventory turns. Let's analyze each.

Increase Days Payable

Most companies allow their customers up to 2 weeks past the due date before they consider the invoice seriously delinquent. Therefore, every entrepreneur should take advantage of these extra days by paying no earlier than 2 weeks after the due date. This shortens the cash gap because it extends payments that may have been due in 30 days to 44 days. Using the information from the Varnadoe Company, if days payable were increased by 4 days, to 44, the cash gap would be

31.5 instead of 35.5. Such a decrease would save the company $23,012 in interest payments (4 days × $5,753).

Decrease Days Receivable

This topic was discussed in great detail in Chapter 3. Some industries historically have lower days receivable than others. For example, manufacturing companies typically expect payment in 30 days, whereas retailers such as Amazon .com usually get paid immediately upon sale. They have no receivables because payment is required at the time of the order. In fact, in 2012, Amazon.com reported 15 days receivables, 76 days payables, and 44 days of inventory. The result was that Amazon.com's cash gap was a beautiful negative 17 days (15 + 44 – 76 = –17), which means that it raised interest-free money from its customers for half a month. Specifically, given its average cost of sales, which at the time was $114 million, the company raised $1.9 billion ($114 million × 17 days), which it used to help pay overhead expenses.[17] Using the Varnadoe Company data again, if the days receivable were reduced from 35 to 29, the effect would be a 6-day reduction in the cash gap and therefore a $34,518 cash savings.

Increase Inventory Turnover

The faster a company can convert its inventory into cash, the less cash it needs because it can reduce its days of inventory carried and decrease its inventory carrying cost, which was discussed in Chapter 3. A company that has successfully increased its inventory turns is Wal-Mart Stores, Inc., known in some circles as the world champion of lean. Its inventory turnover was 4.1 in 1990 and 8.3 in 2012, an average increase of 3.3% per year. Another company, Dell, when it was on its way to its best performing years of sales was successful in improving its cash flow by turning inventory faster. Dell turned its inventory an amazing 83.7 times per year in 2007, compared with less than 5 times for traditional computer manufacturers.[18]

The hope is that, as a result of this rich discussion, it is now clear that every entrepreneur must know why cash gap analysis is important and how to use it as a proactive tool for operating the company. Every entrepreneur should do the complete analysis explained in this section at least annually and use the information for strategic planning for the next year.

TABLE 4-4 **Cash Gaps by Industry**

	Receivables	(+) Inventory	(-) Payables	(=) Cash Gap
Manufacturing				
Bread and bakery	24	19	23	20
Chocolate Candy	23	70	21	72
Semiconductors	76	45	32	89
Wholesale				
Tools, Hardware	40	101	33	108
Automobiles	16	65	12	69
Toys, hobby goods	38	96	38	96
Retail				
Gasoline stations	1	7	5	3
Drugstores	17	31	21	27
Shoes	1	135	48	88
Information				
Software Publishing	58	N/A	N/A	58
Mobile Carriers	27	N/A	N/A	27
Internet Portals	41	N/A	N/A	41

Source: Risk Management Association, Annual Statement Studies: Financial Ratio Benchmarks, 2013.

What is the ideal cash gap? It varies by industry. An industry comparison should be made annually using the Risk Management Association (formerly Robert Morris Associates) guide. A few of the industries are highlighted in Table 4-4.

WORKING CAPITAL

The procurement, maintenance, and management of working capital seem to be some of the most common and challenging tasks facing entrepreneurs. Therefore, let's devote a little more time to the subject.

As was stated earlier in this chapter, the interval between a company's payment and receipt of cash must be financed. The money for this is called *working capital*, which consists of funds invested in all current assets, including inventory, accounts receivable, and cash. Gross working capital is used to finance only the company's current assets. Net working capital, which is a measurement of a company's solvency, is current assets minus current liabilities. The goal is to have positive net working capital. The greater the net working capital, the stronger the company's cash position relative to its ability to service its other expenses, including long-term debt.

Very few companies are able to finance their working capital needs internally. Therefore, external financing in the form of debt or equity is inevitable. How much working capital is ideal? One expert, Skip Grandt, a commercial lender with 20 years of experience, says that he likes to see a company have net working capital levels of 3 to 6 times its annual fixed costs.[19] A great resource for finding working capital levels for different industries is *CFO* magazine's annual working capital survey, which can be found on CFO's website (www.cfo.com).

FINDING CASH

Entrepreneurs have frequently asked me to help them raise external financing from debt and/or equity investors. Most of the time, after reviewing their financial statements, I have told them that they do not need outside capital. They simply need to reduce their inventory and/or accounts receivable levels. That's right. Cash is often readily available to entrepreneurs who carry excessive amounts of these two assets.

What is the ideal level of inventory that an entrepreneur should carry? The formula to make this determination is shown in Equation 4-9.

Ideal Inventory Calculation

Ideal inventory = COGS/targeted inventory turns (4-9)

Let's use the information from the Hoy Company to show how an entrepreneur can raise internal cash by applying this formula. The Hoy Company had the following numbers for 2012:

- Revenues: $30,848,000
- Cost of goods sold (COGS): $13,989,000

- Inventory: $9,762,000
- Inventory turns: 1.43 times
- Average industry inventory turns: 2 times
- Accounts receivable: $5,996,000
- Days receivable: 71
- Average days receivable for industry: 40

If in 2013, the revenues and COGS remained the same as in 2012, but the entrepreneur was able to turn inventory 2 times rather than 1.43 times, the cash savings would be dramatic. The ideal level of inventory is $6,994,500, determined by $13,989,000/2. The actual savings based on the 2012 inventory level would be $2,767,500 in cold, hard cash!

What is the ideal level of accounts receivable that an entrepreneur should carry? The formula to make this determination can be seen in Equation 4-10.

Ideal Level of Accounts Receivable

$$\text{Ideal level of accounts receivable} = \text{average daily sales} \times \text{targeted days receivable} \qquad (4\text{-}10)$$

Using the same information for the Hoy Company, if days receivable can be reduced from 71 to 40 days, the cash savings would be significant. To compute average daily sales, the annual revenue must be divided by 365. Therefore, $30,848,000/365 generates average daily sales of $84,515. This figure multiplied by 40 days receivable shows that the Hoy Company's ideal level of receivables should be $3,380,600. The actual savings based on the 2012 accounts receivable, or $5,996,000, would be $2,615,400 in cold, hard cash!

5

Valuation

INTRODUCTION

When I teach my MBA students about entrepreneurial finance, on Day 1 of the classes, I run through an exercise in which students attempt to value a company. You should know that many of these students have previously sat through high-level finance classes, know about discounted cash flows, and have their heads full of formulas. We look at the numbers. "Tell me what you would pay for the company," I demand. The valuations range from zero to $300,000. Actually, I tell them, when the company was sold, it went for $38,000. It sold for the price of its inventory. There is a story behind the valuation that is not quantitative. The owner had to sell the company because his wife had told him that if he didn't, she was going to leave him and retire to Florida by herself. It had nothing to do with a multiple of cash flows, multiple of revenue, or anything other than that he simply had to get out of the business.

Here's the lesson: valuation is very tricky and can never be done in a vacuum. Entrepreneurs must learn the methods used to value companies and become comfortable with the "ambiguity of valuation" and the fact that the valuation process is not a hard-and-fast science. The story of Bain Consulting highlights this fact. In 1973, Bill Bain, a former vice president at Boston Consulting

Group, and 7 partners founded the consulting firm Bain Consulting. From the mid-1980s through 1993, it was estimated that Bain's revenues had increased from $100 million to $220 million. During this time, the 8 partners decided to sell 30% of the company to a Bain Employee Stock Option Plan (ESOP) for $200 million. This transaction gave the company an implied valuation of $666 million. A few years later, the vice presidents of the company took legal action against these partners, which ended in the partners returning $100 million to the company as well as the 70% of the company's equity that they held. This transaction, in which the 8 partners essentially sold 100% of their equity back to the company, changed the valuation from $666 million to $200 million, a reduction of more than 70%! The point of this story is to show that even a world-class organization such as Bain, filled with brilliant MBA graduates from some of the finest business schools in the country, including Kellogg, Harvard, Stanford, and Wharton, could not initially come up with the "correct" valuation.

Let me repeat this again. The valuation of a company, particularly that of a start-up, is not an exact science. As Nick Smith, a venture capitalist in Minnesota, stated, "Valuation in a start-up is an illusion." Therefore, the true value of a company, be it a start-up or a mature business, is established in the marketplace. Very simply, a company's ultimate value is the price agreed to by the seller and the buyer. This fact can be traced back to the first century BC, when Publilius Syrus stated, "Everything is worth what its purchaser will pay for it."

One of the best examples of this fact is highlighted by the story of Apple Computer and Be, Inc. In October 1996, Apple Computer's CEO, Gil Amelio, began negotiations to buy Be, Inc., from its CEO, Jean-Louis Gassée. Be had developed a new operating system called Be OS that some people in the industry said "put Apple's Macintosh and Microsoft's Windows to shame."[1] Like most opportunistic entrepreneurs, Gassée was more than willing to sell his 6-year-old entrepreneurial venture, which he had financed with $20 million from venture capitalists and other private investors. In 1996, Be, Inc., had 40 employees and approximately $3 million in annual revenues. Amelio offered $100 million for the small company. However, Gassée thought the value of Be, Inc., was much greater and countered with a $285 million asking price, which amounted to approximately 10% of Apple's valuation.

Amelio refused to offer anything over the $100 million price. Instead, he bought the more established NeXt Software, Inc., which, ironically, had been founded by Steve Jobs, Apple Computer's founder and its CEO until shortly before his death. Therefore, what was the value of Be, Inc., in 1996? It was an amount between $100 million and $285 million. And what happened to Be, Inc.? In September 2001, Nasdaq regulators told the company that they were delisting it for failing to maintain a minimum bid price of at least a dollar for 30 consecutive days. Be, Inc.'s shares were trading for about 14 cents. That same month, Be, Inc., announced that it would sell its remaining assets and technology to Palm Inc. for $11 million.

This overvaluation experience taught Gassée the valuable lesson that all entrepreneurs must learn: "Pigs get fat and hogs get slaughtered." He could have been a nice fat, happy pig by accepting the $100 million. Instead, he got greedy, a common trait of hogs, and got nothing.

Despite the fact that business valuation is not an exact science, entrepreneurs should determine a value for their company at least once a year. This process must not intimidate them. As has been repeatedly stated throughout this book, this is not brain surgery. In fact, it can be rather simple, and almost everyone can do it. What is the reason for performing an annual valuation of a company? There are many. If the entrepreneur does not determine the value of his company, then someone else will, and the entrepreneur will not be happy with the result. For example, if the entrepreneur is selling his business and relies entirely on a prospective buyer to determine its worth, the buyer will certainly look out for her own interests and price it low. The entrepreneur must, therefore, look out for his own best interests by establishing a price that he is comfortable with, using logical and acceptable valuation methods. Which methods are correct? As you will see later in this chapter, all of them.

Valuation involves estimating the worth or price of a company. Different industries use different methods to determine this value. Some industries use complicated quantitative models, while others use relatively simple approaches. Regardless of the methodology used, however, the valuation of a business incorporates not only a financial analysis of the company, but also a subjective assessment of other factors that may be difficult to quantify, including:

- Stage of the company
- Management team assessment
- Industry

- Reason the company is being sold
- Other general macroeconomic factors

Ultimately, the value of a company is driven by the present and projected cash flows, which are affected by all the factors just mentioned. As Bill Sutter, a former venture capitalist at Mesirow Partners, said to a class of MBA students, "Where does value come from? Cash flow. It does not come from assets or revenues. It comes from cash flow."

VALUING THE CLARK COMPANY

At the beginning of this chapter, I shared the story about the owner whose selling price had more to do with his wife's threats than with any fancy formula. The company is called the Clark Company, and it is worth examining in a bit more detail. As we discussed in Chapter 3, the Clark Company had 2012 revenues of about $113,000. The cash flow that the business generated was an astonishing $45,000, or 39% of revenues. This was calculated after scrutinizing the income statement and asking the seller questions. Remember, the starting point for calculating cash flow is net profit plus depreciation plus any other noncash item expenditures. In this case, we add the just under $16,000 in net profit and the $835 for depreciation. Cash flow calculations will often also include discretionary expenses that the new owners of the business would not incur if they were to acquire the company. For Clark Company, the additional add-backs include wages, which were in fact wages ($12,214) being paid to the owner's spouse.

In reality, the $8,965 allocated for office expenses covered personal expenditures for a new car that his wife drove that the owner was running through the company. In addition, as the owner of the business also owned the building that the business was renting, he was in effect renting the building to himself. The company was paying about $7,000 more than market value for the rent for this building.

This company is really "a little engine that could." To value this company or any other, many different valuation methods could be used. For example, using a conservative multiple of 3 in the multiple of cash flow valuation method, the company's valuation is approximately $135,000 (3 × $45,015). If another valuation method, such as multiple of revenues, were used, then a different value could be determined. For example, if a conservative 0.9 multiple of revenue was used, Clark Company's value would be $101,700. Clark actually sold for $38,000, which was the value of the inventory on hand. Why did it sell for the price of the inventory? Again, the answer was that the owner had to sell it. His wife had told him that if he did not sell, she was going to leave him and retire to Florida by herself. The price was not determined by using a free cash flow, a multiple of cash flow, or a multiple of revenue method—or, for that matter, any other valuation method that is usually used in determining the value of a business.

Again, this case perfectly highlights two major points. One is that valuation is not a hard-and-fast science. The second is that the valuation of a business can never be done in a vacuum. A myriad of things, both quantitative and qualitative, affect valuation.

Before we proceed further, it is important that we clarify 2 terms that are commonly used when discussing valuation. Those terms are *premoney valuations* and *postmoney valuations*.

PREMONEY AND POSTMONEY VALUATIONS

At the beginning of negotiations, private equity investors routinely ask entrepreneurs for the value of their company. When an answer is given, the usual follow-up question is, is the valuation a premoney or a postmoney valuation? Premoney is defined as the company's value, using whatever method the entrepreneur chooses, before the investment. Postmoney is very simple. It means the premoney valuation plus the amount of the equity investment.

As we will see later in this chapter, there are several ways to determine the value of a company. These methods provide a premoney valuation. Therefore, if the multiple of revenue method creates a $12 million valuation and the company is pursuing $3 million of private equity capital, the postmoney valuation will be $15 million if the equity capital is successfully raised.

The significance of the 2 valuation terms is to ensure that both parties, the entrepreneur and the investor, are viewing the valuation the same way. The other significance is that postmoney valuations determine how much equity the investor gets. This ownership amount is calculated by dividing the investment by the postmoney valuation. Using the previous example, if the premoney value is $12 million, then the person who invests $3 million will get 20% (i.e., $3 million invested divided by the sum of the $12 million premoney valuation plus the $3 million investment).

The problem arises when the investor thinks the value is postmoney and the entrepreneur considers it premoney. In that situation, if the $12 million valuation is thought to be postmoney, the premoney valuation would be $9 million. The investor thinks that his $3 million investment will get him 25% of the equity (i.e., $3 million divided by the sum of $9 million + $3 million), while the entrepreneur wants to give up only 20%.

This is the reason why it is imperative for both parties to quickly agree on what they mean. Therefore, when she is asked by investors whether the valuation is premoney or postmoney, the entrepreneur's answer should be a resounding, "Premoney with the equity amount for the investor determined by the postmoney valuation."

Another major point to be made is that the postmoney valuation of the last financing round is usually where the premoney valuation of the next round begins—unless there is an increase in the valuation using another agreed-upon method. In the earlier example, the first round, the "Series A," was financed at a $15 million postmoney valuation. Therefore, the premoney valuation for the next round of financing, the "Series B," will be $15 million, and if a new investor puts in $3 million, the new postmoney valuation will be $18 million. The Series B investor will receive 17% of the equity for his second round of financing. The Series A investor, who invested $3 million for 20% will now own 20% of 83% (the balance of the equity after Series B), or 16.6% of the company. Finally, the private equity industry has a rule of thumb that Series B financing should never be done at a valuation more than twice the Series A valuation.[2]

WHY VALUE YOUR COMPANY?

There are numerous reasons why an entrepreneur should know the value of his business. These include:

- To determine a sale price for the company
- To determine how much equity to give up for partnership agreements
- To determine how much equity to give up for investor capital

Let us discuss this final point in a little more detail.

How Much Equity to Give Up

It is quite common for entrepreneurs to establish the value of their companies unknowingly when they are raising capital. Many of them will determine the amount of capital they need and at the same time arbitrarily state the level of ownership they wish to retain. Such an act automatically places an implied value on the company. For example, if an entrepreneur is looking to raise $100,000 and says that she wants to retain 90% of the company, the postmoney valuation is $1 million.

The most common minimum level of ownership that many start-up entrepreneurs seek is 51%. They believe that this is the minimum percentage they need in order to maintain their control of the company. Therefore, they are willing to give up 49%. The problem with arbitrarily giving up 49% for an investment is that it typically gives the company too low a valuation and leaves it with little equity to sell to future investors.

Another very simple way to determine the level of equity to give up is by calculating the company's value using the methods that will be cited later in this chapter. This calculation should be done prior to undertaking any fund-raising action. After the valuation has been logically, rather than arbitrarily, calculated, the amount of equity capital needed, as explained in Chapter 8 should be determined. Once these two numbers have been identified, the entrepreneur is prepared to actively pursue investors because he can now tell investors what they will get for their capital. For example, if the company has a postmoney value of $2 million and the entrepreneur is raising $200,000, then the investor will get 10% of the company.

The entrepreneur should be aware of the fact that sophisticated and experienced investors will want to use a more complex formula to determine their future equity position. Investors may determine the equity stake that they want using calculations that factor in the company's present and future valuations along with time and their desired rate of return. In this instance, 4, not 2, variables are needed: the future expected value of the company, the amount of capital invested, the investors' desired annual return, and the number of years that the capital will be invested. This approach is shown in Equation 5-1.

Equity Stake

$$\frac{\text{Amount of investment} \times (1 + \text{Year 1 expected return}) \times (1 + \text{Year 2 expected return}) \times \cdots}{\text{future expected value of company}} \qquad (5\text{-}1)$$

Using this formula, an entrepreneur who is seeking an equity investment of $400,000 for a company valued at $5 million can calculate the amount of equity she should expect to give up to an investor who wants to cash out in 4 years with an annual return of 30%. See for example, the calculation shown in Figure 5-1.

This shows that the entrepreneur should expect to give up 23% of the company.

The final way to determine the amount of equity to give up requires knowing the equity investment amount, knowing the investor's desired return, and placing a value on the company before and after the investment. In the example in Figure 5-2, the entrepreneur established the company's value at the time of the investment at $10 million, and forecasted that the company's value would be $40 million in 5 years. The entrepreneur also found out, by asking the investor, that the investor expected an internal rate of return (IRR) of 38%, which is the same as 5 times the investment in 5 years. The $5 million investment would generate a $25 million return. Therefore, the $25 million return that the investor would be entitled to equals 63% of the company's future projected value of $40 million.

$$\frac{\$400{,}000 \times (1 + 0.30) \times (1 + 0.30) \times (1 + 0.30) \times (1\ \ 0.30)}{\$5{,}000{,}000}$$

or

$$\frac{\$400{,}000 \times 2.86}{\$5{,}000{,}000} = 0.23$$

Figure 5-1 **Equity Stake Calculation: Method 1**

	Today	Five Years Later
Company value	$10 million	$40 million
Investors' equity	$5 million	$25 million
Investors' ownership	50%	63%

Figure 5-2 **Equity Stake Calculation: Method 2**

Regardless of the reason, however, every entrepreneur who owns a business, or who intends to own one, should have some idea of its worth. Thomas Stemberg, founder of Staples, Inc., gives excellent advice when he notes, "No one will ever value your business as highly as you do. No one really knows how a new business will fare. A company's valuation is very much a test of your own conviction."[3]

KEY FACTORS INFLUENCING VALUATION

As noted earlier, the value of a business is influenced by a multitude of factors, qualitative as well as quantitative. Before a final value for any company can be determined, the entrepreneur must identify and review these factors. This procedure is commonly referred to as completing a "contextual factor analysis." In other words, what is the general context in which the valuation is taking place? A proper valuation of a company does not occur in a vacuum. A solid valuation contextual factor analysis should include the following factors:

- The company's historical, present, and projected cash flow.
- Who is valuing the company?
- Is it a private or a public company?
- The availability of capital.
- Is it a strategic or a financial buyer?
- The company's stage of entrepreneurship.
- Is the company being sold at an auction?
- The state of the economy.
- The reason the company is being valued.

- Tangible and intangible assets.
- The industry.
- The quality of the management team.
- Projected performance.

Let's discuss each factor in more detail.

Cash Flow Status

Historically, the value of a company has been largely driven by its present and projected cash flow. Contrary to this historical practice, however, over the last few years, technology companies, particularly Internet and e-commerce businesses, have created immense value without the existence or even the projection of positive cash flow in the foreseeable future. Despite this fact, which we will analyze and discuss in more detail later in this chapter, the argument of this book is that all entrepreneurs should focus on creating and maximizing value by aggressively pursuing positive cash flow.

The idea that value comes from positive cash flow is rather simple and direct. The entrepreneurial pursuit of business opportunities usually comes with one basic goal in mind: to make more money than you spend—also known as positive cash flow. The other issues involved in why people choose to become entrepreneurs, including to create jobs, nurture an idea, and get rich, are simply by-products of the successful attainment of the goal of making more money than you spend.

Thus, the company's cash flow is where its true value lies. This cash flow can be used to reward employees with special bonuses, reward owners and investors, or reinvest in the company to make it even stronger in the future. It should be noted that the timing of a company's cash flows can also affect its value, depending on who is valuing the company. For example, an entrepreneur who is buying a company should give the greatest importance to the targeted company's present, not future, cash flows. The reason is that future cash flows are uncertain. They are merely projections, with no assurance of achievement. Experienced entrepreneurs like Wayne Huizenga correctly refuse to pay for the unknown. When asked about valuation, Huizenga said, "We pay for what we know, today's cash flow, not tomorrow's."[4]

The other reason that buyers should base their valuation on today's cash flow is that future cash flow will come from the work put in by the new buyer. Paying the seller for the company's future performance would be rewarding the seller for the work that the buyer will do. By doing so, the buyer would essentially be giving away the value that she will create. The craziness of the practice of valuing a company and paying the seller based on a company's future cash flow is something akin to the following. A prospective home buyer sees a house for sale in Beverly Hills that has been appraised at $10 million in its present condition and needs a lot of repairs. The buyer does due diligence and finds that once the repairs have been completed, the value of the house will be $30 million. With this information, the buyer makes an offer of $30 million, paying the seller for the work that he is about to do!

Obviously, such a scenario is utterly ridiculous, and the same should hold true with a business. The value of a business to a buyer should be based on the company's most recent cash flow, not on the future. The difference between the present and future cash flows belongs to the buyer. On the other hand, if the person valuing the company is the seller, she will want the valuation to be based on future cash flow because the future is always projected to be rosier than the present, which would lead to a higher valuation. In the case of a start-up, a valuation based on cash flow projected for the future is acceptable to investors and the entrepreneur because there is no historical or present cash flow.

Finally, the cash flow of a company directly affects its value based on the amount of debt it can service. This can be determined by working backward. The idea is that, for the buyer, the value of a company is primarily based on the amount of debt that the company's cash flow can service in 5 to 7 years (the typical amortization period for a commercial loan) under the worst-case scenario (the worst-case scenario should be the actual for the most recent year). Most highly leveraged acquisitions have capital structures consisting of 80% debt and 20% equity. Therefore, if an entrepreneur were able to get a 7-year commercial loan for 80% of the value of a company that had a worst-case projected cash flow of $100,000 for the first year, the company's value would be $875,000.

This valuation is based on the fact that 80% of the company's value equals $700,000 cumulative cash flow projected over 7 years. Thus, each percentage of ownership of the company is valued at $8,750, or 100% equals $875,000. This relationship between value, debt serviceability, and present cash flow is supported by a comment made by Sam Zell after he purchased the *Chicago Tribune* newspaper in 2007 with $8.2 billion in debt. Regarding the 2006 cash flow of $1.3 billion, Sam said, "I don't think you need it to go up, you need for it not to go down."[5]

Who Is Valuing the Company?

Are you an entrepreneur who is selling the business or raising capital? Are you the buyer of the entire company or an equity investor? As Stemberg aptly points out:

> The central tension in a venture capital deal is how much the new company is worth. The company's valuation governs how much of it the entrepreneur will own. Venture capitalists yearn to keep the valuation low and take control. Entrepreneurs want to push the number up to raise the maximum amount of cash and keep control themselves.[6]

Stemberg's experience with venture capitalists highlights the tension that often exists between financiers (both venture capitalists and others) and the entrepreneur. He notes:

> I thought Staples was worth $8 million post-money when I went out to raise capital. I wanted to raise $4 million for 50% of the company. Relative to the company's value, are you the insurance company who has to pay a claim, or are you the claimant? The former wants a lower company valuation than the latter. Are you the party in a marriage divorce trying to minimize payments to your spouse as assets are being divided or are you the spouse? The venture capitalists wanted to value the company at $6 million. On January 23, 1986, I struck a deal: The venture capitalists would pay $4.5 million for 56% of the company. Staples was worth $8 million.[7]

The value placed on a business will depend on which side of the table you sit on. If you are the entrepreneur, you will want as high a valuation as possible so that you give up as little equity as possible. If you are the investor (e.g., the venture capitalist), you will want a low valuation because you will want to get as much equity as possible for your investment. As Scott Meadow, a 20-year veteran of the venture capital industry, said, "I'm going to pay you as little as possible for as much of your company as I can get."[8] This point is best illustrated by Stemberg's experience that was just cited. The venture capitalists initially wanted 66% of Staples for their investment, compared with the 56% they received. Not all investors are as aggressive as Scott Meadow. Another venture capitalist is quoted as saying, "The key to valuing a company is to do it in a way that enables the investor to get his desired return, while keeping the entrepreneur happy and motivated." Obviously, this venture capitalist seeks a valuation that creates a "win-win" situation for the investor and the entrepreneur.

Public Versus Private Company

Two companies of similar age, operating in the same industry, producing exactly the same products or services, and achieving the same level of revenues, profits, and growth rates will have significantly different values if one is publicly traded (i.e., listed on the NYSE or Nasdaq stock exchange) and the other is privately owned. A publicly owned company will always have a greater value than a private one. Specifically, private companies have historically been valued at 15 to 25% less than similar companies that are publicly traded.[9] This difference in valuation is explainable by the following factors:

- According to Securities and Exchange Commission (SEC) rules, all public companies are required to disclose all details regarding the company's financial condition, past and present. These disclosures allow investors in public companies to base their investment decisions on more information. As private companies do not have to adhere to SEC disclosure rules and regulations, investors in private companies do not have access to this type of information.
- Investors in publicly owned companies have a ready market to buy and sell shares of stock. As you will see in more detail in Chapter 6, "Raising Capital," anyone can buy and sell the stock of public companies. That is not the case with the stock of private companies. Legally, private companies are supposed to sell stock only to

> "sophisticated" investors whom they know directly or indirectly. *Sophisticated* is loosely defined to mean individuals with a certain minimum net worth who understand the risks associated with equity investing. Investors who are known "directly" means those who are associates, family members, or personal friends. Investors who are known "indirectly" are people known through others, for example, through a banker, lawyer, or accountant.

Therefore, publicly owned companies have greater value because they provide greater and more reliable information regularly to investors than do private companies. This fact supports the axiom "information is valuable." Publicly owned companies also have greater value because of the liquidity opportunities available to investors.

Availability of Capital

As seen in Table 5.1, purchase price multiples of EBITDA on transactions under $250 million in value reached 13.2 in 2008, then retreated to 6.1 by 2012, somewhat below the mean of 7 for the 19-year historical period. The availability of capital was one of the main reasons for this increase. Between 2002, when multiples reached a 7-year low, and 2008, a number of factors converged to make this a golden era for sellers. First and foremost, the amount of credit available to investors reached historic levels. Low interest rates and the explosion of securitization of loans opened the spigot, enabling financial buyers to use leverage to target acquisitions. The proliferation of private equity firms, flush with new capital, was another factor driving valuations higher. Armed with overflowing coffers and easily accessible credit, for 5 years, between 2004 and 2008, buyout firms pumped out nearly $40 billion per year on 3,446 deals, an average of $58 million per deal.[10] Corporate buyers, traditionally the most lucrative exit option for sellers, contributed their share to the multiple increase.

As noted in Chapter 3 and shown in Table 5.2, corporate profitability was at a historic high in the mid-2000s, riding a strong economy and years of cost cutting. This left firms flush with cash and looking for ways to spend it. In 2006, cash and cash equivalents for S&P 500 firms were more than 6 times as high as in 1995 and even twice as high as they had been in the dot-com era. While profits sagged

TABLE 5-1 **Purchase Price Multiples**

Year	Price/Adjusted EBITDA
1995	5.5
1996	6.1
1997	7.0
1998	7.0
1999	6.3
2000	6.2
2001	6.1
2002	3.6
2003	7.5
2004	6.1
2005	8.6
2006	6.7
2007	8.0
2008	13.2
2009	7.9
2010	8.2
2011	7.3
2012	6.0
2013	6.1

Source: Carter Morse & Mathias, "Strategic Buyers in Perspective," November 2, 2006; *PitchBook Decade Reports 2001–2010*, Vol. 2, Investments, p. 5; PitchBook Deal Multiples and Trends Report, 2013.

from 2006 to 2008, they later recovered and have since risen to new record highs. Additionally, other factors such as the entrance of hedge funds and second-tier lenders into the market and the increasing presence of foreign buyers as a result of a weaker dollar also supported these higher multiples.

In 2008, the international credit markets tightened significantly as a result of the increasing fallout from the U.S. home mortgage crisis. The reduction in liquidity resulting from the softer credit markets led to a decline in purchase

TABLE 5-2 **U.S. Corporate Profits**

Year	U.S. Corporate Profits (Billions of Dollars)
1995	769
1996	835
1997	809
1998	842
1999	803
2000	744
2001	851
2002	988
2003	1,239
2004	1,428
2005	1,627
2006	1,530
2007	1,383
2008	1,252
2009	1,655
2010	1,755
2011	1,980
2012	2,020

Source: Federal Reserve Bank of St. Louis, Economic Research Division, Federal Reserve FRED Graph Observations, Federal Reserve Economic Data, Corporate Profits with Inventory Valuation Adjustment (IVA) and Capital Consumption Adjustment (CCAdj) (CPROFIT), Billions of Dollars, Quarterly, Seasonally Adjusted Annual Rate, http://research.stlouisfed.org/fred2.

price multiples, as seen in Table 5-1. As Scott Sperling, co-president of buyout firm Thomas H. Lee Partners, said in an interview, "Prices have gotten much higher than historical trading levels for many of these companies. That's probably not sustainable if debt markets adjust to more normalized levels."[11] The results of a survey of investment bankers lent support to a more difficult environment for financing in 2008 and beyond: 68% of the bankers in the survey said that the availability of financing was getting worse, and only 11% said that it was getting better.[12] Moreover, corporate profits and the economy were slowing, and both factors were working to bring down acquisition prices.[13]

Venture capital fund-raising levels tend to track both the economy and the stock market. Typical of this historical pattern, venture capital funds were awash with investable capital in the years leading up to 2007 and early 2008. While annual fund-raising at this point in time was a third of the $101 billion raised in 2000, venture capital fund-raising became more plentiful during those years. In the period from 2007 to 2013, investments by venture capital funds into venture firms (known as "deals") reflected changes in available capital. As indicated in Tables 5-3 and 5-4, average deal sizes dropped from 2008 to 2009 and have remained below 2008 for 5 years, with the exception of investments in the energy industry and very late stage investments. Average deal size amounts are widely available from sources like Prequin and Crunchbase and approximate premoney valuations. Firms in hotter industries and later stages get greater deal sizes and higher premoney valuations.

TABLE 5-3 **Average Deal Size by Industry, All Rounds, $millions**

Industry Group	**2007**	**2008**	**2009**	**2010**	**2011**	**2012**	**2013**
Healthcare	13.8	11.7	9.6	9.2	10.3	9.3	10.3
Internet	6.3	7.3	4.5	6.0	10.3	7.2	7.3
Consumer	8.8	8.4	6.4	4.5	7.9	4.6	5.1
Energy	20.8	7.8	9.4	7.1	10.7	14.0	7.3
Telecommunications	9.4	8.22	6.3	6.7	6.7	6.2	6.5

Source: Prequin.

TABLE 5-4 **Average Deal Size by Round of Investment, $millions**

By Round	**2007**	**2008**	**2009**	**2010**	**2011**	**2012**	**2013**
Seed	1.3	1.0	1.0	0.9	0.9	0.9	1.1
Series A	7.7	7.4	6.2	5.9	7.0	6.4	6.8
Series B	12.3	12.5	10.1	11.7	12.8	11.6	12.0
Series C	18.1	18.6	13.3	18.5	24.4	20.3	21.0
Series D+	22.5	24.3	21.5	21.3	35.9	30.3	36.4

Source: Prequin.

Strategic or Financial Buyer

The value of a company is also affected by who the buyer is. Corporations, such as those in the Fortune 500, have historically valued companies at higher prices than financial buyers, entrepreneurs with financial backing from leveraged-buyout funds (i.e., leveraged buyouts, or LBOs), and other private equity sources. As stated previously, a significant reduction in the amount of available credit typically reduces the buying power of private equity firms and returns the spread between financial and strategic buyers closer to historical norms. In situations where financial buyers have an abundance of available funds, they often pay higher prices for attractive companies; in these instances, financial buyers will often pay higher prices than strategic buyers. Table 5-5 shows the average EBITDA multiples by sectors, and Table 5-6 shows the multiples by year.

Speculation

There are some companies that gain all of their value based on their projected future performance. This was the case with the vast majority of Internet and e-commerce companies, which we will examine in more detail later in this chapter, which typically had modest revenues and no history of profits.

TABLE 5-5 **Average EBITDA Multiples 2004-2013 by Sector**

	Financial Buyers	Strategic Buyers
Materials & Industrials	8.7	10.4
Information Tech	9.9	10.6
Energy	8.3	8.8
Consumer	9.4	10.4
Healthcare	9.4	10.6
Telecommunications	7.3	7.2
Overall	9.4	9.9

Source: S&P Capital IQ.

TABLE 5-6 **Average EBITDA Multiples by Year, All Sectors**

	Financial Buyers	Strategic Buyers
2007	10.4	10.1
2008	10.8	9.5
2009	8.2	9.5
2010	9.0	9.2
2011	9.7	10.5
2012	9.4	10.2
2013	9.4	9.1

Source: S&P Capital IQ.

In response to the question, "Are Internet stocks overvalued?" one business writer responded, "Let's put it this way: They sell more on hype and hope than on real numbers."[14] That is the reason why Amazon.com, at the end of March 1999, had a 27% greater market value than Sears, a company with revenues more than 15 times greater—and, more important, with actual profits compared with losses for Amazon.com, as Figure 5-3 shows. After the market crash in 2001, both companies took a huge hit from investors, but Amazon.com was crushed. Later that year, Sears's market capitalization was listed at $11.2 billion, while Amazon was valued at just over $2 billion—a 91% drop from its value in 1999. In mid-2007, the picture shown in Figure 5-4 suggests that maybe

	Sears	Amazon.com
Value	$18.6 billion	$23.6 billion
Revenues	$9.0 billion	$293 million
Net profit (loss)	$144 million	($62 million)

Figure 5-3 **Valuation Comparison (1999)**

	Sears	Amazon.com
Value	$22.6 billion	$28.4 billion
Revenues	$52.7 billion	$11.4 billion
Net profit (loss)	$1.5 billion	$0.25 billion

Figure 5-4 **Valuation Comparison (2007)**

	Sears Holding Co.	Amazon.com
Value	$6.6 billion	$166 billion
Revenues	$39.9 billion	$61.1 billion
Net profit (loss)	($1.1 billion)	$0.12 billion

Figure 5-5 **Valuation Comparison (October 2013)**

the speculators in Amazon were on to something, as Amazon.com had become one of the world's most successful online retailers, only to further dominate on both a revenue and a market value basis by October 2013, as seen in Figure 5-5.

Stage of Company Development

The earlier the stage of the company's development, the lower its value. A company that is in the early seed stage will have a lower value than a company that is in the more mature growth stage. The reason is that there is less risk associated with the later-stage company. It has a history. Therefore, entrepreneurs are generally advised to develop their products and companies as much as possible before they seek outside private equity financing. Unfortunately, many entrepreneurs learn this lesson too late. They procure equity financing in the company's earliest stages, when its valuation is extremely low and the leverage is on the side of the investors.

This problem is further exacerbated by the fact that early-seed-stage entrepreneurs typically need relatively little money to start their company and/or develop prototypes. It is not uncommon for these entrepreneurs to need as little as $25,000 or as much as $200,000. When equity investors come in at this stage, they want to own at least 50% of the company in return for their investment. Their investment of $25,000 to $200,000 for half the company results in a postmoney company valuation of only $50,000 to $400,000. This creates major problems for the entrepreneur later because he is left with little stock to sell to future investors.

Another common problem that arises is the "seller's remorse" that entrepreneurs feel once they realize that they have given up so much of their company for so few dollars. This was the feeling that Joseph Freedman had with the company he founded in 1991, Amicus Legal Staffing, Inc. (ALS). He raised $150,000 by selling 65% of the company, thereby giving the company a value of only $230,769. In 1997, Freedman sold ALS to AccuStaff, and his investors received $13 million, or 65% of the price, for their initial $150,000 investment.[15]

Auction

When a company is being sold via an auction process, it theoretically will ultimately be valued based on what the market will bear. This process typically has multiple potential buyers bidding against one another. The result is usually a nice high price for the seller. For example, in 2007, Microsoft outbid Google and Yahoo! for the right to buy a portion of Facebook. Microsoft's $240 million investment for 1.6% of Facebook gave the company a value of $15 billion! At the time, Facebook's revenues were less than $50 million.

State of the Economy

The condition of the country's and possibly even the world's economy can dramatically affect the valuation of a company. As stated earlier in this chapter, the value of companies being started up or purchased increased annually for 5 years until 2000. It is not merely a coincidence that this occurred at the same time that the U.S. economy experienced the longest period of continuous economic growth without a recession.

A strong economy translates into an increased availability of investor capital, which, in turn, as we mentioned earlier in this chapter, translates into leverage for the entrepreneur. Obviously, the converse is true. The value of companies typically declines as the economy worsens because investors have less money to invest. Therefore, the economy affects the availability of capital, which in turn affects the value of companies.

This is not just economic theory, but a fact, evidenced by the periods 1991–2003, and 2003–2010, as the data in Table 5–7 show. The recession in 2001 in the United States cut in half the amount of capital raised (i.e., available for investing) by all private equity firms (venture capital, LBO, and mezzanine funds) from an all-time peak in 2000 of $182.0 billion to $91.4 billion in 2001. The next year, 2002, was the first full year of the recession. Capital raised in that year plummeted again to $46.9 billion, a 49% decrease from a year earlier. Fund-raising in 2003 revealed the bottom of the data series for this period, at $46.5 billion, after which time the economic recovery was reflected in gradually increasing capital raises up to and including 2007 of a new all-time high of $272.6 billion. Once again the economic slowdown showed up in fund-raising results as $206.5 billion (a 24% drop) was logged in 2008, after which capital vanished in a 213% drop in 2009 to $66.1 billion, finally bottoming at $65.2 billion in 2010 before resuming a climb upwards in 2011 and 2012.

Reason for Selling

The value of a company that is being sold is directly related to the reason behind the sale. A company has its greatest value if the entrepreneur is not selling as a result of personal or business pressures. For example, the value of a company that is being sold because of the threat of insolvency brought on by cash shortages will be much less than the value of the exact same kind of company that does not have financial problems.

The same holds true for personal reasons. The value of a company that is being sold, for example, to settle the estate of divorcing owners will be lower than it would be if that circumstance were not driving the sale. Other personal

TABLE 5-7 **Commitments to Private Equity Partnerships**

Year	Total Funds (Number)	Amount Raised (Millions of Dollars)	Average per Fund (Millions of Dollars)
1990	150	12,054.3	80
1991	67	6,142.4	92
1992	138	15,975.6	116
1993	174	21,451.0	123
1994	236	28,093.7	119
1995	269	36,428.0	135
1996	272	44,531.3	164
1997	378	60,544.9	160
1998	463	92,665.4	200
1999	596	107,318.5	180
2000	805	182,032.7	226
2001	461	91,446.4	198
2002	326	46,944.0	144
2003	282	46,500.1	165
2004	370	78,015.6	211
2005	439	138,877.1	316
2006	452	183,937.9	407
2007	499	272,642.3	546
2008	446	206,501.1	463
2009	310	66,065.9	213
2010	348	65,194.6	187
2011	395	89,399.6	226
2012	400	126,315.7	316

Source: National Venture Capital Association, 2013.

reasons that may negatively affect the value of a company include, but are not limited to, the illness or death of the owner(s) or members of the owner's family and internal conflict (business or personally related) among the owners.

Because these personal and business problems can negatively affect the value of a company that is being sold, it is common for owners to disclose as little as possible about the real reasons for the sale. That is why it is essential for any entrepreneur who is buying a company to do thorough due diligence to determine the reason that the company is being sold before valuing the company and making an offer. The major lesson to be learned from this section is that information is valuable. The same lesson was the highlight of an earlier section in this chapter, which discussed the reason why public companies have greater value than private companies.

Tangible and Intangible Assets

The tangible and intangible assets of a company will also affect the company's value. Most of the value of manufacturing companies typically lies in their tangible assets. The age and condition of these assets—such as machinery, equipment, and inventory—will have a direct impact on the company's value. For example, if the equipment is old and in poor condition as a result of overuse or lack of maintenance, the company will have a lower value than a similar company with newer and better-maintained equipment.

The same holds true for intangible assets, including a company's customer list, patents, and name. For example, if a company's name is damaged, the company will have less value than another company in the same industry with a strong, reputable name. That is the reason why AirTran Airways changed its name from Value Jet Airlines. The latter's name had been severely damaged as a result of a disastrous plane crash in 1996.

Type of Industry

The industry that a company competes in is also very important to its valuation. It is not uncommon for 2 companies with similar revenues, profits, and growth, but in different industries, to have significantly different valuations. As we will see later in this chapter, that was most certainly the case a few years ago when Internet and e-commerce companies were compared with companies in almost any other industry. Based on the price/earnings ratio (P/E ratio) valuation method, which we will also discuss in more detail later in this chapter, the industries with the highest and lowest valuations were the ones shown in Figure 5-6.

Highest P/E Ratios		Lowest P/E Ratios	
Industry	**Ratio (Trailing 12 Months)**	**Industry**	**Ratio (Trailing 12 Months)**
Diversified Capital Markets	91.9	Photographic Products	4.0
Residential REITs	73.0	Mortgage REITs	8.2
Internet Retail	49.4	Asset Management and Custody Banks	8.9
Healthcare Technology	43.6	Reinsurance	9.1
Internet Software	42.4	Consumer Finance	10.2
Systems Software	41.1	Oil & Gas Refining	11.4

Source: S&P Capital IQ, 12 months 1/1/2013–12/31/2013

Figure 5-6 **Highest and Lowest Industry P/E Ratios**

The reasons why some industries had greater value than others were the sexiness of the industry and its growth potential. Those companies that were viewed as being sexier, with high and rapid growth potential, typically had higher valuations than those companies that were in staid, conservative, and moderate-growth industries, despite the fact that—as we saw earlier in this chapter when comparing Sears and Amazon.com—the conservative industries were immensely more profitable.

Quality of Management Team

The quality of the management team, which is primarily measured by the number of years of experience that each member of the team has and the individual members' success and failure rates, will affect the value of a company that is being sold or is raising capital from external investors. In the situation where a company is being sold and the existing managers require the new owners to retain them, the value of the company will be negatively affected by the evaluation of the management team. If the new owner views the old management team as being poor, then she will be less willing to pay a high price for the company because she will have to pay to further train or replace the team members. The chance that the management team may need to be replaced adds risk to the future of the company, which in turn decreases the value of the company.

Private equity investors will give greater value to a company that has experienced management. The reason is exactly the same as that just mentioned: risk.

The greater the risk, the lower the valuation. For example, 2 start-up companies looking for the same amount of investor capital will have significantly different valuations if one company's management is composed of people with start-up experience and the other's management has none.

VALUATION METHODS

There are numerous ways to value a company, and seemingly, almost no 2 people do it the same way. Methods may differ from industry to industry, as we will see later in this chapter, as well as from appraiser to appraiser. It is important to know that there is no single valuation methodology that is superior to all the others; each has its own benefits and limitations. But ultimately, most business appraisers prefer one method and use it rather than the others. Typically, the commitment to one method comes after experimenting with several methods and determining which consistently provides the valuation that the person is most comfortable with.

Candidly, valuation is part gut and part science, and simply saying that you believe in one valuation method is all well and good. However, the rubber hits the road when you actually risk your own capital when using one or more of these methods to value a business. The point is that an entrepreneur's valuation method is determined by experience; without that valuable experience, it is strongly recommended that the entrepreneur use at least 2 different valuation methods to determine a company's range of valuations.

Valuation methods basically fall into 3 categories: (1) asset-based, (2) cash flow capitalization, and (3) multiples. In the world of entrepreneurship, if there is a most popular and commonly used valuation category, it is multiples, and within this category, the most popular method is the multiple of cash flow.

Multiples

Multiple of Cash Flow

The cash flow of a company represents the funds available to meet both its debt obligations and its equity payments. These funds can be used to make interest and/or principal payments on debt, and also to provide dividend payments, make share repurchases, and reinvest in the company. One way of valuing a company is by determining the level of cash available to undertake these activities. This level of cash is determined by calculating earnings before interest, taxes, depreciation, and amortization—EBITDA.

In this valuation methodology, EBITDA is multiplied by a specified figure (i.e., the multiplier) to determine the value of the company. In general, as shown here, a multiplier of between 3 and 10 is used. However, whether it is a buyers' market or a sellers' market, sales growth, industry growth potential, variability in a company's earnings, and exit options available to investors are all factors that affect the level of the multiplier used in valuation. The multiple is not static, but evergreen. It can change for a myriad of reasons. As venture capitalist Bill Sutter, a graduate of Yale University and Stanford Business School, stated:

> Virtually every conversation about a company's valuation in the private equity industry starts with a 5 times cash flow multiple discussion. The multiple will go up for qualitative reasons like super management and higher growth and will go down for other types of industries that are recessionary, where risk and volatility is perceived to be higher.[16]

Another means of reducing or improving valuations based on cash flow multiples is to adjust EBITDA. The adjusted EBITDA should be calculated after the entrepreneur's salary has been deducted. The reason is that the entrepreneur is entitled to receive a market-rate salary. This salary should be treated as a legitimate expense on the income statement. If the owner's salary is not recognized, then the company's EBITDA will be artificially inflated, resulting in an overvaluation of the company. This result would not be in the best interest of a buyer, who would pay more for a company, nor would it be in the best interest of an investor, who would get less equity for his investment. In the case of a buyer, the proper way to determine EBITDA is to replace the seller's salary with the new salary anticipated by the buyer, as long as it is at a justifiable market-rate level. The calculation is shown in Equation 5-2.

EBITDA Salary Adjustment

$$\text{Adjusted EBITDA} = \text{EBITDA} + \text{seller's salary} - \text{buyer's salary} \qquad (5\text{-}2)$$

For example, if a company in an industry that commonly uses a multiple of 7 had an EBITDA of $500,000, one would assume a valuation of $3.5 million. But suppose further analysis of the seller's financial statements shows that he took a salary of only $50,000 when similar-size companies in the same industry paid their owners $125,000. If the buyer intends to pay himself the market rate of $125,000, then the company's value, using the EBITDA multiple of 7, should be $2,975,000 [i.e., ($500,000 + $50,000 – $125,000) × 7]. This $525,000 difference is an 18% overvaluation!

Please note that the change in the owner's salary would also affect the amount of taxes paid by the company. Since the new salary would decrease the operating profit, the taxes would also decrease.

As stated earlier, multiples of EBITDA up to 10 are not uncommon. For example, in 2008, Mars, the candy manufacturer, agreed to buy Wrigley, the gum company, for $23 billion, or 19 times EBITDA, whereas the packaged food industry generally averages a 12 multiple.[17] But the acceptance of such multiples is discouraged unless you are the seller of the entire company or a portion of it. For a buyer, it is suggested that you should accept multiples no greater than 5. The reason is that the valuation should be such that under the worst-case scenario, cash flow will be able to completely service the debt obligation in the typical 5- to 7-year amortization period.

At a 5 multiple, if the capital structure is 60 to 80% debt, as is common, then it can be serviced within 7 years. For example, if the Grant Company's EBITDA is $1 million, a buyer should pay no more than $5 million. With an 80%, or $4 million, loan at 7%, if the cash flow over the next 7 years remained the same and no major capital improvements were needed, the total $7 million could comfortably service the debt obligation.

Multiple of Free Cash Flow

Finally, for companies that require major investments in new equipment in order to sustain growth, it is common to use a multiple of the company's free cash flow (FCF) instead of just EBITDA. This is a more conservative cash description that yields a lower valuation. For multiple purposes, FCF is calculated as shown in Equation 5-3.

Free Cash Flow

FCF = EBITDA – capital expenditures (5-3)

Manufacturing companies are usually valued based on a multiple of FCF. On the other hand, media companies such as television stations are usually valued based on a multiple of EBITDA. For example, in 1995, Westinghouse and Disney purchased CBS and ABC, respectively. Westinghouse paid 10 times EBITDA, and Disney paid 12. In fact, a quick review of the television broadcasting industry (see Table 5-8) will highlight the earlier point regarding the "evergreen" aspect of multiples.

It should be noted that the EBITDA and FCF multiple methods correctly value a company as if it is completely unleveraged and has no debt in the capital structure. The adding back of interest, taxes, and depreciation to the net earnings eliminates the relevance of whatever debt the company presently carries. This is the proper way to value a company, especially if you are a buyer, because the seller's chosen capital structure has nothing to do with the buyer and the capital structure that she ultimately chooses. The company's present capital structure could be loaded with debt because the owner wants his balance sheet to look dreadful as he begins asset settlement negotiations as part of his upcoming divorce. Therefore, the company should be valued without regard to its existing debt. Once the buyer determines the value that she wants to pay, she can agree to inherit the debt as part of her payment. For example, if the company's value is $5 million, the buyer can agree to pay it by assuming the $1 million of long-term debt that the seller owes and paying the $4 million balance in cash.

TABLE 5-8 **Television Broadcasting Industry Multiples**

Years	Selling Multiple
1980s	10–12
Early 1990s	7–8
1996	16
2007	15
2012	7–8

Multiple of Sales

This multiple is one of the more widely used valuation methods. Sales growth prospects and investor optimism play a major role in determining the level of the multiple to be used, and different industries use different multiples. In the food industry, businesses generally sell for 1 to 2 times revenue, but sales growth prospects can have an impact on raising or lowering the multiplier. For example, Quaker Oats, a strategic buyer, paid $1.7 billion, or 3.5 times revenue, for Snapple in 1995 at a time when similar companies were being sold for a sales multiple of 2 or less. Quaker's rationale: it expected rapid growth from Snapple.

However, that rapid growth did not happen. Two years later, Quaker sold Snapple to Triarc Cos. for $300 million, or a little more than 50% of its annual revenues of $550 million. Quaker's obvious overvaluation of Snapple was instrumental in the CEO's departure from the company. On the other hand, Triarc's owners were given the greatest compliment after buying Snapple when someone said, "They stole the company!"[18] In 2001, PepsiCo acquired Quaker for $13.4 billion.

Other industries that are commonly valued on a multiple of revenues include the radio station industry. Typical valuations are 2.0 to 2.5 times revenues for small-market stations, 3 to 3.5 times for middle-market stations, and 4 times for large-market stations. Another such industry is professional services firms, which are typically valued at 1 to 3 times revenues. But the most prominent industry that uses the multiple of sales model is technology, especially the Internet industry, which will be discussed in more detail later in this chapter.

The shortcoming of this method is that it ignores whether the company is generating cash. The focus is entirely on the top line. Therefore, this valuation method is best suited for those entrepreneurs who are focusing on growing market share by acquiring competitors. The idea is to buy new customers and rely on your own operational skills and experience to make each new customer a cash flow contributor. This method is best carried out by entrepreneurs who are quite experienced in operating a profitable venture in the same industry as that of the company being acquired.

Multiple of Unique Monthly Visitors

This valuation method has surfaced primarily in the Internet space. In 2005, News Corporation purchased MySpace for $580 million, or $2.93 per unique monthly visitor. The next year, Google purchased YouTube for $1.65 billion, or $4 per unique monthly visitor. Additionally, in 2008, NBC Universal agreed to buy the Weather Channel for $3.5 billion. At the time of this purchase, the Weather Channel's website had 37 million unique monthly visitors, making it a top 15 website. This purchase price translates into a price of $9.40 per unique monthly visitor.[19]

P/E Ratio Method

Another common valuation method that falls into the multiples category is the price/earnings ratio. This model is commonly used when valuing publicly owned companies. The P/E ratio is the multiplier used with the company's after-tax earnings to determine its value. It is calculated by dividing the company's stock price per share by the earnings per share (EPS) for the trailing 12 months. For example, a company with a stock price of $25 per share, 400,000 shares outstanding, and trailing 12 months' earnings of $1 million will have a P/E ratio of 10, calculated as shown in Figure 5-7. In the figure, the P/E of 10 means that it costs $10 to buy $1 in profit, or conversely, that an investor's return is 10%. This return compares very favorably with the 3.4% historical average returns on long-term bonds.[20]

The average historical P/E multiple for the Dow Jones Industrial Average is 15,[21] and for the Standard & Poor's 500 is 15.[22] In 1998, during the heart of the stock market rise, the S&P multiple was 28 and the Dow 22.20. In late 2001, during the heart of the market crash, the S&P multiple was 23.5 and the Dow multiple was 57.3. If you excluded Honeywell (with a P/E of 731, due in large part to GE's attempted acquisition), the Dow multiple was 32.9. That multiple was higher than the historical averages for some good reasons. The

P/E = price per share/EPS
EPS = earnings/number of shares outstanding
P/E = $25/($1,000,000/400,000)
P/E = $25/$2.5 = 10

Figure 5-7 **Price/Earnings Calculation**

Dow consists of larger blue-chip companies that tend to have less volatility, and during the economic downturn, investors were migrating to these safer companies. Consequently, the P/E multiples of these companies tended to be higher than normal.

P/E multiples are published daily on finance websites and in the business sections of some newspapers, showing the ratios for publicly traded companies in comparable businesses. Companies in the same industry may have different P/E multiples despite the fact that they have similar annual earnings and a similar number of outstanding shares. The difference may be related to the price of the stock. Investors may be willing to pay a higher stock price for one company because of its higher forecasted growth rate, the presence of more experienced management, the settlement of a recent lawsuit, or the approval of a new patent. In this situation, the company with the higher stock price would have a higher P/E multiple and therefore a higher valuation. Thus, it can be concluded that when a company has a P/E multiple that is higher than the industry average, it's primarily because investors have a positive view of the company's growth opportunities and expect relatively reliable earnings. Conversely, lower P/E multiples are associated with low growth, erratic earnings, and perceived future financial risk.

Be mindful of the fact that P/E multiples are ideally used to value publicly owned companies. However, P/E multiples are sometimes used to value private companies.

The ideal way to value a private company using a P/E multiple is to find the public company that is the most comparable. The most important criterion to look for is a company with exactly the same, or as close as possible, products or services. The objective is to select a company that is in the same business. The other important criteria are as follows:

- Revenue size
- Profitability
- Growth history and potential
- Company age

After the best comparable company has been determined, the P/E multiple should be discounted. The reason? As stated earlier in this chapter, the value of a publicly owned company will always be higher than that of a private company with exactly the same revenues, profits, cash flow, growth potential, and age, as a result of liquidity and access to information. The result is that private companies are typically valued at 15 to 25% less than public companies. Therefore, the P/E multiple of a public company that is selected as the best comparable should be discounted by 15 to 25%.

Multiple of Gross Margin

As a rule of thumb, the multiple of gross margin should be no higher than 2. Therefore, a company with revenues of $50 million and gross margin of 30% has a value of $30 million (i.e., $50 million × 0.30 = $15 million; $15 million × 2 = $30 million).

Different Industries Use Different Multiple Benchmarks

Before we close out the discussion of multiples, it is important to highlight the fact that different industries use not only different multiple numbers, but also different benchmarks. They include the following:

- Distribution companies in the soft drink and alcoholic beverages industry are valued at a multiple of the number of cases sold.
- The pawnshop industry, which provides loans averaging $70 to $100 at annual interest rates ranging from 12 to 240%, typically uses one of two valuation methods: the multiple of earnings model or the multiple of loan balances model. There are more than 9,100 pawnshops in the United States,[23] and approximately 6% of them are publicly owned. These public pawnshops are valued at a multiple of 18.5 times earnings, which is significantly higher than the figures for private shops, which are valued at between 4 and 7 times earnings.

While this multiple of earnings valuation model is not unique to pawnshops, the model of a multiple of loan balance is. A pawnshop's loan balance provides evidence of the number of its customer relationships, which is its greatest asset. Thus, the multiple range commonly used to value a pawnshop is 2 to 4 times its outstanding loan balance.

Rules of thumb are often used to make quick estimates of business values. The 2010 *Business Reference Guide*, published by the Business Brokerage Press, is a great resource for anyone who is involved in valuing, buying, or selling a privately held business. Table 5-9 is a sample of some businesses and the "rule-of-thumb" multiples outlined in the guide.

As one further point of reference, the *Newsletter of Corporate Renewal* suggests that the value of any company should be no more than 2 times its gross

TABLE 5-9 Rule-of-Thumb Valuations

Industry	"Rule-of-Thumb" Valuation
Accounting firms	100–125% of annual revenues
Auto dealers (new cars)	0–10% of annual sales + inventory
Bookstores	15% of annual sales + inventory
Coffee shops (gourmet)	40% of annual sales + inventory
Daycare centers	45–50% of annual sales including inventory
Dental practices	60–65% of annual revenues including inventory
Dry cleaners	70–80% of annual sales + Inventory
Engineering services	40–45% of annual revenues
Flower shops	30–35% of annual sales + inventory
Food shops (gourmet)	30% of annual sales + inventory
Gas stations (without convenience store)	15–20% of annual sales + inventory
Gift/Card shops	35% of annual sales including inventory
Grocery store (supermarket)	15% of annuals sales + inventory
Hardware stores	45% of annual sales including inventory
Insurance agencies	125–150% of annual revenues
Landscape businesses	45% of annual sales
Law practices	90–100% of annual revenues
Liquor stores	40–45% of annual sales + inventory
Restaurants (full-serve)	30–35% of annual sales + inventory
Restaurants (limited-serve)	30–40% of annual sales + inventory
Sporting goods stores	25% of annual sales + inventory
Taverns/Bars	40% of annuals sales + inventory
Travel agencies	35–40% of annual commissions
Veterinary practices	70% of annual revenues + inventory

Source: Business Brokerage Press via bizstats.com.

margin dollars.[24] In conclusion, when valuing a company using any one of the aforementioned multiple models (that is, revenues, cash flow, earnings, or gross margins), it should be noted that the multiples are not static. They are constantly changing and should be adjusted up or down, depending on several factors.

If an industry is experiencing a downturn, thereby making it a buyer's market, then the multiples will typically decline. The television industry is a perfect example. During the 1980s, television stations were selling for 10 to 12 times EBITDA. By the end of the decade, however, the multiples had gone down to 7 to 8. The reason? The country was in the early stages of a recession. Fewer advertising dollars were going to television stations because there was more competition from the new cable industry. Also, the major networks decreased the amount of payments they were making to their affiliate stations. The combination of these factors created a buyer's market for network-affiliated television stations. By 1995, the multiples had changed again. The reason for the increase was aptly described in a *Chicago Tribune* article:

> Television stations normally sell for 8 to 10 times cash flow. But some of the recent [1995–1996] sales sold at multiples of 15 to 20. A strong economy and an even more robust advertising market helped make TV stations virtual cash cows, producing profit margins ranging from 30 to 70%. The approach of a presidential election year in 1996 and the Olympic Games in Atlanta should provide further stimulus to the ad market.[25]

Another interesting example is the newspaper industry. Since 1940, the number of U.S. daily newspapers has steadily declined. In addition, more recently, advertising revenue for newspapers has come under siege from other media, including the Internet. As Warren Buffett said at his annual investors' meeting in May 2006, newspapers appear to have entered a period of "protracted decline." To illustrate, Google's market capitalization in October 2013 was approximately 14 times that of the 5 largest newspapers, yet Google's EBITDA of $16.2 billion was just 6 times the $2.8 billion generated by these newspapers. Table 5-10 demonstrates this point.

There are many factors that may justify an increase or decrease in a company's multiple relative to the industry's typical multiple. An example of multiples

TABLE 5-10 **Valuation Comparison**

	Top Five Newspapers	Google
Total EBITDA	$2.8 billion	$16.2 billion
Market capitalization	$24.6 billion	$346.3 billion
Multiple of EBITDA	8.9	21.4

Source: Company financials via Google Finance, October 2013.

increasing occurred in the funeral home industry. Historically, this industry was characterized primarily by small "mom-and-pop" family owner/operators. These small businesses were selling for 2 to 3 times EBITDA. But in the early 1990s, the value of companies in this fragmented industry of more than 25,000 funeral homes began to change dramatically. Four companies, which are now publicly owned, began a fierce battle, competing with one another to grow their companies rapidly by consolidating the industry. The 4 companies, Service Corporation International, Stewart Enterprises Inc., Loewen Group Inc., and Carriage Services, Inc., in many instances sought the same funeral homes, so that by the end of 1998, funeral homes were selling for 8 to 10 times EBITDA.

In 1997, the industry saw the beginning of a decline in these multiples because the growth began to slow. As one business analyst said, this industry is suffering from overvaluation of companies financed by too much debt that cannot be repaid because of an "out-break of wellness"—fewer people are dying.[26] About 2.3 million people die each year in the United States, with a typical average annual increase of 1%. But in 1997, for the first time in a decade, that number decreased. There were 445 fewer deaths in 1997 than in 1996. One interesting reason for this decline was the weather. Most people die during the harsh winter. The previous few winters in the United States had been relatively mild. The industry's growth was also hurt by the increasing popularity of cremations, which cost half the price of traditional burials.[27]

The final example of an ever-changing multiple was that applied to high-growth Microsoft. From 1994 to 1996, Microsoft's multiple of revenues more than doubled, from 6 to 14.[28]

Asset Valuation

In the past, the value of a company's assets had great significance in determining the company's overall valuation. Today, most American companies do not have many tangible assets because each year fewer things are produced in the United States. Most are produced overseas in low-wage-paying countries like China, India, and Taiwan.

The result is that, over time, the value of a company has come to be dependent less on its assets than on its cash flow. Asset value tends to be most meaningful in cases in which financially troubled companies are being sold. In that case, the negotiation for the value of the company typically begins at the depreciated value of its assets.

Capitalization of Cash Flows

Free Cash Flow Model

The most complicated and involved valuation model is the free cash flow model, also known as the discounted cash flow or capitalization of cash flow model. It is a model that relies on projections filled with assumptions, because there are so many unknown variables. Therefore, it is the model that is least commonly used to value high-risk start-ups.

Simply stated, free cash flow is the portion of a company's operating cash flow that is available for distribution to the providers of debt (i.e., interest and principal payments) and equity (i.e., dividend payments and repurchase of stock) capital. This is the cash that is available after the operating taxes, working capital needs, and capital expenditures have been deducted.

Using this valuation method, one approach is to forecast the FCF as the Japanese do: for 25 years without regard to what happens later, because its discounted value will be insignificant. Another similar, and more commonly used, approach is to separate the value of the business into two time periods: during and after an explicitly forecasted period. The "during" period is referred to as the planning period. The "after" period is referred to as the residual.

The FCF valuation formula, Equation 5-4, is the sum of the present value (PV) of the free cash flow for the planning period and the present value of the residual value.

Free Cash Flow Valuation

PV for the FCF planning period + PV residual value = FCF value (5-4)

To calculate the PV of the FCF for the planning period, the following steps must be followed:

1. Determine the planning period. It is customarily 5 years.
2. Project the company's earnings before interest and taxes (EBIT) for five years. The use of EBIT assumes that the company is completely unleveraged—it has no debt in its capital structure.
3. Determine the company's EBIT tax rate. This will be used to calculate the exact amount of adjusted taxes to be deducted. These are "adjusted" taxes because they ignore the tax benefits of debt financing and interest payments, since this model, as stated previously, assumes a capital structure that does not include debt.
4. Determine the amount of depreciation expense for each of the 5 years. This expense can be calculated in several ways:
    a. Assume no depreciation expense because the capital expenditures for new assets and the corresponding depreciation will cancel each other out. If this assumption is made, then there should also be a zero for capital expenditures for new assets.
    b. Using historical comparables, make the future depreciation expense a similar constant percentage of fixed assets, sales, or incremental sales.
    c. Using the company's actual depreciation method, forecast the company's value of new assets from capital expenditures and compute the actual depreciation expense for each of the forecasted years.
5. Determine the needed increase in operating working capital for each year. The working capital required is the same as the net investment needed to grow the company at the desired rate. The working capital can be calculated as shown in Figure 5-8. The increase in working capital would simply be the change from year to year.

Current operating assets excluding cash
−current liabilities
=**working capital**

Figure 5-8 **Working Capital Calculation**

6. Determine the investment amounts for capital expenditures. Capital expenditures are made for two purposes. The first is to repair the existing equipment in order to maintain the company's present growth. The other is for new equipment needed to improve the company's growth. As was stated in step 4a, the cost of new assets can be zeroed out by the depreciation expense. Therefore, only the capital expenditures needed for maintenance would be highlighted. As stated earlier, that amount can be determined by using historical comparables.
7. Determine the company's expected growth rate (GR).
8. Determine the discount rate (DR). This rate should reflect the company's cost of capital from all capital providers. Each provider's cost of capital should be weighted by its prorated contribution to the company's total capital. This is called the *weighted average cost of capital* (WACC). For example, if a company is financed with \$2 million of debt at 10% and \$3 million of equity at 30%, its WACC, or discount rate, can be determined as follows:
   a. Total financing: \$5 million
   b. Percent of debt financing: 40% (\$2 million/\$5 million)
   c. Percent of equity financing: 60% (\$3 million/\$5 million)
   d. (Debt amount × debt cost) + (equity amount × equity cost)
   e. $(0.40 \times 0.10) + (0.60 \times 0.30) = 0.22$

   A final point: please note that the tax-shield benefit of the debt financing is incorporated in the WACC.
9. Input all the information into the FCF planning period formula, Equation 5-5.

Free Cash Flow for the Planning Period

EBIT
− taxes
+ depreciation
− increase in operating working capital
− capital expenditure
= FCF for the planning period (5-5)

10. Once the FCF for each year has been determined, a present value of the sum of the periods must be calculated. The discount rate is required to complete the calculation, shown in Equation 5-6.

Present Value of Free Cash Flow for the Planning Period

$$\text{PV of FCF planning period} = \frac{\text{Year 1 FCF}}{(1+\text{DR})} + \frac{\text{Year 2 FCF}}{(1+\text{DR})^2} + \frac{\text{Year 3 FCF}}{(1+\text{DR})^3} + \frac{\text{Year 4 FCF}}{(1+\text{DR})^4} - \cdots \quad (5\text{-}6)$$

Next, the present value of the residual must be determined. To do so, the first year's residual value must be calculated by simply forecasting the FCF for Year 6, the first year after the planning period. Then all the information should be put into the PV of residuals formula, Equation 5-7.

Present Value Residuals

$$\text{PV of residuals} = \frac{\text{first year residual value/(discount rate} - \text{growth rate)}}{(1 + \text{discount rate}) \times \text{number of years to discount back}} \quad (5\text{-}7)$$

The final number from this calculation should then be added to the PV of the FCF number to determine the company's value.

Let's determine the value of Bruce.com using the FCF model. The company is forecasting a conservative 10% growth rate. Its WACC is 13%, and its tax rate is 52%. The forecasted annual FCF is presented in Figure 5-9.

The PV of the FCF planning period is determined as shown in Figure 5-10. With an estimated Year 6 FCF valuation of $960,300, the PV residual can

	2013	2014	2015	2016	2017
EBIT	$1,398	$1,604	$1,789	$1,993	$2,217
Tax (52%)	727	834	930	1,036	1,152
Depreciation	—	—	—	—	—
Increase in working capital	56	144	158	175	191
Capital expenditure	16	18	20	21	24
Forecasted annual FCF	**599**	**606**	**681**	**761**	**850**

Figure 5-9 **Forecasted Annual Free Cash Flow Calculation, in Thousands of Dollars**

be calculated using the equation in Figure 5-11. Now we can determine the value of Bruce.com. As you can see in Figure 5-12, Bruce.com's value is $19,798,746.

It should be noted that 88% of the company's value comes from the residual value. Also, this FCF valuation formula is very sensitive to slight changes in the growth and discount rates. For example, if the discount rate were 0.17 instead of 0.13, an 18% difference, the value of Bruce.com would decrease by 57%, to $8,430,776. The PV of the residual would be $6,264,187, and the PV of the FCF would be $2,166,589.

The criticisms of this model are that it is too theoretical and complex and that it is filled with uncertainties. The three major uncertainties are the FCF projections, the discount rate, and the growth rate. Nobody truly knows any of these. It is all educated speculation. As Bill Sutter, the venture capitalist at Mesirow Partners and a Stanford Business School graduate with a major in

PV of FCF for the planning period =

$$\frac{599}{(1+0.13)^1} + \frac{606}{(1+0.13)^2} + \frac{681}{(1+0.13)^3} + \frac{761}{(1+0.13)^4} + \frac{850}{(1+0.13)^5}$$

$530,088 + $473,437 + $469,655 + $466,871 + $461,956 = $2,402,007

Figure 5-10 **Present Value of Free Cash Flow for the Planning Period Calculation**

PV of the residual =

$$\frac{\$960{,}300/(0.13 - 0.10)}{(1 + 0.13)^5} = \frac{\$960{,}300/0.03}{1.84}$$

$$= \$17{,}396{,}739$$

Figure 5-11 **Present Value of the Residual Calculation**

$17,396,739	PV of the residual
2,402,007	PV of the FCF
$19,798,746	Bruce.com valuation

Figure 5-12 **Valuation Calculation**

finance who was mentioned earlier in this chapter, noted in a lecture to graduate business school students:

> Valuation is remarkably unscientific. You can take out your FCF models, Alcar models, talk about your capital asset pricing model and betas until you are blue in the face. I have not used any of those since I got out of business school. Frankly, that is not the way we operate. You can use it for your finance class but you are not going to use it out in the real world.

VALUING TECHNOLOGY AND INTERNET COMPANIES

In most cases, the valuation methods discussed in this chapter were not applicable when valuing start-up Internet and related technology companies during the 1990s. The P/E ratio method could not be used because the companies had no "E." Until 2000, Internet companies that had negligible or no present cash flow streams, and in most instances did not expect to get positive cash flow streams for years to come, were valued at extremely high prices at the time they went public. Examples of this include Netscape, Yahoo!, and Amazon.com, to name just a few of the better-known brand names.

When Netscape, the Internet browser company, went public in 1996, the value of its stock went from $28 to $171 per share over a 3-month period, despite the fact that the company had never made a profit. AOL eventually acquired Netscape.

In 1995, 2 Stanford Ph.D. students founded Yahoo!, the Internet search engine company. In 1996, with annual revenues of $1.4 million and profits of only $81,000, the company went public at a valuation of $850 million. In 1999, Yahoo!'s $19 billion market value was equivalent to that of television broadcaster CBS, which had 37 times Yahoo!'s revenues. At year-end 2012, Yahoo!'s revenue of just under $5 billion generated a market value of $23.9 billion.

Finally, another famous e-commerce company, Amazon.com, which went public in May 1997 at a value of $500 million despite the absence of any historical, present, or near-term projected profits, once had a value greater than profitable Fortune 500 companies such as Sears, as noted earlier in this chapter. Another example: the Internet firm Epigraph had expected revenues of $250,000 in 1999 and $1.4 million in 2000. When asked when his company might become profitable, the founder responded, "Oh, come on. We're an Internet company!"[29]

In the late 1990s, the prices of Internet and technology companies soared enormously: Dell Computer rose 249% in 1998, Amazon.com went up 966% during the same year, and Yahoo! went up 584%, while eBay rose 1240% from its initial offering price. These valuations raised the question of whether conventional valuation methods were applicable in estimating the worth of Internet stocks. As one stockbroker noted, "I don't know how you value these things. It's a new set of rules. The Internet stocks are bizarre and outrageous."[30] And as we all discovered, many of those high-flying Internet stocks could be hazardous to one's health.

A prominent investor, Warren Buffett, the CEO of Berkshire Hathaway, who has forgone any significant investment in technology-related stocks, was also baffled by these stocks' valuations. At a 1999 news conference, he cheerfully closed a discussion of how he thought business schools should teach the principles of valuing companies by saying, "I would say for a final exam, here's the stock of any Internet company; what is it worth? And anybody who gave an answer, flunks."

Warren Buffett and others who believed that Internet stocks were being valued more on hope and on hype than on real numbers were justifiably concerned that most Internet companies had high debt levels, few assets, and, most important, a limited, if any, history of profits. Despite this, investors were more than willing to pay premium prices for these stocks, with the expectation that the companies would eventually produce significant earnings.

Therefore, given all this controversy, what was (were) the best method(s) to use for valuing technology and Internet companies? Quite frankly, all of them had major drawbacks. The least practical method seemed to be a multiple of earnings or cash flow. As stated earlier, most of these companies had not only negative earnings but also negative cash flow. For example, in 1998, *Forbes* magazine identified what it called "the Internet landscape," which included 46 companies that covered the breadth of the Internet market, from semiconductor chips to sports commentary. Only 14 (or 35%) of the companies had had at least a breakeven net income for the previous 12 months. Despite this fact, the value of the lowest company was $182 million.[31]

Using the comparable valuation method also created problems. The process of borrowing a valuation from a similar company that had been priced by an acquisition or some other event did not work very convincingly either, said columnist Jim Jubak, especially given the fact that all Internet companies might be overpriced.[32] For example, 2 Internet service providers, Mindspring Enterprises Inc. and EarthLink Network Inc., were sold in 1998. Their selling prices translated into a value of $1,500 per subscriber. In mid-1998, America Online (AOL), the largest and most prominent Internet service provider—at one time operated by Time Warner—had 14 million subscribers. If AOL were valued based on comparable subscriber rates, the company's value at the time would have been $21 billion, not the actual $14 billion. Thus, using the comparable method would have foolishly suggested that AOL was 33% undervalued.

Even the most popular and seemingly acceptable valuation method for the Internet industry, the multiple of revenues, had many justifiable criticisms. The rule of thumb was to use a multiple of between 5 and 7 times a company's projected, not current, revenues to determine valuation. The multiple would go up or down depending on the company's revenue growth rates and gross margins.

Criticisms of this model included the fact that a 5 to 7 multiple for companies that had low or no profits seemed excessively high when a company like Sears was valued at a revenue multiple of 1 and a profitable media company such as Gannett was valued at a multiple of 5. The other problem was that the value was based on projected, not present, revenues. If Amazon.com as of the third quarter of 1999 had been valued based on present revenues, the multiplier would have been an astonishing 20 times. Even more astounding is that, because of the use of projected revenues, a company like Yahoo! had a $19 billion market value, similar to that of CBS television, despite the fact CBS had revenues 37 times those of Yahoo!.

Another example of the craziness of the revenue valuation model that was previously used to value Internet companies was a company called Rhythms NetConnections, a high-speed Internet access firm. Rhythms NetConnections, with revenues of $5.8 million, was valued at $3.1 billion, or 539 times revenues. In defense of this multiple, the founder said that it was justified because Rhythms NetConnections was growing exponentially, doubling its size every quarter.[33] On August 1, 2001, Rhythms NetConnections and all of its wholly owned U.S. subsidiaries voluntarily filed for reorganization under Chapter 11.

To get a sense of perspective, let us look at the Standard & Poor's MidCap 400. If the market capitalization of the companies on this list were valued based on multiple of revenues, their historical median from 1995 to 2013 was 1.1 times.[34] This multiple's top value of 1.36 has been reached three times: 1) April, 1998; 2) March, 2000; 3) January, 2006 and its low of 0.50 was touched in March 2009. In 2013, the mean value was 1.17.

The final criticism of the revenue method was based on the discovery that many Internet companies were reporting "virtual revenue." The revenue was not real. For example, the companies recognized as revenues the value of the ad space that they exchanged with each other for space on their sites. While the recognition of revenue in such a situation had to be offset by an expense on the income statement, the expense became irrelevant because the valuation was based only on revenues. Since the expense was irrelevant, this practice encouraged companies to inflate the price of their bartered ad space. Another problem with this practice was the fact that there was no guarantee that if the ad space had not been bartered, it would have been sold. Thus, bartering was very important to a company's reported revenue. Internet.com did not include bartered ads in its revenues. Its CEO, Alan Meckler, says that this hurt the value of his company's stock, because competitors that included barter appeared to be doing better.[35] Figure 5-13 lists several public companies that, according to their company reports, included bartered ads in their revenue in 1998.

Not surprisingly, private companies that were planning to go public realized the value of recognizing barter. Deja.com, an online chat site that went

Company	Percent of Revenue from Barter
CNet	6
Yahoo!	10
EarthWeb	11
SportsLine USA	20

Figure 5-13 **Bartered Advertisements**

public in 1999, reported 1998 revenues of $5 million. More than 25% of that reported revenue came from barter. After 6 years of no profits, Deja.com went out of business in 2001 and sold its assets to the search engine Google.

Given the fact that most Internet and e-commerce companies did not have earnings or positive cash flows, the commonly used and accepted valuation model was a multiple of revenues. Therefore, the companies were in constant aggressive pursuit of increased revenues to bolster their valuations. As stated earlier, this practice of rewarding revenues without regard for profit seemingly encouraged more companies to recognize "virtual revenue." The standard accounting rules, which have now been revised, vaguely stated that retailers that do not assume the risk of holding inventory are "business agents" and should book as revenue only the difference between what the retail customer pays and the wholesale price. Therefore, if a retailer charges a customer $200 for a bike that will be shipped to the customer directly from the manufacturer (i.e., drop-shipped), and the manufacturer charges the retailer $100, the amount of revenue recognized by the retailer should be the $100 difference, not $200.

The vagueness of the accounting rules resulted in Internet companies recognizing revenues differently. This inconsistency made some companies seem significantly larger than others. For example, Preview Travel's CFO, Bruce Carmedelle, said that rival Priceline.com appeared to be 10 times larger even though it "sells only a few more tickets than we do." At that time, Priceline.com counted as revenue what customers paid for airline tickets, whereas Preview counted only the commissions it got from carriers.

This virtual revenue phenomenon also occurred when a company generated sales both by shipping inventory from its warehouse and by having the products shipped directly from its supplier's warehouse to the end customer.

Ideally, the revenue amounts should have been recognized differently. In the former case, the amount of revenue that should have been recognized was the total price that the customer paid. In the latter case, where the product was being drop-shipped, the revenue recognized should have been only the difference between the retail and wholesale prices. Xoom.com, now part of Comcast, was one of the companies that adhered to this practice. But many other companies, such as Theglobe.com, booked revenue the same way in all cases, although some items came from company warehouses and others from suppliers.[36]

Theglobe.com would soon see its world come crashing down. While its opening-day high was $97 in 1998, the stock was delisted and trading for just 7 cents a share in late 2001. The technology industry, which came under justifiable criticism for overvaluation of companies without profits, began using the multiple of gross margin method. This method became more popular after it was realized that the multiple of revenues method had encouraged these companies to generate revenue without regard to gross, operating, or net profits. The result of the revenue method was the creation of companies, such as Buy.com, that sold products at prices below cost. This was sheer madness.

Beginning in April 2000, the valuation of technology companies began declining rapidly. For example, IWon purchased the web portal Excite.com in 2001 for $10 million. In 1997, Excite.com had been worth $6.1 billion. As a comparison to their lofty status in 2000, Table 5-11 lists the current P/E ratio (where it exists) for the five firms with the highest P/E ratios in the 2000 USA Today Internet 100 (now the Internet 50). As you can see, only 2 of the firms

TABLE 5-11 **Current Status of Firms with Highest P/E Multiples in the 2000 USA Today Internet 100**

Firm	2000 P/E	2008 P/E	2013 P/E
Infospace.com	599.3	22.8	33.1 (now Blucora)
Exodus Communications	634	N/A (bankrupt)	
Vertical Net	854	N/A (acquired for $15 million in 2007)	
Covad Communications	922	N/A (acquired for $1.02 per share)	
CMGI	1,228	18.77	N/A (now ModusLink)

are still publicly traded today—at P/E ratios significantly lower than they were traded at in 2000; one firm, Exodus Communications, went bankrupt; and 2 firms were acquired at fractions of their market values just 8 years earlier.

Another thing that positively affected the value of publicly traded Internet companies was the fact that they had "thin floats." This means that most of the company's stock was controlled by insiders, such as the management team and other employees. Therefore, public investors held very little stock. The result was that it did not take a lot of buying by the public to increase the share price. Examples of companies that had thin floats are listed in Table 5-12. In contrast, companies with typical levels of stock held by the public include those listed in Table 5-13.

While we correctly criticized the looniness of valuations during the Internet craze, it is important that the lesson learned be greater than a few jokes. The primary lesson learned is that whether one operates in a new economy, an old economy, or a future economy, financial fundamentals related to profitability and valuation will always be important because they have passed the test of time.

TABLE 5-12 Companies with Thin Floats, >200m Shares Outstanding, 2014

Company	Held by Insiders	Public Float
Clear Channel Outdoor (NYSE:CCO)	89%	11%
Santander Consumer USA (NYSE:SC)	88%	12%
Valhi, Inc (NYSE:VHI)	97%	3%
CNA Financial (NYSE:CNA)	90%	10%
Crown Media Holdings (NasdaqGS:CRWN)	90%	10%

Source: S&P Capital IQ.

TABLE 5-13 Companies with High % of Publicly Held Stock, >200m Shares Outstanding, 2014

Company	Held by Insiders	Public Float
Safeway Stores (NYSE:SWY)	1%	99%
UnitedHealth Group (NYSE:UNH)	2%	98%
Starbucks (NasdaqGS:SBUX)	3%	97%
KKR (NYSE:KFN)	5%	95%
Adobe Systems (NasdaqGS:ADBE)	6%	94%
Google (NasdaqGS:GOOG)	17%	83%

Source: S&P Capital IQ.

6

Raising Capital

Money is always dull, except when you haven't got any, and then it's terrifying.
Sheila Bishop, *The House with Two Faces* (1960)

INTRODUCTION

As Gene Wang, a successful business owner, noted, for the entrepreneur who is in the capital-raising stage, there are 4 important things to do:

1. Never run out of money.
2. Really understand your business or product.
3. Have a good product.
4. Never run out of money.[1]

These are great words of advice, but for many entrepreneurs, accomplishing points 1 and 4 is easier said than done.

Several of the most common complaints about entrepreneurship concern money. Entrepreneurs repeatedly lament the fact that raising capital is their greatest challenge because there seemingly is never enough and the fund-raising process takes too long. These are not groundless complaints. Thomas Balderston, a venture capitalist, said, "Too few entrepreneurs recognize that raising capital is a continuing process."[2] Also, it is extremely tough to raise capital, be it debt or equity, for start-ups, expansions, or acquisitions. The process typically takes several years and multiple rounds.

The founding and funding of Google is a classic example of this process. Initially, college friends Sergey Brin and Larry Page maxed out their credit cards to buy the terabytes of storage that they needed in order to start Google. Next, they raised $100,000 from Andy Bechtolsheim, one of the founders of Sun Microsystems, and another $900,000 from their network of family, friends, and acquaintances. Subsequently, Google raised $24 million from two venture capital firms and $1.67 billion from its initial public offering (IPO). The company was 3½ years old when it raised venture capital, and 8½ when it had its IPO.[3]

Why is it so difficult to raise capital? The most obvious reason is that capital providers are taking major risks when they finance entrepreneurial ventures. Roughly 50% of businesses fail within the first 4 years, and more than 7 out of 10 fail within 10 years.[4] Over a long time window, the success rate is low. Given this fact, capital providers are justified in performing lengthy due diligence to determine the creditworthiness of entrepreneurs. It may seem sacrilegious for me to say this, but it must be said: those who become entrepreneurs are not entitled to financing simply because they joined the club.

One of my objectives for this book is to supply you with information, insights, and advice that will, I hope, increase your chances of procuring capital. Here are some words on the advice front: since it is so tough to raise capital, the entrepreneur must be steadfast and undeviating in this pursuit. Successful high-growth entrepreneurs are not quitters. They are thick-skinned; hearing the word *no* does not completely deter or terminate their efforts. A great example of an entrepreneur with such perseverance is Howard Schultz, the CEO of Starbucks. When he was in search of financing for the acquisition of Starbucks, he approached 242 people and was rejected 217 times. He finally procured the financing, acquired the company, and today boasts a public company that has 19,200 locations and more than 160,000 employees.[5]

VALUE-ADDED INVESTORS

Howard Schultz and all other successful high-growth entrepreneurs know not only that it is important to raise the proper amount of capital at the best terms, but that it is even more important to raise it from the right investors. There is an old saying in entrepreneurial finance: whom you raise money from is more important than the amount or the cost. The ideal is to raise capital from "value-added" investors. These are people who provide you with insights in addition to their financial investment. For example, value-added investors may give the company legitimacy and credibility because of their upstanding reputation.

Value-added investors also include those who can help entrepreneurs acquire new customers, employees, or additional capital. A great example of an entrepreneur who understands the importance of value-added investors is the founder of eBay, Pierre Omidyar, who accepted capital from the famous venture capital firm Benchmark. Ironically, eBay did not really need the money. It has always been profitable. It took $5 million from Benchmark for two reasons. The first was that it felt that Benchmark's great reputation would give eBay credibility. The second was that it wanted Benchmark, which had extensive experience in the public markets, to help eBay make an IPO.

Another great example of an entrepreneur who understood the importance of a value-added investor is Jeff Bezos of Amazon.com. When pursuing venture capital financing, Bezos rejected money from two funds that offered a higher valuation and better terms than Kleiner Perkins Caufield & Byers (KPCB), which he accepted. When asked why he took KPCB's lower bid, he responded, "If we'd thought all this was purely about money, we'd have gone with another firm. But KPCB is the gravitational center of a huge piece of the Internet world. Being with them is like being on prime real estate."[6]

In addition to investing $8 million, KPCB also helped persuade Scott Cook, the chairman of Intuit at the time, to join Amazon.com's board. KPCB also immediately helped Bezos recruit 2 vice presidents and, in May 1997, helped him take Amazon.com public.

While these 2 examples highlight only venture capitalists, it must be made perfectly clear that there are several other sources of value-added capital.

SOURCES OF CAPITAL

The source of capital that gets the most media attention is venture capital funds. But in reality, as Figure 6-1 shows, these funds have been a small contributor to the total annual capital provided to entrepreneurs. According to the 2014

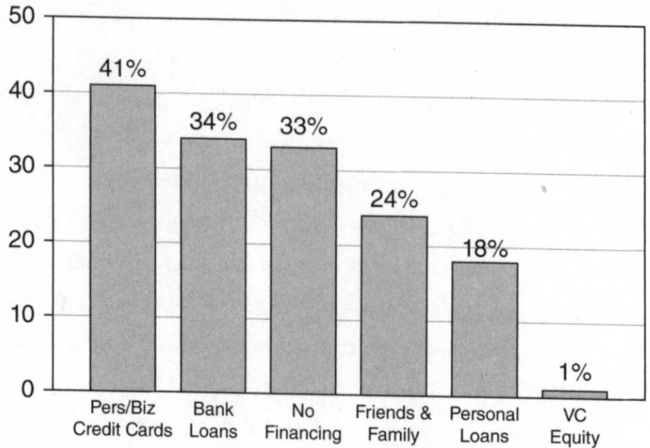

Figure 6-1 **Sources of Small-Businesses' Financing**

Pepperdine Private Capital Markets Project, current financing comes from multiple sources mixed together. Venture capital is the *least* common at 1%! Combined personal and business credit cards are the most common at 41%, business loans supply 34%, friends and family provide 24%, and 18% of business capital is supplied by the entrepreneur himself through personal loans. Notably, 1/3 or 33% of small business owners have no financing at all.[7] The former director of this annual research project on U.S. private capital, Dr. John Paglia, made it clear in a verbal summary of his findings: "Basically, American Express cards are the most common source of start-up capital in America!"

According to the 2012 Global Entrepreneurship Monitor (GEM) United States report on financing entrepreneurship, eliminating venture capital would not make a perceptible difference in entrepreneurial activity overall because fewer than 1 in 10,000 new ventures has venture capital in hand at the outset, and fewer than 1 in 1,000 businesses ever has venture capital at any time during its existence. According to the GEM, across the world, 73% of start-up funds come from the entrepreneurs themselves, with the remaining 27% coming from external sources.[8]

Money from friends, family, and the owners themselves is a bit more difficult to track. Table 6-1 shows data from a study conducted a few years back that examines the more formal sources of financing for entrepreneurs, and it shows that banks, with $179 billion in annual loans to small businesses at that time,

TABLE 6-1 **Sources of Outside Capital for Entrepreneurs**

Banks	$179 billion	53%
Nonbanks	96 billion	29%
Angels	30 billion	9%
Venture capitalists	10 billion	3%
Other	20 billion	6%
Total capital	**$335 billion**	

were the most active backers of entrepreneurs. The number 2 providers, with $96 billion, were nonbank financial institutions such as GE Capital and Prudential Insurance. Venture capital was less than one-tenth of the amount of capital provided by banks. These relative levels have not changed drastically today.

The fact that banks are more important to entrepreneurship than venture capitalists can be further highlighted by the fact that even the most active venture capitalist will finance only 15 to 25 deals a year after receiving as many as 7,000 business plans. The result is that in 2012, after receiving an estimated 8 million business plans, the entire venture capital industry invested in a total of 3,143 companies, of which fewer than two-fifths (1,174) were new ventures; most were reinvestments in known entrepreneurs and later-stage ventures.[9] This is akin to a pebble in the ocean compared with banks. For a business loan in 2013, business owners approached on average 2.4 banks and achieved a 69% success rate. Owners approached 4.8 VC funds through which only 19% were successful. Business credit cards provided the best success as owners approached 1.6 sources with an 83% success rate.[10]

The financing spectrum in Figure 6-2 best depicts the financing sources typically used by start-up entrepreneurs. In Chapter 7, "Debt Financing," we will discuss each of these sources in greater detail. And at the end of Chapter 8, we will show how one entrepreneur became successful by using almost all the sources. Using all the sources is quite common among successful high-growth entrepreneurs.

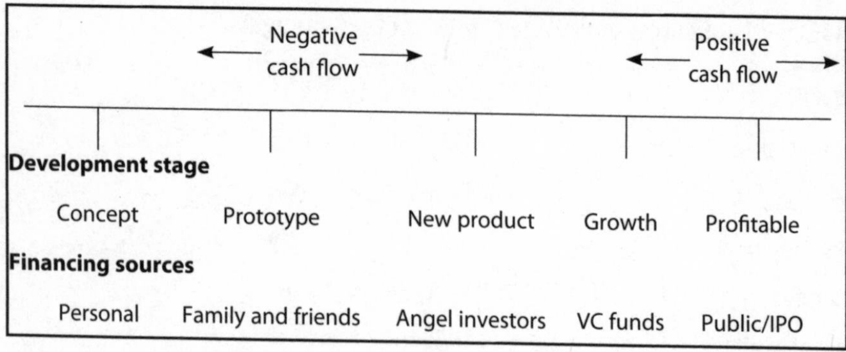

Figure 6-2 **Financing Spectrum**

7

Debt Financing

INTRODUCTION

Bill Gates has a rule that Microsoft, rather than incurring debt, must always have enough money in the bank to run for a year with no revenues.[1] In 2013, Microsoft had $77 billion in cash on its balance sheet.[2] Unfortunately, 99.9% of entrepreneurs will never be able to emulate this financing plan. Therefore, they must be willing to pursue and accept debt financing.

Debt is money provided in exchange for the owner's word (sometimes backed up by tangible assets as collateral as well as the personal guarantees of the owner) that the original investment plus interest at a predetermined fixed or variable rate will be repaid in its entirety over a set period of time.

As we saw in Chapter 6, banks have been by far the biggest source of capital for entrepreneurs on an annual basis. In June 2012, commercial banks had a total of $2.5 trillion in business loans outstanding (in other words, total loans, not just the notes written that year). Of that, 24%, or $588 billion, was in small-business loans (loans of less than $1 million).[3]

In today's environment, lenders reportedly want to see a company's capital structure with debt equivalent of 1.5 to 3.7 times EBITDA (earnings before interest, taxes, depreciation, and amortization).[4]

TYPES OF DEBT

There are basically four types of debt: senior, subordinated (sometimes called sub debt), short-term, and long-term. The first two refer to the order of entitlement or preference that the lender has against the debt recipient. Holders of senior debt have top priority over all other debt and equity providers. The senior holders are the "secured creditors," who have an agreement that they are to be paid before any other creditors. If the company is dissolved, the senior holders are entitled to be paid first and "made whole" as much as possible by selling the company's assets. After the holders of senior debt have been completely repaid, the remaining assets, if there are any, can go to the providers of subordinated debt.

A lender does not automatically get the senior position simply because it made the first loan. The lender must request this position, and all other present and future lenders must approve it. This can sometimes be a problem because some lenders may refuse to subordinate their loan to any others. If the other lenders will not acquiesce, then the loan is generally not made.

Sub debt, also referred to as mezzanine debt, is subordinated to senior debt, but ranks higher than equity financing. The term *mezzanine* comes from a reference to the design of theaters, where there are often three levels, with the middle level being called the mezzanine. Both types of debt are used for financing working capital, capital expenditures, and acquisitions. Mezzanine financing usually occurs after senior lenders exhaust their lending capabilities. Finally, because it is in a subordinate position, mezzanine debt is typically more expensive than senior debt.

Mezzanine and senior debt, in addition to equity, constitute a company's capital structure, which describes how the company finances itself. Therefore, when a company's capital structure is said to be highly leveraged, this means that it has a large amount of long-term debt.

Debt that is amortized over a period longer than 12 months is considered long-term debt (LTD). It can be senior or mezzanine. It is found in the balance sheet in the long-term liabilities section. Loans for real estate and equipment are usually multiyear, long-term debt obligations.

In contrast, short-term debt (STD) is that which is due within the next 12 months. STD comes in two forms: revolver debt, which is used for working capital, and current maturity of long-term debt. It is found in the balance sheet in the current liabilities section. This debt typically has a higher cost than does long-term debt. Short-term debt is usually used to buy inventory and to fund day-to-day operating needs.

Let's look at the strengths and weaknesses of debt financing.

Pros

- The entrepreneur retains complete ownership.
- The cost of capital is low.
- Loan payments are predictable.
- There is a 3-, 5- or 7-year payback period.
- It can involve value-added lenders.
- It provides tax benefits.

Cons

- Personal guarantees are required.
- The lender can force the business into bankruptcy.
- Amounts may be limited to the value of the company's assets.
- Payments are due regardless of the company's profits.

SOURCES OF DEBT FINANCING

The major sources of debt financing are personal savings, family and friends, angels, foundations, government, banks, factors, customer financing, supplier financing, purchase order financing, and credit cards. Let's review these sources in more detail.

Personal Savings

An entrepreneur often uses her own money to finance the company. This is especially true in the early stages of a start-up. The Global Entrepreneurship Monitor's "2012 Financing Report" showed that 73% of the funds available to start-ups across the globe came from the entrepreneurs themselves.[5] The primary reason for this is that banks and other institutional debt providers do not supply start-up capital because it is too risky. Start-ups have no history of cash flow that can be used to repay the debt obligation.

Using the entrepreneur's own capital is commonly referred to as "bootstrapping." This is how, for example, Ernest and Julio Gallo started their wine business in a rented warehouse in Modesto, California, in 1933, at the height of the Depression. After researching the industry at the local library, they decided to start their business using what little capital they had, and they convinced local farmers to provide them with grapes and defer payment until the wine was sold. They also bought crushing and fermenting equipment on 90-day terms. Today, the company started by these two bootstrappers enjoys annual worldwide sales of $896 million.[6] Other examples of bootstrapping include Domino's Pizza, Hallmark Cards, Black & Decker, and Ross Perot's EDS.[7]

Often these start-up investments are made in the form of equity rather than debt. But there are no rules that require such an equity investment. An entrepreneur's ownership stake does not have to come from his capital investment. In fact, it should come from his hard work, called "sweat equity." My advice is that all investments that the entrepreneur makes in his company should be in the form of debt at a reasonable interest rate. The repayment of this debt allows the entrepreneur to receive capital from the company without the money being taxed because it was simply the return of the original investment. The interest payment would be deductible by the company, reducing its tax liability. The entrepreneur would be required to pay personal taxes on the interest earned.

All of this is more favorable to the entrepreneur than if the capital were invested as equity. In that case, if it were repaid by the company, it would be taxed at the investor's personal tax level, and any dividends would also be taxed. Unlike interest payments, dividends paid are not tax deductible. Therefore, the company would receive no tax reduction benefits.

Family and Friends

As stated earlier, it is virtually impossible to procure debt financing for prerevenue start-ups. Therefore, an obvious viable alternative is family members and friends. The benefit of raising debt capital from this source is multifold. Raising money may be easier and faster because the lenders are providing the capital for emotional rather than business reasons. They want to support the family member or friend. That was the case with Jeff Bezos's first outside lenders, who were his parents. Another benefit, especially with debt, is that if repayments cannot be made, these lenders may be more conciliatory than institutional lenders. Unlike the latter, they are not likely to force the entrepreneur into bankruptcy if she defaults on the loan.

The negative aspects of procuring money from family members and friends exceed the positives, however. First, these are typically not value-added investors. Second, they may not be "sophisticated investors," which we will discuss in more detail later in this chapter. They may not understand either the risk of the investment or its form. Regarding the first point, they may not really comprehend the fact that they might lose such an investment completely, yielding no capital return at all. They expect to be repaid no matter what happens. They also may not realize that as debt investors, they are not entitled to any ownership stake, but only a predetermined interest payment and the return of their original investment. This usually becomes an issue when the entrepreneur is extremely successful in increasing the company's value. In such a case, many family members and friends may not be content with simply having their principal returned and earning interest on that money. They expect to share in the firm's value appreciation. In essence, they expect their debt to be treated as equity. If it is not, they feel that they have been cheated by their own child, grandchild, niece or nephew, or childhood friend.

This final point leads to the greatest problem with raising debt capital from family members and friends: there is a risk of irreparably damaging or losing important personal relationships. As one professor said, "Remember these are people whom you eat Thanksgiving with, and it may not be safe to sit next to your uncle if you have lost all his money and he has sharp utensils in his hands."

In closing, my advice is to refrain from raising debt capital from family and friends. If this cannot be avoided, adhere to the following recommendations:

- Raise money only from those who can afford to lose the entire amount. Do not get money from a grandparent who has no savings and lives on a fixed government income. Make it clear to the family members that they are putting their entire investment at risk, and that therefore, there is a chance that it may not be repaid.

- Write a detailed loan agreement, clearly highlighting the interest rate, the payment amounts, and the expected payment dates.
- The agreement should give the investor the right to convert any or all of the investment into company stock, thereby giving the investor an ownership stake if desirable. Alternatively, the agreement should be that the investment is mezzanine financing, which is debt with equity. The investor receives all of the investment back, interest, and an equity stake in the company.
- Personally guarantee at least the amount of the investment and at most the investment plus the amount of interest that the investment could have gained had it been put in a safe certificate of deposit. Today that would yield approximately 0.1%.

Angel Investors

Angel investors are typically busy professionals who invest in companies as a side business. (The term was originally coined to describe individuals who were patrons of the arts.) They are different from family and friends in that they usually have not had a long-term relationship with the entrepreneur prior to the investment. In addition, they are active investors who understand the risks of private investment; they should have the capacity to comfortably absorb a complete loss of their investment. Angel investors are typically former entrepreneurs who focus on industries in which they have experience. Prominent examples of large corporations that received angel investing at their start are the Ford Motor Company, Facebook, and Amazon.

With venture capital (VC) increasingly looking toward later-stage investments, money from angels has come to provide the bulk of seed and start-up capital in the United States. An estimate made in 2005 by the Angel Capital Association ("ACA"), sponsored by the Kauffman Foundation, and remains as a current benchmark, places that percentage at as much 90% of all early-stage capital provided in the country.[8] A study by the Center for Venture Research at the University of New Hampshire estimated that in 2012, there were 268,160 active angel investors in the United States who annually provided $341,800 per deal in debt and equity to entrepreneurs. In 2012, angels funded

67,030 businesses at a dollar value of $22.9 billion. These numbers grew by 1.2% and 1.8%, respectively, from 2011.[9] While available capital from angels obviously delights entrepreneurs, angels generate the opposite response from many people in the institutional venture capital community, since they create more competition for deals and provide a floor for valuations. Some venture capitalists call money from angels "dumb money," alleging that it is far less than value-added money. In my opinion, such insulting comments are simply sour grapes.

For many years, angel investing has been an important part of the financial support and mentoring available to entrepreneurs that assists them in bridging the financing gap between the individual investments of friends and family members and the institutional venture capital provided by traditional VC firms. Increasingly, though, angel investors are banding together into angel investor groups in order to attract better deals; provide infrastructure and support for the tax, legal, and other issues that arise from angel investing; and provide more formal support systems that allow them to increase their real and perceived "value added."[10] In 2013, there were 170 angel investor groups affiliated with the most widely known U.S. trade association, the ACA, up from just under 100 groups in 1999.[11]

While most angels demand equity for their investments, there are some who have invested debt in companies that had "shaky credit" and had been dumped by their banks. In those instances, the angels restructured the loans at significantly higher interest rates.

The positive aspect of getting debt financing from angels is that they can be more flexible in their terms than an institution like a bank. For example, the angel can make a 10-year loan, whereas the maximum term of a bank's commercial loan is typically 5 to 7 years. Also, angel investors, unlike banks, make their own rules for lending. A bank may have a rule that a loan will not be provided to any applicant who has declared personal bankruptcy. The angel, on the other hand, uses her own discretion in determining whether she wants to make a loan to such a person.

On the negative side, the cost of debt capital from angels is usually higher than that of institutional financing. It is not unusual for these investors to charge entrepreneurs 2% per month, which equals an astounding annual rate of 24%. Not only is such a rate higher than the 2 to 3% over prime that banks usually charge their best customers, but it is also greater than the 18% that some credit cards charge their customers. The other negative is that, unlike banks, which cannot legally interfere with their customers' day-to-day business operations or strategy, the angel typically expects to be involved. For some entrepreneurs, this may ultimately cause problems.

When most people think about formal organizations that provide debt capital, banks are the first ones that come to mind. But as stated earlier, there are other types of debt providers. Let's review and discuss a few of these nonbank sources of capital.

Foundations

Another interesting source of capital for entrepreneurs is philanthropic organizations, including the Ford Foundation, the MacArthur Foundation, the Wieboldt Foundation, and the Retirement Research Foundation. Historically, these organizations have provided grants and loans only to not-for-profit entities. But since the beginning of the 1990s, they have broadened their loan activity to include for-profit companies that provide a social good. Eligible companies are those that explicitly state their charitable or educational intention to improve society by doing such things as employing former convicts, building homes in economically deprived areas, providing childcare services to single mothers, or offering computer training to low-income families. Specific examples include the MacArthur Foundation's loan to a Washington, DC, publisher that tracks the economic policies of states. The company used the loan to purchase additional technology hardware. Another example is the inventory loan that the Wieboldt Foundation made to a Chicago company called Commons Manufacturing that made window blinds to install in public housing.[12]

Foundations also provide grants to community development corporations (CDCs), which, in turn, use the money to provide business loans. The objectives of the CDCs are the same as those of the foundations, which is to lend capital to businesses that provide a benefit to society. An example of such a CDC is Coastal Enterprises, an organization that provides capital to companies that employ low-income people in Maine.

These loans from foundations and CDCs are an example of program-related investments (PRIs). More than 790 organizations throughout the world have provided nearly 5,400 PRIs,[13] including those listed in Figure 7-1.

For entrepreneurs, one of the attractive aspects of PRI loans is that interest rates can be as low as 1% with a 10-year amortization period. Another positive

Bhartiya Samruddhi Investments and Consulting Services

Hyderabad, India

BRIDGE Housing Corporation

San Francisco, California

Cooperative Housing Foundation

Silver Spring, Maryland

Corporation for Supportive Housing

New York, New York

Enterprise Corporation of the Delta

Jackson, Mississippi

MBA Properties

St. Louis, Missouri

MacArthur Foundation

Chicago, Illinois

Peer Partnerships

Cambridge, Massachusetts

Shorebank

Chicago, Illinois

Wieboldt Foundation

Chicago, Illinois

Figure 7-1 **Organizations Providing PRIs**

element is that the foundations can be considered to be value-added investors. The ALSAM Foundation in Utah and the Ford Foundation in New York City were the top PRI funders, each issuing investments of more than $70 million in 2006–2007 (latest data available).[14] If more information about PRIs is desired, two sources are *Program Related Investments: A Guide to Funders and Trends* and *The PRI Directory: Charitable Loans and Other Program Related Investments by Foundations*, 3rd ed. (2010).

Government

Local, state, and federal government agencies have programs for providing loans to entrepreneurs. These programs are typically part of a municipality's economic development or commerce department. Some government loans are attractive because they offer below-market rates. SBA and CAP (capital access program) loans, which we will discuss later, are usually market-priced. They are provided to companies that are geographically located in the municipal area, that can prove their ability to repay, and, just as important, that will use the money to retain existing jobs or create new jobs. Regarding the retention of jobs, entrepreneurs in Chicago have accessed capital from the city for the acquisition of a company based on the fact that if they did not buy the company, someone else might do so and move it, along with the jobs, to another city. Other entrepreneurs have procured expansion debt capital with the agreement that for every $20,000 that the city provides, 1 new job will be created in 18 to 24 months. Practically every town, city, and state provides such job-related debt financing.

The negative aspect of these loans on the local and state levels is that they often take a long time to procure. The applicant has to complete a lot of paperwork, and the process can take as long as 12 months.

A great periodical for identifying federal, state, and local government economic programs is *The Small Business Financial Resource Guide*, which can be received free by writing to the U.S. Chamber of Commerce Small Business Center at 1615 H Street, NW, Washington, DC 20062. It can also be ordered online through MasterCard's website at www.mastercard.com.[15]

Another drawback for some entrepreneurs is that the applicant must personally guarantee the loans. Personal guarantees will be discussed in more detail at the end of the discussion of debt.

Capital Access Programs

One local government program that does not take as long is your state or municipality's capital access program (CAP). There are currently 25 states and several cities that operate CAPs, which were first introduced in Michigan in 1986.[16] By 1998, CAPs had provided more than 25,000 loans totaling nearly $1.5 billion. While this is a pittance compared with the $19.1 billion guaranteed by the SBA, CAPs have become popular, as they compete with SBA loans.

The CAP loan product is a "credit enhancement" that induces banks to consider loan requests that they might otherwise have rejected because of deficiencies in collateral or cash flow. The mechanism for a CAP loan typically involves the bank and the borrower paying a fee ranging from 3 to 7% of the loan amount to a loan-loss reserve account held at the bank. This loan reserve contribution is then matched by state or local money, with the total reserve ranging from 6 to 14% of the loan. This amount is used to cover any loan losses.[17]

Banks seemingly like this state– or local government–sponsored loan program because the banks, not the government agency, set the terms, rates, fees, and collateral. They do not have to get approval from any other organization or agency. Entrepreneurs like it for the same reason. The bank has the flexibility to approve a loan that may not qualify for SBA financing for one reason or another. Another attraction is that entrepreneurs have stated that CAP financing is faster than SBA loans. CAPs differ in the size of the eligible loans, the nature of eligible borrowers, and the size of the loan-loss reserve. Check with your state or municipality's economic development agency to determine whether a CAP exists.

Small Business Administration Loan Program

Federal business loan programs fall under the authority of the U.S. Small Business Administration, which is the largest source of long-term small-business lending in the nation. Each year, the SBA guarantees loans totaling more than $17.9 billion. And since its inception in 1953, the agency has helped fund approximately 20 million businesses. There are two primary reasons for the popularity of SBA loans. First, the length of an SBA loan can be longer than that of a regular commercial loan. For example, an SBA-guaranteed loan can be for as long as 10 years for a working capital loan, compared with 1 to 5 years normally. Second, the SBA guarantees loans to borrowers who cannot get financing elsewhere.

It should be made perfectly clear that the SBA does not provide loans directly to entrepreneurs. It uses other financial institutions, banks and nonbanks, to do the actual lending. The SBA gives these approved institutions the authority to represent it as a lender and will guarantee up to 85% of the loan. For example, with the SBA's approval, a lender may provide a $100,000 loan to an entrepreneur. If the recipient defaults on the loan, the lender has only 15% at risk because the SBA guarantees the balance of the loan.

Most of these loans go to established businesses. About one-third ($4.9 billion in FY2013) of SBA loans are made to new businesses each year. A few start-ups that received SBA loans are Ben & Jerry's, Nike, Federal Express, Apple Computer, and Intel.

Some people foolishly believe that they can default on these loans with minimal consequences. Nothing could be further from the truth. Remember, all SBA loans are personally guaranteed. Also, the lender, despite the SBA guarantee, will doggedly pursue the payment of as much of the loan as possible before requesting SBA reimbursement. The lender's reputation is on the line, and if the lender's loan default rate becomes too high, the SBA will discontinue that bank's participation in the program.

SBA lenders fall into three categories: general, certified, and preferred lenders. General lenders are those that have a small volume of deals or very little experience in providing SBA loans. Therefore, they must submit all of an applicant's loan information to the national SBA office to obtain its approval before they can approve a loan. The process can take several weeks and even months. In contrast, the other types of SBA lenders can act faster.

The most active and expert lenders qualify for the SBA's streamlined lending programs. Under these programs, lenders are given partial or full authority to approve loans, resulting in faster service from the SBA. Certified lenders are those that have been heavily involved in regular SBA loan-guarantee processing and have met certain other criteria. They receive a partial delegation of authority and are given a 3-day turnaround on their applications by the SBA (they may also use regular SBA loan processing). Certified lenders account for 4% of all SBA business loan guarantees. Preferred lenders are chosen from among the SBA's best lenders and enjoy full delegation of lending authority in exchange for a lower rate of guarantee. This lending authority must be renewed at least every 2 years, and the SBA examines the lender's portfolio periodically. Preferred loans account for more than 29% of SBA loans.[18]

To find a list of the SBA lenders in any state, go to www.sba.gov or contact the SBA hotline at 800–827–5722. There is a publication available for each state that is updated at least every 2 years. It lists all the lenders and shows whether they are general, preferred, or certified. The SBA also posts a state-by-state listing of SBA preferred or certified lenders online.

The SBA's most popular lending programs are the 7(a) Loan Guaranty, Micro Loan, and 504 (CDC) Loan programs. Before we look at each of these programs, let's discuss a few of the general highlights of SBA financing terms.

Depending on the program, loans can be amortized for as many as 25 years. Interest rates vary. The SBA charges the lender a fee between 2 and 3.5% of the loan, which is usually passed on to the loan recipient. And all investors with a stake in the company of 20% or more must personally guarantee the loan. Finally, if the loan is to be used to purchase another company, the seller must subordinate his financing of the company to the SBA. In fact, the SBA might require the seller to agree to "absolute subordination." In this case, no payments can be made to the seller as long as SBA money is outstanding.

To be eligible for an SBA loan, the business must qualify as a small business, be for-profit, not already have the internal resources to provide the financing, and be able to demonstrate repayment ability. The SBA uses varying requirements to determine whether a business is small; these requirements depend on various factors, including the industry in which the company operates. For example, because the SBA targets smaller companies, the applicant can't have a workforce the size of GE's. If the company is in manufacturing, it cannot employ more than 1,500 people, and the maximum number of employees for a wholesale business is 100. The SBA's requirements and guidelines can be found at www.sba.gov.

A few types of businesses that are ineligible for SBA financing are not-for-profit organizations and institutions, lending companies, investment firms, gambling companies, life insurance companies, religion-affiliated companies, and companies that are owned by non-U.S. citizens.

7(a) Loan Guaranty program. The majority of SBA loans are made under this program. In 2013, $17.9 billion was guaranteed through 46,399 loans, with an average loan of $385,000.[19] [Figure 7-2 shows the top five 7(a) loan markets by state.[20]] Essentially, the 7(a) program is a conventional bank loan of up to $5 million that receives an SBA guarantee. The SBA guarantees 85% of these loans up to $150,000 and 75% above $150,000. The proceeds can be used to purchase commercial real estate, business equipment, and machinery. They can also be used to refinance existing debt, for construction financing, and for working capital.

There are personal net worth eligibility criteria for 7(a) loans. For example, for a $250,000 loan, the owner's net worth must be less than $100,000.

SBA Express Loan program. Express loans allow lenders to offer revolving credit lines that are renewable annually for up to 7 years and are administered within 36 hours. They are meant to overcome the difficulties that lenders face in making smaller loans that are too expensive to underwrite as part of the traditional 7(a) program. Under this program, loans under $25,000 do not require collateral. Lenders use their own application forms. The maximum loan amount is $350,000, with a 50% SBA guaranty. In some areas, there are special versions of this program for

Top States	Total Loans, in Millions
California	$2,310
Ohio	1,782
Texas	$796
New York	$677
North Carolina	$675

Source: Small Business Administration data compiled by National Association of Government Guaranteed Lenders.

Figure 7-2 **Top Five SBA 7(a) Loan Markets by State, FY Ending 9/2011**

veterans (Patriot Express Pilot Loan Initiative) and those doing business in low- and moderate-income areas (Small Loan Advantage and Community Advantage).

Loan prequalification. Business applicants with needs of less than $250,000 can be reviewed and potentially authorized by the SBA before the loans are taken to lenders for consideration. The program employs intermediary organizations to assist borrowers in developing a viable loan application. Small Business Development Centers (discussed later in this chapter) provide this service for free. For-profit organizations will charge a fee. The application is expedited by the SBA after submission. Interest rates, maturities, and guarantee percentages follow the 7(a) guidelines.[21]

Micro Loan program. Nonprofit groups such as community development corporations are the primary issuers of micro loans. These are the smallest loans guaranteed by the SBA, at levels as small as $450. The maximum is $50,000, with the average loan being $13,000. Since 1992, the SBA has provided loans totaling more than $321 million to more than 28,000 borrowers. Interest rates on these loans are generally between 8 and 13%. In 2012 the Micro Loan program provided an estimate $45 million in loans to borrowers.[22] There are 150 intermediaries that disburse these loans.[23]

504 (CDC or Real Estate and Equipment) Loan program. This loan program is a long-term financing tool for economic development within a community that is offered through certified development companies in an area. The program provides growing businesses with long-term, fixed-rate financing for major fixed assets, such as land and buildings. The funds cannot be used for working capital or inventory, consolidating or repaying debt, or refinancing. CDCs are nonprofit corporations set up to contribute to the economic development of their community and retain jobs. CDCs work with the SBA and private-sector lenders to provide financing to small businesses.

There are 270 CDCs nationwide, each covering a specific area. Loan amounts vary, but can be as large as $4 million. In 2013, the SBA approved 7,708 loans totaling $5.23 billion under this program.[24]

Nonbank SBA Lenders

As stated earlier, the SBA guarantees loans made by both banks and other financial institutions. These other lenders compete with banks by offering lower rates and faster loan approval. The SBA refers to these firms as small business lending companies (SBLCs).

One of the largest nonbank lenders is CIT Small Business Lending, a division of CIT Group Inc., which is a publicly traded global commercial finance company. CIT was one of the top named SBA 7(a) lenders for 9 consecutive years prior to 2008 and remains one of the top lenders to minorities, women, and veterans in the country. The following are examples of some of CIT's primary lending criteria:

- Adequate historical cash flow to cover the debt.
- Business debt to net worth ratio must meet industry average.
- Borrowers must be actively involved in the day-to-day operation of the business.
- Satisfactory personal credit histories are required for all principals and guarantors.
- No past bankruptcies or felony arrests.

Other prominent large nonbank SBA lenders include the Small Business Loan Source and Loan Source Financial. Unfortunately, as of this writing, the number of nonbank lenders is decreasing. Banks have lowered their rates to a point where the nonbanks can no longer compete. One reason that banks have been able to do this is that their cost of capital is lower than that of nonbanks. Banks can use the deposits that they have, whereas nonbanks must get their money from the public capital markets. Another reason is that banks are using their commercial loans as "loss leaders." They will sacrifice returns on business loans to increase the number of customers who use many of their other services, such as online banking, personal savings, loan accounts, and cash management programs. Nonbanks that have departed from or significantly decreased their loan business include Heller Financial, Transamerica Finance, and The Money Store.[25]

Banks with SBA Loan Programs

Approximately 6,639 of the 6,940 banks in the country (down from 14,000 in 1997) use the SBA's guaranteed loan program. Certified lender status is held by 850 banks, and preferred lender status by 450 banks. The Small Business Administration produces an annual report on the small-business lending activities of the nation's leading commercial banks. It analyzes lending patterns and ranks "small-business-friendly" banks in every state and on a national level. The SBA says that its goal is to give small businesses an easy-to-use tool for locating likely loan sources in their communities. It also aims to nudge banks to compete more aggressively for small-firm customers. The report is a great resource for entrepreneurs who are trying to determine which banks will be more likely to lend a sympathetic ear and, more important, some cash for their business. The most recent report is titled "Small Business Lending in the United States 2012," and it can be found at http://www.sba.gov/advocacy/7540/719311. This report covers micro lending (under $100,000) and small-business lending (between $100,000 and $1 million).

Advice for Getting an SBA Loan

It has been estimated that the SBA will approve fewer than 50% of requested loans. Some advice for improving your chances of obtaining an SBA-guaranteed loan is provided here:

- *Clean up your personal financial problems.* Most of the rejected loans are rejected because of the applicants' poor personal credit history. Before applying, the entrepreneur should reduce her credit card debt, and also the number of credit cards she has. Financiers are aware of these numbers and view holding too many credit cards negatively. It is especially important for loan applicants to know their three-digit credit or FICO score, which ranks their creditworthiness on a scale from 300 to 850. Finally, before applying, the entrepreneur should check with the major credit bureaus and make sure there are no errors on her credit reports. The bureaus are Equifax (www.equifax.com),

TransUnion (www.transunion.com), and Experian (www.experian.com). Americans are entitled to one free credit report per year.

- *Define your goals realistically.* Apply for a specific dollar amount, and identify in detail how the funds will be used. Develop realistic, logical financial pro formas that show that even under the worst-case scenario, the debt can be repaid. At a minimum, most lenders want to see that a company's annual cash flow is 1.25 times its total annual loan obligations (principal and interest). Do not plug in numbers. Do not ask for money that you cannot forecast being paid back.
- *Begin early.* Apply for financing at least 6 months before the money is needed.
- *Work with experienced lenders.* Apply to institutions that have certified or preferred lender status.
- *Submit an excellent business plan.* Make sure that the entire plan, especially the executive summary, is well written, clear, and thorough. Just as important, check and recheck all numbers, making sure that they are correct and that the math is perfect. All numbers must add up.
- *Collect preapplication information.* Loans for existing and start-up businesses require much of the same information, including:
  - The personal tax returns of all investors with at least 20% ownership for the past 3 years.
  - The personal financial statements for all investors with at least 20% ownership.
  - The ownership documents, including franchise agreements and incorporation papers.
- A few pieces of information are needed for an existing business that are not needed for a start-up, and vice versa.

For an Existing Company:

- Tax returns for the past 3 years
- Interim financial statements
- Business debt schedule

For a Start-up Company:

- Business plan

    - Potential sources of capital
    - Available collateral
- *Do not lie.* Never lie. An entrepreneur's greatest asset is his reputation.

Other SBA Programs

Small Business Development Centers (SBDCs). There are more than 1,000 SBDCs, most of which are located in universities throughout the country. This program is a collaborative effort between the SBA, the academic community, the private sector, and state and local governments. The centers provide management and technical assistance as well as assistance in the preparation of loan applications. The services are tailored to the local economies they serve.

SCORE. This advisory group has 340 chapters and 11,000 retired and active senior executives and small-business owner-volunteers. They provide marketing advice, business plan preparation, and business planning, and they handle approximately 10,000 cases per month. Information can be found at www.score.org.

Small Business Learning Center. This network is an online training resource for small-business owners. The resource offers online courses, workshops, publications, information resources, and learning tools; direct access to electronic counseling; and other forms of technical assistance. It can be found at www.sba.gov/training.

Banks Without SBA Loan Programs

Historically, banks without SBA programs (those that use personal guarantees as their primary collateral), including some community development banks, have not been viewed as great friends to entrepreneurs. The reason is that most of them were asset-backed lenders that determined the loan amount using a strict formula, such as 80% of the value of accounts receivable plus 20% of inventory and 50% of fixed assets. Given this formula, start-ups could never get loans, and companies with tangible assets were limited to the amount mandated by the formula, regardless of the true amount they needed.

With the "entrepreneur generation" of the mid-1990s came the advent of an increasing number of banks that were cash flow lenders, like the SBA for small businesses. Recent research from the SBA suggests that, much like other dot-com phenomena, this type of lending has waned. A study of banking and small and medium enterprise financing by the SBA showed that in 2006, 90% of loans under $1 million by small domestic banks required collateral.[26] The focus on small business has remained, however, and credit is generally more available to small firms than was the case many years ago. Large banks like Bank of America, JPMorgan Chase, Citigroup, and Wells Fargo have taken aim at the small-business market. While it is true that much of this focus is on credit lines or credit cards of under $100,000, these banks are increasingly focusing on small business.

Overall, the traditional rules of bank financing still apply. Entrepreneurs will need to pass a full credit analysis, including a detailed review of financial statements and personal finances, to assess their ability to repay. Banks will require collateral and will want to understand what kind of assets you can liquidate to pay them. They will also want to get comfortable with your business plan and how it fits within the larger macroeconomic conditions. In general, the bigger your business, the easier it will be for you to secure financing. The Federal Reserve Bank of New York refers to this as the "Five Cs."[27] These are Capacity to repay; the Capital you have committed; your personal Commitment to the business; the Collateral you have to secure the loan; the conditions of the loan, such as economic climate and the purpose of the loan; and your Character in terms of the general impression that you make.[28] As stated earlier, the SBA report on small-business and micro-business lending in the United States provides statistics on the top lenders to small businesses in each state and nationally.

Community Banks

Unlike the large banks, community banks have usually been seen as a friend to the entrepreneur. As Larry Bennett, director of the Center for Entrepreneurship at Johnson & Wales University, notes, "There is a huge difference in banks' receptivity to lending to entrepreneurs." The biggest difference is that local and regional banks will more readily agree to customize loans to fit entrepreneurs' needs.[29] These are typically small independent banks that specialize in certain types of targeted lending. After years of consolidation, community banks are making a comeback. There are almost 7,000 such banks in the country, some of which are listed in Figure 7-3. To find out who and where they are, contact the Independent Community Bankers of America at 1–800–422–8439 or visit www.icba.org.

Entrepreneurs should choose the bank that best fits their needs. Bill Dunkelberg, chief economist at the National Federation of Independent Business and chairman of a small bank in Cherry Hill, New Jersey, explains how entrepreneurs should think about choosing a bank. He says that small businesses should "figure out if they fit better with the point scoring model [or] if playing golf with the loan officer would help." In short, Dunkelberg is saying that larger banks will look more at the numbers behind your business, whereas small community banks will get to know the entrepreneur and may be more willing to work a bit more with her.[30]

Community Development Financial Institutions (CDFIs)

CDFIs primarily provide loan financing to businesses that are generally unbankable by traditional industry standards. They are typically community development loan funds, banks, credit unions, and community development venture

Community Bank	Investment Focus
Mechanics and Farmers Bank Durham, North Carolina	African Americans
Michigan Heritage Bank Novi, Michigan	Equipment leasing
United Commercial Bank San Francisco, California	Asian small-business community
Legacy Bank Milwaukee, Wisconsin	Urban families and entrepreneurs
First Truck Bank Charlotte, North Carolina	Small and women-owned businesses

Figure 7-3 **Various Community Banks**

funds. The pricing on these loans is a bit higher to reflect the additional risk: from 0.5 to 3.0% above normal loan rates. There are about 1,000 CDFIs nationwide. In 2012, CDFIs supplied $175 million to 4,102 small and medium-size businesses, and since 1994, they have supplied $1.7 billion.[31] CDFIs can make riskier loans because they are not restricted by FDIC regulations in the same way as depository institutions are. CDFIs can also be value-added investors. There is no listing of every CDFI, but the Treasury Department has a partial list at www.cdfifund.gov, and more resources can be found at www.cdfi.org.

CDFIs can be useful for starting up or growing a business when bank financing is not an option and your returns are not high enough to attract the interest of angel investors or venture capital firms. CDFIs also can be useful for owners with less than perfect credit. CDFIs typically fund businesses in economically depressed or rural areas.

Personal Guarantees

For many entrepreneurs, one of the greatest drawbacks to debt financing from banks is the personal guarantee, which is collateralized by all one's assets, including one's home. While such a guarantee is not required for loans from all capital sources, it is for any SBA financing. Leslie Davis, a former commercial lender, said that it is not unusual for entrepreneurs to say, "I cannot agree to personally guarantee the loan because my spouse will not let me." In those cases, she immediately rejects the loan, because, as she explains, "If the spouse does not completely believe in the entrepreneur, why should we?"

One of the greatest fears that entrepreneurs have is losing their homes. Bankers estimate that at least 90% of first-time business owners use their homes as collateral. These are the entrepreneurs and spouses who are completely committed. Should they worry? Yes and no. If the borrower defaults and a personal guarantee is backed partially or completely by his home, the lender has the legal right to sell the home in order to recoup its investment. But private banks and the SBA typically attempt to work with the entrepreneur to develop a long-term repayment plan that does not include selling the house. This point was supported by an SBA director who said, "Our position as far as personal residences is to try to work with the individual borrower as much as possible. We look at the home as collateral of the last resort. We certainly don't want to retain assets, especially not residential real estate."[32]

Therefore, it is good advice to communicate regularly with the lender after providing a personal guarantee, so that if the loan becomes a problem, it can be restructured prior to default. Loan officers have been trained to receive bad news. They do not necessarily like it, but they like surprises even less. Keep the loan officer informed. The loan officer wants you to repay the loan and succeed, and will help you if you try to deal with the problem early. Even when default is inevitable or occurs, the loan officer will still help you as long as you communicate, are open with information, are willing to negotiate, and agree to a payment plan that could take 10 to 15 years. Most important, demonstrate a "good-faith effort" to work things out.

The worst thing you can do when you are facing default is to become difficult, noncommunicative, or threatening. Do not attempt to negotiate by threatening to declare bankruptcy if the lender does not give you what you want. Such threats usually upset the lender, and if you carry out the threat, it will be more harmful to your future than to the lender's. In such combative cases, the lender will not only pursue the home that was used as collateral, but also seek to garnish any future earnings that the entrepreneur may have to eliminate the entire debt obligation.

Try to work things out. Most successful high-growth entrepreneurs fail at least twice. Give yourself another chance by making the bad experience a win-win situation for both you and the financier. The financier wins by receiving payment, and you win by keeping a strong reputation and putting yourself in a position to receive financing from the same lender for future deals. As one bank executive explained, "If you've had some financial trouble in the past, it doesn't mean that I'll turn you down. I'll be curious about how you responded to the trouble."[33]

Nonbank Financial Institutions Without SBA Loan Programs

Many nonbank financial institutions without SBA programs also provide long-term debt financing to entrepreneurs. Included in this group are national insurance companies, such as Northwestern Mutual and Prudential. Their loans can be used for working capital, business acquisitions, and equipment and machinery.

These institutions tend to have higher minimum loan levels than banks that service entrepreneurs. For example, Prudential's loan level ranges between $10 and $15 million. Another difference from traditional bank lending is that if the insurance company were a subordinated lender, the loan would be for only 1 to 1.5 times EBITDA. As the senior lender, nonbank financial institutions will be similar to banks, lending as much as 3 times EBITDA. Another attraction is that these institutions are not asset lenders, they are cash flow lenders. As one supplier said, "We don't look at collateral upfront. We look at management's work history, and then the cash flow of the business. Banks don't usually do that."[34] The final significant difference is one of their main attractions: be it senior or subordinated debt, they can amortize the loan over 15 years. This compares very favorably with the maximum 7 years that banks traditionally offer.

Person-to-Person (P2P) Lending

For prospective entrepreneurs who have had difficulty qualifying for traditional commercial or SBA loan products because of poor credit ratings and/or an unproven track record, an increasingly popular alternative for start-up capital is person-to-person (P2P) lending. At websites like Prosper.com, Zopa (www.zopa.com), Lending Club (www.lendingclub.com), and GlobeFunder (www.globefunder.com), entrepreneurs are able to connect with people across the globe who want to lend small sums of money to strangers in exchange for the promise of higher returns than they might see with their traditional personal banking products. P2P lending allows individuals to lend to each other at a set rate for a fixed period of time, offers built-in solutions for loan repayment and tracking, and employs social networking capabilities that allow borrowers to tell the stories associated with their need for capital.[35]

The maximum loan amount at a P2P site is $35,000 (although maximum loan amounts are expected to increase higher in the future), with loans often syndicated among several lenders. Each of the major sites employs a slightly different model, but all typically require that borrowers register on their site, submit to a basic credit check (with required minimum credit scores of 640–660), and have a debt/equity ratio of around 30%. Currently, roughly 5–7% of the loans on Prosper are for business purposes.[36]

While rates on P2P sites can be more attractive than using credit card debt to finance a business, there are downsides to consider. These loans typically require both principal and interest to be paid down every month (whereas several types of bank loans allow only interest payments at first). Additionally, the fixed payment periods associated with these loans can often be difficult to manage for seasonal businesses. Finally, it is almost impossible to renegotiate these loans once their terms are set.[37]

P2P lending will not replace traditional commercial lending anytime soon, but it is a growing niche. Entrepreneurs are especially cautioned to carefully consider their overall debt levels and ability to repay before obtaining a P2P loan, since these products do not come with the built-in sanity checks that a commercial banker brings to the traditional bank loan process.

CREATIVE WAYS TO STRUCTURE LONG-TERM DEBT

Debt is usually structured so that it is amortized over 5 to 7 years, with interest and principal payments due each month. For the first-time or inexperienced entrepreneur, it is recommended that you ask for more lenient terms. The purpose is to give you a little breathing room immediately after you procure the loan, so that your entire focus can be on operating the company, rather than becoming a slave to servicing debt. The options for repaying the debt could include:

- Making payments quarterly or semiannually.
- Making only interest payments each quarter, with a principal balloon payment at the end of Year 5 or Year 7.
- Making no payments at all until 3 to 6 months following the loan closing, then paying interest only for the balance of the fiscal year, followed by quarterly payments of interest and principal for 4 to 6 years.
- With SBA loans, structuring fixed principal and interest monthly payments, even with a variable rate. If interest rates go down, you pay down the principal faster. If interest rates rise, you'll have a balloon payment at maturity.

These are only a few suggestions that every entrepreneur should consider pursuing. As is obvious, these structures free up a lot of cash in the early stages—cash that the entrepreneur can use to solidify the financial foundation of the company. These options, or any variation of them, are not typically offered automatically by the lender. The entrepreneur must ask for them during negotiations.

LONG-TERM DEBT RULES TO LIVE BY

In summary, here are a few final pieces of advice relative to debt financing:

- Always take the maximum number of years allowable for repayments. Try to include a no-prepayment-penalty clause in the agreement.
- Get a fixed rather than a floating rate of interest. Always know what your future payments will be.
- Expect loan application rejection. Do not be thin-skinned.
- After getting the loan, keep your investors informed. Send them monthly or quarterly financial statements, and, if possible, send out a quarterly status report. Invite lenders to visit your business at least once a year. A few of these suggestions may actually be stipulated as required in your loan documents.
- When things go wrong, renegotiate.
- Keep excellent and timely financial statements. Historical statements should be readily available at any time. They should be neatly stored in an organized filing system.
- Once the loan application has been submitted, expect to hear from a loan officer by telephone before or after normal working hours. This is one of the ways that bankers evaluate the entrepreneur's working habits. Does he come in early and stay late? Or is he an 8:00 a.m. to 5:00 p.m. person? (To prove you are not the latter, call the loan officer at 6:00 a.m. or 9:00 p.m. and leave a message on his voice mail that you are in your office and working and thought he might be doing the same, because you had a question for him.)

DEBT FINANCING FOR WORKING CAPITAL

Up to this point, the sources of capital discussed could have been used for business acquisitions, start-ups, or working capital. As stated before, most entrepreneurs find access to working capital their greatest problem. Therefore, in addition to the aforementioned sources, here are other sources of debt financing specifically for working capital.

Factors

Factoring firms, or factors, are asset-based lenders. The asset that they use for collateral is a company's accounts receivable (AR). By way of example, a company sells its AR, at a discount, to a factor. This allows the company to get immediate cash for the products shipped or services rendered. Factoring is one of the oldest financial tools available, as it dates back to the Mesopotamians. It was also a tool of the American colonists, who would ship furs, lumber, and tobacco to England. Eventually, the U.S. garment industry became a user. In 2012, worldwide, factoring volume is $477 billion annually.[38]

The usual agreement is that when the product is shipped, copies of the shipping document, called the bill of lading, and the invoice are faxed to the factor. Typically, within 48 hours, the factor deposits 70 to 90% of the invoice amount into the client's account. When the customer pays the bill, which is usually remitted to the factor in accordance with instructions on the invoice, the factor takes the 70 to 90% that it had advanced to the client plus 2 to 4% for the use of its capital. The balance is sent to the client.

There are 2 types of factors, recourse and nonrecourse. The former buys accounts receivable with an agreement that it will be reimbursed by the client for receivables that cannot be collected. The latter type takes all the risk of collecting the receivables. If a receivable is not paid, the client has no obligations to the factor. Obviously, the fees charged by nonrecourse factors are greater than those charged by recourse factors.

Regardless of the type of factor, before reaching an agreement with a client, the factor investigates the creditworthiness of the client's customers. In most instances, the factor will "cherry-pick," or select certain customers while rejecting the accounts of others. The rejected customers are those that have a history of slow payment.

The factoring industry has continued to grow for a number of reasons. First, factors provide immediate access to cash. This can be particularly helpful for fast-growing companies or companies that are in immediate need of liquidity. Alton Johnson of Bossa Nova Beverage Group used factoring to avoid giving up equity during the early stages of the firm's growth. This got the firm to profitability without giving up precious equity. In some industries, factoring is actually the most profitable way to go. For example, Roger Shorey, president of Accurate Metal Fabricators, a Florida-based kitchen-cabinet company, receives discounts for immediate payment that exceed the costs of factoring. Another force driving the growth in the factoring industry has been globalization. Factoring is an excellent way for small companies to manage the uncertainty of a new export market.[39]

On the flip side, there are some clear negatives associated with factoring, and it should almost always be viewed as a stopgap or temporary measure. The primary negative associated with factoring is that it is very expensive. At 2 to 4% per 30-day period, the annual cost of factoring is between 24 and 48% interest. There are very few businesses that can generate returns at these levels for sustained periods of time. Factors also typically prefer to engage in longer-term contracts. Finally, a company's existing debt covenants may forbid it from using this source of capital because it involves the selling of assets.

How can an entrepreneur find a factor? Usually the factor will find you. Once you go into business, factors will begin mailing you unsolicited requests to use their services. The postcard or letter will not call it factoring; instead, it will call it working capital or inventory financing.

There are hundreds of factoring firms in the country. Some online resources on factoring include Factors Chain International (www.factor-chain.com) and the International Factoring Association (www.factoring.org). Also, Alana Davidson, the principal of IBC Funding, a factoring broker, has written a paper entitled "Ten Frequently Asked Questions about Factoring." It can be obtained free of charge by writing to IBC Funding, 3705 Ingomar Street, NW, Washington, DC 20015.[40]

Advice for Using Factors

- Factors are ideal for businesses in industries with inherent long cash gaps, such as the healthcare industry, where insurance companies are notoriously slow in paying claims, or the apparel industry, where producers must buy fabric 6 to 9 months before they use it.
- Factors are also ideal for companies that are experiencing or forecasting rapid growth.
- Factors are also ideal for companies that are first experimenting with exporting goods to foreign countries with unfamiliar regulations.
- They are ideal for companies that cannot get capital from anywhere else.
- However, factors should be used only by companies that have included the cost of factoring in their prices. Otherwise, the cost of factoring could eliminate all of the company's profits. In fact, one factor suggested that the only firms that should use this financing method are those with at least 20% gross margins.[41]
- Companies with many small customers should not use factoring, as it is cumbersome for factors to deal with checking the credit of so many customers.
- Ultimately, cheaper forms of capital should replace factor financing. It is too expensive to use on a long-term basis.

Customer Financing

The idea that a customer could be a provider of debt may seem odd, but it is indeed possible and has happened many times. Customers are willing to provide capital to suppliers who provide them with a high-quality or unique product that they may not be able to buy somewhere else. This financing can be a direct loan or a down payment on a future order. That is the type of financing that Robert Stockard, the owner of Sales Consultants of Boston (SCB), an executive recruiting firm, received from his largest customer, MCI. When the telecommunications giant needed a temporary sales force of 1,200 people to launch its new calling plan, Friends and Family, nationally, it hired SCB. Rather than approach a bank for additional working capital to finance this larger-than-usual job, Stockard persuaded MCI to make a 10% down payment on the $2.5 million contract.[42]

Entrepreneurs like Stockard who successfully procure working capital from customers show that anything is possible if you simply ask. An investor who is also a customer is a value-added investor.

But raising capital from a customer has a few drawbacks that should be considered first. One is that you may risk losing customers who are competitors of your investor. Another is that, as an investor, your customer could get access to key information about your company and use it to become your competitor.

Still another negative is that once a customer is an investor, the customer knows more about the true state of the company's operations. This exposure to the company's internal operations may cause the customer to seek another supplier if the customer thinks the company is poorly managed.

Finally, the additional insight that a customer has may make it tough for a supplier to increase prices, since the customer now knows the cost of the product. Therefore, be careful when accepting capital from customers.

Supplier Financing

Suppliers are automatically financiers if they give their customers credit. The simplest way for entrepreneurs to improve their supplier financing is by delaying the payment of their bills. This is called "involuntary extended supplier financing." But sometimes a supplier will graciously agree to extend its invoice terms to help a customer finance a large order that, in turn, helps the supplier sell more goods.

And there are other instances where a supplier will give a customer a direct loan. That was the case when Rich Food Holdings, a grocery wholesaler in Richmond, Virginia, loaned $3 million to Johnny Johnson, a grocery chain owner, "to buy my buildings, equipment and groceries. In exchange, I agreed to purchase 60% of my inventory from them."[43]

Like customer financing, supplier financing has a few negative aspects. The first is that the supplier may require you to purchase most or all of your products from it. This causes a problem when the supplier has poor delivery, poor quality, and higher prices.

Another problem may be that because your supplier is an investor, other suppliers that are the supplier's competitors may refuse to continue to do business with you.

Purchase Order Financing

Although they may seem alike, factoring and purchase order financing are 2 different things. The first provides financing after the order has been produced and shipped. The latter provides capital at a much earlier stage—when the order has been received. There are many businesses that have orders that they cannot fill because they cannot buy inventory. This working capital is used to pay for the inventory needed to fill an order. It is a great resource for companies that are growing fast but do not have the capital to buy additional inventory to maintain their growth.

That was the case with Jeffrey Martinez, the president of Ocean World Fisheries USA in Florida. His company is an importer of shrimp and crab from Latin America. His customers were giving him purchase orders at a rapid pace. He, in turn, was generating orders to his supplier faster than he was collecting receivables, which created a cash shortage and diminished the speed with which he could buy more inventory. In addition, his suppliers expected to be paid immediately upon delivery. He had to pay for inventory before he got paid. Martinez explained his working capital problem this way: "We're able to sell all the shrimp and crab we could import and more. But when suppliers put the product in a container, they expect to be paid immediately."[44] His solution? He procured inventory using purchase order financing from Gerber Trade Finance in New York, which allowed him to pay for his inventory upon delivery.

This type of financing is designed for companies that cannot get a traditional loan from a bank or finance company, perhaps because they are carrying too much long-term debt. It is ideal short-term financing for companies that do not hold inventory for long, such as importers, wholesalers, and distributors.

Like factoring, purchase order financing is not cheap. The lender charges fees that range from 5 to 10% of the purchase order's value, and payment is due in 30 to 90 days.[45]

Purchase order financing is riskier than factoring because the collateral is inventory, which may get damaged, be poorly produced, or spoil. Therefore, banks and other traditional financiers have not wholeheartedly embraced this type of debt financing.

In addition to Gerber, 2 additional purchase order financiers are Bankers Capital and Transcap Trade Finance. Both are located in Northbrook, Illinois.

Credit Cards

The final source of debt working capital is from credit cards. But before proceeding, let me offer a stern warning about using credit cards. Be careful! The abuse of credit cards can be one of the entrepreneur's easiest and quickest ways to go out of business.

Americans owe more than $3.0 trillion on their credit cards.[46] The top 4 cards are Visa, MasterCard, American Express, and Discover, which collectively hold approximately 70% of market share. It is estimated that 138 million Americans have at least 1 credit card.[47] In 2010, the Federal Reserve Survey of Consumer Finances found that the median balance for household credit card debt was $3,100. The credit card industry is cashing in on this debt, with $18.5 billion in profits in 2011.[48] Not surprisingly, with all this money to be made, the number of credit card offers has skyrocketed. The number of credit card solicitations in the mail has increased from 1.1 billion in 1990 to an annual rate of 4.8 billion in 2010.[49] There are approximately 314 million men, women, and children in the entire country. This is equivalent to 15 solicitations for every person in the country!

One group that has been receptive to these solicitations is entrepreneurs. A 2012 survey done by Pepperdine University showed that credit cards were the most common financing option that entrepreneurs used to meet their capital needs. Entrepreneurs have embraced credit card use for several reasons. First and foremost, credit cards are very easy to get, as proved by the statistics just cited. Second, these cards allow easy access to as much as $100,000 in cash advances without having to explain how the money will be spent. Small businesses that don't qualify for bank loans also look to credit cards to finance their growth. The final reason is that if they are used methodically and strategically, credit cards can provide inexpensive capital. Regarding this final point, there are 2 ways in which this source of capital can be cheap. The first is by using cards that offer introductory rates as low as 0%. The second is a situation in which the capital can be provided as an interest-free short-term loan. That occurs when the bill is paid off each month during the grace period.

This second method highlights one of several negative aspects of using credit cards for working capital: one large bill comes due every month, as opposed to small bills from many suppliers when you pay by check. When cash is short, it is easier to juggle the payments of a number of small bills than 1 large bill.

This problem leads to the next issue, and that is the assessment of expensive late-payment penalties. In 1997, the government lifted restrictions on maximum penalty charges, resulting in credit card issuers charging whatever late fee they wanted, even if the bill was paid only 1 day after the grace period. Until that ruling, most banks charged an annual fee of about $25, used fixed rates for all borrowers, and had late fees of $10 or less. Furthermore, most cards came with a grace period. Since that ruling, late fees have jumped to $39, and in some cases the grace period has been eliminated. Moreover, credit card companies have begun increasing rates on borrowers for reasons ranging from being late on a house payment to using too much of their available credit. The Durbin Amendment to the Dodd-Frank Wall Street Reform and Consumer Protection Act of 2010 has had only a mixed set of benefits to consumers and entrepreneurs. For more on the debate on these benefits, see www.americanbanker.com.[50]

One thing that has not changed is the high interest rates. While many credit card companies use low introductory rates to lure new customers, once these rates expire in 3 to 6 months, the traditionally high credit card rates of 12 to 20% or even more take effect. This is very expensive money because of the high rates and the fact that the interest charges are compounded. Getting behind on credit card payments can put an entrepreneur in a deep financial hole. The worst situation is that in which the debt is so far past due that the interest costs are being compounded and late penalties are being added, so that payments never decrease the principal. A situation like this can harm the entrepreneur's personal credit because she is liable, not the business.

Another challenge in using credit cards other than for cash advances is finding suppliers that will accept them. Suppliers that might have credit card payment capabilities have an aversion to accepting credit cards because the suppliers have to pay the issuing institution 1.5 to 3.0%. This in effect reduces the price they are charging you.

The final negative is that the use of personal credit cards for business purposes is a violation of the customer-cardholder agreement that you sign.

If you are not dissuaded from using a credit card, here are a few suggestions:

- Pay the entire bill before the end of the grace period to eliminate interest charges or late fees. Payment means that the money must actually be received, not simply be "in the mail."
- Not all cards have grace periods. Use only those that do.
- Know how long your grace period is. That is the amount of time a lender allows before charging interest on the balance due. Some grace periods are as few as 20 days. If the bill is paid in full before the end of the grace period, no interest is charged. You should know that federal law says that credit card bills must be mailed or delivered no later than 21 days before the payment is due.
- Refrain from getting cash advances if interest is charged immediately after the money is given, regardless of whether the account is paid in full during the grace period. In addition to interest charges, most credit card companies charge a fee of 2 to 5% of the total cash advance. Use only cards that treat cash advances like other charges that you make.
- Find out the closing date of your credit card statement. This is the date in every month when billing for that month ends. For example, if your statement closing date is the tenth of every month and you have a 20-day grace period, complete payment must be made and received by the thirtieth of the month in order to avoid interest charges.
- When using the card to pay suppliers, get an agreement with them that no matter when you make the actual purchase, they will bill the credit card on the day following your statement closing date. Using the example in the previous item, that date would be the eleventh of the month. Therefore, that charge will not show up until you receive the bill that closed on the tenth of the next month. With a 20-day grace period added to that, you could get a 50-day interest-free loan.

Let's use a more detailed example to illustrate this point. The Perkins Company purchases 60 widgets from the Steinharter Company for $1,000 on

October 14. The Perkins Company's closing statement date is the twenty-ninth of each month. Therefore, the Steinharter Company submits the charge on October 30. On November 29, the charge is sent to the Perkins Company by the issuer. The 20-day grace period ends December 18. The Perkins Company pays the entire bill at the bank on December 17. The result is that the Perkins Company received an interest-free $1,000 loan for 62 days, from October 14 to December 17.

In closing—be careful! Credit card companies are constantly changing things. One such change could be your closing statement date or the number of days in your grace period. Unnoticed changes in either could result in your owing a complete month's worth of interest because your payment was 1 day late. Finally, just as with any other contract, make sure to read the fine print and know what obligations you and your business must fulfill.

8

Equity Financing

INTRODUCTION

Equity capital is money provided in exchange for ownership in the company. The equity investor receives a percentage of ownership that ideally appreciates in value as the company grows. The investor may also receive a portion of the company's annual profits, called dividends, based on his ownership percentage. For example, a 10% dividend yield or payout on a company's stock worth $200 per share means an annual dividend of $20.

Before deciding to pursue equity financing, the entrepreneur must know the positive and negative aspects of this capital.

Pros

- No personal guarantees are required.
- No collateral is required.
- No regular cash payments are required.
- There can be value-added investors.
- Equity investors cannot force a business into bankruptcy.
- On average, companies with equity financing grow faster.

Cons

- Dividends are not tax-deductible.
- The entrepreneur has new partners.
- It is typically very expensive.
- The entrepreneur can be replaced.

SOURCES OF EQUITY CAPITAL

Many of the sources of debt capital can also provide equity capital. Therefore, for those common sources, what was said about them elsewhere in the book also applies here. When appropriate, a few additional issues might be added in this discussion of equity.

Personal Savings

When an entrepreneur personally invests money in the company, it should be in the form of debt, not equity. This will allow the entrepreneur to recover her investment with only the interest received being taxed. The principal will not be taxed, as it is viewed by the IRS as a return of the original investment. This is in contrast to the tax treatment of capital invested as equity. Like interest, the dividend received would be taxed; however, so would the entire amount of the original investment, even if no capital gain is realized.

The entrepreneur's equity stake should come from her hard work in starting and growing the company, not her monetary contribution. This is called *sweat equity.*

Friends and Family

Equity investments are not usually accompanied by personal guarantees from the entrepreneur. However, such assurances may be required of the entrepreneur when he receives capital from friends and family members in order to maintain the relationship if the business fails.

But this may be a small price to pay in order to realize an entrepreneurial dream. Start-up capital is difficult to obtain except through friends and family.

Dan Lauer experienced this firsthand when he was starting his company, Haystack Toys, in 1988. He raised $250,000 from family and friends after quitting his job as a banker. He went to family and friends after 700 submission letters to investors went unanswered.[1]

Angel Investors

Wealthy individuals usually like to make their investments in the form of equity because they want to share in the potential growth of the company's valuation. There is at present and has always been a dearth of capital for the earliest stages of entrepreneurship—the seed or start-up stage. Angel investors have done an excellent job of providing capital for this stage. Their investments are typically between $150,000 and $300,000. In exchange, they expect high returns (ranging from 25 to 38% IRR),[2] similar to that expected by venture capitalists.[3] Since they are investing at the earliest stage, they usually also get a large ownership position in the company because the valuation is so low.

As stated in Chapter 7, many angel investors are former successful entrepreneurs. One of the prominent former entrepreneurs who has gone on to become an angel investor is Mitch Kapor, who in 1982 founded Lotus Development, the producer of Lotus 1-2-3 software, which he sold to IBM in 1995 for $3.5 billion. Kapor became an angel investor, placing 18 investments annually in a range of $100,000 to $250,000; among his recent investments are Uber, Mozilla and Twilio.[4] He was also an early investor in UUNet, the first Internet access provider.

But angel investing has never been limited to former entrepreneurs. In fact, Apple Computer got its first outside financing from an angel who had never owned a company. He was A. C. "Mike" Markkula, who gained his initial wealth from being a shareholder and corporate executive at Intel. In 1977 he invested $91,000 in Apple Computer and personally guaranteed another $250,000 in credit lines. When Apple went public in 1980, his stock in the company was worth more than $150 million.[5]

This is one of several reasons why the number of angel investors has increased so dramatically: returns. The publicity surrounding successful entrepreneurial ventures often includes stories about the returns that investors received. These stories, coupled with research, have led many wealthy individuals to the private equity industry. And while the anecdotal stories themselves are quite impressive, the more seductive story is empirical research that compares the returns of private equity firms with returns on several other investment options. Table 8-1 shows that over all investment windows, average annual returns for private equity firms were greater than those for all other investment options.

The second reason for the increase in angel capital was an increase in the number of wealthy people in the country who had money to invest. For example, from 1995 to 2012, the number of U.S. households with million-dollar incomes increased from 3 million, or 3% of households, to 7.65 million, or 6.5% of households.[6] Many of these millionaires gained their wealth through successful technology entrepreneurial ventures.

The final reason for the explosion in angel capital was the change in federal personal tax laws. In May 1997, the statutory capital gains tax rate on long-term gains was decreased from a maximum of 28% to 20%; this rate was further reduced to 15% starting in May of 2003. During these years, people were able to keep more of their wealth, and they used it to invest in entrepreneurs.

TABLE 8-1 **Average Annual Returns, 1987–2012**

Sector	**Returns, %**
Private equity	14.5
Russell 3000	13.8
Growth	11.9
S&P 500	11.8
Gold	11.9
Oil	11.8
10-Year Treasury	8.4

Source: Steven DeKlerck, "Value vs. Growth, S&P 500, Oil, Treasuries, & Gold," *ValueWalk*, September 16, 2012, http://www.valuewalk.com/2012/09/value-vs-growth-sp-500-oil-treasuries-gold/; and Timothy Pollard, "Private Equity Outperforms Public Counterpart by 70 Basis Points Annually When Comparing Median Returns," *Pensions & Investments*, July 12, 2013, http://www.pionline.com/article/20130712/CHARTOFDAY/130719960.

Interestingly, it was rumored that one of the groups that lobbied strongly against reductions in the long-term capital gains tax rate was institutional investors. These are private equity firms, not individual investors. They challenged the change because they correctly predicted that it would hurt their business. They believed that as more money became available to entrepreneurs, a company's valuation would inevitably increase, and there would be more competition. Rich Karlgaard, the publisher of *Forbes* magazine, made this observation:

> In my cherubic youth I used to wonder why so many venture capitalists opposed a reduced capital gains tax. Then I woke up to the facts. Crazy as it sounds, even though venture capitalists stand to benefit individually by reduced capital gains taxes, the reduced rates would also lower entry barriers for new competition in the form of corporations and angels. That might lead to—too much venture capital.[7]

Beginning in January 2013, this group got its wish when the maximum long-term capital gains tax rate was increased to 25%.

Even though the amount of capital invested by venture capitalists and angel investors is traditionally on a similar scale, according to the Center for Venture Research at the University of New Hampshire, in 2012, there were significantly fewer companies funded by venture capital firms (3,796)[8] than by angel investors (67,030). In 2012, there were an estimated 268,160 active angel investors. The current yield on angel investments, or the percentage of investments shown that ultimately receive investments by angels, is 21.3%. This is up from 18.3% in 2011, and also up from the 10% yield after the Internet bubble burst in 2000. In 2012, 23% of angel investments were directed to software, 14% to health services and medical devices and equipment, and 11% to biotechnology firms.[9]

Despite private equity firms' complaints, the increase in available capital was clearly a huge positive for entrepreneurs. A few other positive aspects of angel equity capital for entrepreneurs are as follows:

- Seed capital is being provided. Most institutional investors do not finance this early stage of entrepreneurship.

- Many of the angels have great business experience and therefore are value-added investors.
- Angel investors can be more patient than institutional investors, who have to answer to their limited partner investors.

But there are also a few negative aspects to raising money from angels:

- *Potential interference.* Most angels want not only a seat on the board of directors, but also a very active advisory role, which can be troublesome to the entrepreneur.
- *Limited capital.* The investor may be able to invest only in the initial round of financing because of limited capital resources.
- *The capital can be expensive.* Angels typically expect annual returns in excess of 25%.

Regarding this final point, here is what an angel investor said about his expectations:

> I expect to make a good deal of money—more than I would make by putting my capital into a bank, bonds, or publicly traded stocks. My goal, after getting my principal back, is to earn 33% of my initial investment every year for as long as the business is in operation. My usual understanding is that for my investment I own 51% of the stock until I am paid back, whereupon my stake drops to 25%. After that we split every dollar that comes out of the business until I earn my 33% return for the year.[10]

Despite the drawbacks, most entrepreneurs who raise angel capital successfully do not regret it. As one entrepreneur said, "Without angel money, I wouldn't have been able to accomplish what I have. Giving up stock was the right thing to do."[11]

Gaining access to angel investors is not an easy task. Cal Simmons, an Alexandria, Virginia–based angel investor and coauthor of *Every Business Needs an Angel*, says, "You need to have networks. If someone I know and respect refers me, then I'm going to always take the time to take a meeting." Angel groups are another mechanism for getting access to angel investors. There are currently 170 angel groups registered with the Angel Capital Association (www.angelcapitalassociation.org), an angel capital industry trade group supported by the Ewing Marion Kauffman Foundation. Many of these groups accept applications to present to their angels. Some of them charge entrepreneurs a nominal fee of $100 to $200 to present.

There are forums in almost every region of the country similar to the Midwest Entrepreneurs Forum in Chicago. At this event, held the second Monday of each month, entrepreneurs make presentations to angel investors. There are also several angel-related websites, including the AngelList (www.angel.co) in Silicon Valley, SourceCapitalnet.com (www.sourcecapitalnet.com) in New York, and Gust (www.gust.com).

PRIVATE PLACEMENTS

When entrepreneurs seek financing, be it debt or equity, from any of the sources mentioned up until now, that financing is called a *private placement offering*. That is, capital is not being raised on the open market via an initial public offering, which will be discussed later in this chapter. The capital is being raised from specific individuals or organizations that meet all the standards set by Section 4(2) of the U.S. Securities Act of 1933 and Regulation D, an amendment to this act that clarified the rules for those seeking a private placement exemption. The rule says, "Neither the issuer nor any person acting on its behalf shall offer or sell the securities by any form of general solicitation or general advertising. This includes advertisements, articles or notices in any form of media. Also, the relationship between the party offering the security and the potential investor will have been established prior to the launch of the offering."[12] All of this simply means that an entrepreneur cannot solicit capital by standing on the corner trying to sell stock in his company to any passerby. (A very recent law, which is discussed in Chapter 12, allows for general solicitation by small companies to "accredited investors," a term defined on the next page.) He cannot put an ad in a newspaper or magazine recruiting unaccredited investors. He must know his investors, either directly or indirectly. Potential investors in the latter category are known through the entrepreneur's associates, such as his attorney, his accountant, or his investment banker.

Fund-raising efforts must be restricted to "accredited investors only." These investors are also known as "sophisticated investors." Such an investor has to meet one of the following three criteria:

- An individual net worth (or joint net worth with a spouse) that is greater than $1 million
- An individual income (without any income of a spouse) in excess of $200,000 in each of the two most recent years and reasonably expects an income in excess of $200,000 in the current year
- Joint income with a spouse in excess of $300,000 in each of the two most recent years and reasonably expects to have joint income in excess of $300,000 in the current year

Prior to accepting investments, the entrepreneur must get confirmation of this sophisticated investor status by requiring all the investors to complete a form called the Investor Questionnaire. This form must be accompanied by a letter from the entrepreneur's attorney or accountant stating that the investors meet all the accreditation requirements.

Violation of any part of Regulation D could result in a 6-month suspension of fund-raising or something as severe as the company's being required to return all the money to the investors immediately. Therefore, the entrepreneur should hire an attorney experienced with private placements before raising capital. Figure 8-1 summarizes the Regulation D rules and restrictions.

As stated earlier, sources of capital for a private placement are angel investors, insurance companies, banks, family, and friends, along with pension funds and private investment pools. There are no hard-and-fast rules regarding the structure or terms of a private placement. Therefore, private placements are ideal for high-risk and small companies. The offering can be for all equity, all debt, or a combination of debt and equity. The entrepreneur can issue the offering or use an investment banker.

The largest and most prominent national investment banks that handle private placements are Bank of America/Merrill Lynch, JPMorgan Chase, and Credit Suisse. These 3 banking firms raise a total of more than $30 billion for entrepreneurs each year. Regional investment bankers are better suited for raising small amounts of capital.

		Amount of Offering	
	$1 million	**$1 million–$5 million**	**Unlimited (Emphasis on Nonpublic Nature, Not Small Issue!)**
Number of investors	Unlimited	35 plus unlimited accredited investors	35 plus those purchasing $150,000
Investor qualification	None required (no sophistication requirement)	• Accredited—presumed qualified • 35 nonaccredited—no sophistication requirement	Nonaccredited purchasers must be sophisticated—must understand risks and merits of investment; accredited presumed to be qualified
Manner of offering	General solicitation permitted	No general solicitation	No general solicitation
Limitations on Resale	No restrictions	Restricted	Restricted
Issuer qualifications	No reporting companies; no investment companies; no "blank-check" companies; no "unworthy issuers"	No investment companies; no issuers disqualified under Reg. A no "unworthy; issuers" (Rule 507)	None (except for Rule 507 "unworthy issuer")
Information requirements	No information specified	If purchased solely by accredited investors, no information specified; for nonaccredited, info required: (a) Nonreporting companies must furnish information similar to that in a registered offering or Reg. A offering, but modified financial statement requirements (b) Reporting companies must furnish specified SEC documents, plus limited additional information about the offering	
SEC rules	Rule 504	Rule 505	Rule 506

Figure 8-1 **Regulation D Rules Restrictions**

When hiring an investment banker, the entrepreneur should expect to pay either a fixed fee or a percentage of the money raised (which can be up to 10%), and/or give the fund-raising professional a percentage of the company's stock (up to 5%). One important piece of advice is that the entrepreneur should be extremely cautious about using the same investment banker to determine the amount of capital needed and to raise the capital. There is a conflict of interest when the investment banker does both for a variable fee. Whenever only one investment banker is used for both assignments, the fee should be fixed. Otherwise, use different companies for each assignment.

Shopping a Private Placement

After the private placement document has been completed, it must be "shopped" to potential investors. The following describes the process of shopping a private placement:

1. Make an ideal investor profile list (those who have met the net asset requirement).
2. Identify whom to put on the actual list:
    - Former coworkers with money
    - Industry executives and salespeople who know your work history
    - Past customers
3. Call the candidates and inform them of the minimum investment amount.
4. Send a private placement memorandum outlining the investment process only to those who are not intimidated by the minimum investment indicated during the call.
5. Contact other companies in which your investors have invested.

CORPORATE VENTURE CAPITAL

In the late 1990s, large corporations embraced entrepreneurship with the same interest as individuals. This was surprising because it was assumed that corporations, with their reputations for stodgy bureaucracy and conservatism, were "anti-entrepreneurship." Their primary relationship with the entrepreneurship world came as investors. This began to change in the late 1990s, as corporations began to realize the opportunities associated with investing in companies that had products or services related to their industry. Such strategic investments became a part of corporations' research and development programs as they sought access to new products, services, and markets. For example, cable television operator Comcast Corp. established a $125 million fund to invest in companies that would "help it understand how to capitalize on the Internet." Comcast wanted to bring its cable TV customers online, and also saw the potential to put its QVC shopping channel on the Internet.[13]

The final reason that such prominent corporations as Intel, Cisco, Time Warner, and Reader's Digest created their funds was to find new customers. As one person described it, "Corporations are using their venture-backed companies to foster demand for their own products and technologies."[14] Two companies implementing that strategy were Andersen Consulting and Electronic Data Systems. Both companies invested in customers that used their systems integration consulting services.

Traditional venture capitalists love it when their portfolio companies receive financing from corporate venture capitalists. The primary reason is that the latter are value-added investors. In fact, three of the most successful venture capital firms—Accel Partners, Kleiner Perkins Caufield & Byers (KPCB), and Battery Ventures—have wholeheartedly endorsed the use of corporate funds. This point was made by Ted Schlein, a partner with KPCB, who said, "Having a corporation as a partner early on can give you some competitive advantages. The portfolio companies are after sales and marketing channels."[15]

When the stock market crashed in 2000, corporate venture capital dried up. Total investment dollars dropped from $16.8 billion in 2000 to under $2 billion in 2002. This 88% drop was faster than the 75% drop in the overall markets. This faster rate of decline makes sense. Venture capital is not the primary business of corporations, and it can be expected that, in times of economic hardship, these firms will pull back their financing. Moreover, many of these firms need to manage short-term earnings expectations, so investment funding gets cut when quarterly earnings figures are threatened. Table 8-2 shows corporate venture capital investments from 2002 through early 2011.[16]

TABLE 8-2 **Corporate Venture Capital Investment, 2002 to 2011**

Year	Number of Companies Receiving CVC Dollars	Percent of All Companies Receiving CVC Dollars	Total CVC Investment (Millions of $)	Percent of All VC $
2002	551	17.3%	$1,905.90	9.1%
2003	447	14.9%	$1,296.00	7.0%
2004	528	16.6%	$1,548.70	6.9%
2005	535	16.4%	$1,557.20	6.8%
2006	636	16.6%	$2,031.50	7.6%
2007	777	18.8%	$2,609.40	8.5%
2008	783	19.0%	$2,263.50	7.4%
2009	390	12.7%	$1,428.40	7.2%
2010	481	13.6%	$1,999.80	8.6%
2011	551	14.9%	$2,331.70	8.2%

PRIVATE EQUITY FIRMS

Many of the sources of equity financing that have been discussed up to this point are individuals. But there is an entire industry filled with "institutional" investors. These are firms that are in the business of providing equity capital to entrepreneurs, with the expectation of high returns.

This industry is commonly known as the venture capital industry. However, venture capital is merely one aspect of private equity. The phrase *private equity* comes from the fact that money is being exchanged for equity in the company and that this is a private deal between the 2 parties—investor and entrepreneur. For the most part, all the terms of the deal are dependent on what the 2 parties agree to. This is in contrast to public equity financing, which occurs when the company raises money through an initial public offering. In that case, all aspects of the deal must be in accordance with Securities and Exchange Commission (SEC) rules. One rule is that the financial statements of a public company must be published and provided to the investors quarterly. Such a rule does not exist in private equity deals. The 2 parties can make any agreement they want; for example, financial statements can be sent to investors every month, quarterly, twice a year, or even once a year.

Private Equity: The Basics

It is important to note that the owners of private equity firms are also entrepreneurs. These firms are typically small companies that happen to be in the business of providing capital. Like all other entrepreneurs, they put their capital at risk in pursuit of exploiting an opportunity and can go out of business.

Legal Structure

Most private equity firms are organized as limited partnerships or limited liability companies. These structures offer advantages over general partnerships by indemnifying the external investors and the principals. They also have advantages over C corporations because they limit the life of the firm to a specific amount of time (usually 10 years), which is attractive to investors. Furthermore, the structures eliminate the double taxation of distributed profits.

The professional investors who manage the firm are the general partners (GPs). The GPs invest between 1 to 5% of their personal capital in the fund and make all the decisions. External investors in a typical private equity partnership are called limited partners (LPs). During the fund-raising process, LPs pledge or commit a specified amount of capital for the new venture fund. For most funds formed today, the minimum capital commitment from any single LP is $1 million; however, the actual minimum contribution is completely at the discretion of the firm. The commitment of capital is formalized through the signing of the partnership agreement between the LPs and the venture firm. The partnership agreement details the terms of the fund and legally binds the LPs to provide the capital that they have pledged.

Getting Their Attention

GPs rely on their proprietary network of entrepreneurs, friendly attorneys, limited partners, and industry contacts to introduce them to new companies. They are much more likely to spend time looking at a new opportunity that was referred to them by a source they find trustworthy than one referred to them by other sources. A business plan that is referred through their network is also less likely to be "shopped around" to all the other venture capitalists focused on a particular industry segment. GPs want to avoid getting involved in an auction for the good deals because bidding drives up the valuation. In the course of a year, a typical private equity firm receives thousands of business plans. Less than 10% of these deals move to the due diligence phase of the investment.

Choose Investors Wisely

It is very important that you choose potential investors carefully—you will be establishing an important long-term relationship with them. Do your research on each potential investor before sending your business plan to ensure a better rate of acceptance. Find out what types of deals the investor pursues. What is the firm's investment strategy, and what are its selection criteria? What is its success rate? How have the investors reacted during critical situations, such as a financial crisis? Do the investors just bail out, or are they in for the long haul? One good source of information in this regard is other companies that have received backing from that particular investor. Will the "value-added" investors provide useful advice and contacts, or will they provide only financial resources?

It is extremely important that you know your audience so that you can limit your search to those who have an affinity for doing business with you. If your company is a start-up, then you should send the plan to those who provide "seed" or start-up capital rather than later-stage financing. For example, it would be a waste of time to send a business plan for the acquisition of a grocery store to a technology-focused lender, such as Silicon Valley Bank.

It is always advisable to get what Kellogg clinical professor and venture capital professional Bill Sutter calls "an endorsed recommendation," preferably from someone who has had previous business dealings with the investor, before submitting your business plan. John Doerr at KPCB stated, "I can't recall ever having invested in a business on the basis of an unsolicited business plan."[17] This endorsement will guarantee that your business plan will be considered more carefully and seriously. If a recommendation is not possible, then an introduction by someone who knows the investor will be helpful. In most instances, unsolicited business plans submitted to venture capital firms without a referral have a lower chance of getting funding than those submitted with one. If you are submitting an unsolicited business plan, it is important that you write it so that it is consistent with the investor's investment strategy.

A good example of someone who did this correctly is Mitch Kapor, the founder of Lotus Development Corporation, who, in 1981, sent his business plan to only one venture capital firm. Recognizing that his business plan was somewhat different—it included a statement saying that he wasn't motivated by profit—he knew himself and his company well enough to know that not all venture capitalists would take him seriously. He carefully selected one firm—Sevin and Rosen. Why? Because this firm was used to doing business with his "type"—namely, computer programmers. They knew him personally, and they also knew the industry. It was a good decision. He got the financing he sought, even though he had a poorly organized, nontraditional plan.

Investor Screening Process

Most firms use a screening process to prioritize the deals that they are considering. Generally, associates within a firm are given the responsibility of screening new business plans based on a set of investment criteria, developed over time by the firm. These criteria are communicated in the partnership agreement submitted by the fund manager to their LPs, and to which fund managers must strictly adhere. LPs rely on fund managers to stay within the proposed "investment thesis" or investment characteristics, so that the LPs can measure and manage financial risk down to the portfolio level at each of their fund investments. Straying from the thesis leads to significant criticism by the LPs.

Several of the parameters used to screen investments are:

- Management: financial acumen, integrity, and experience
- Market size
- Growth expectations
- Phase in the industry life cycle
- Differentiating factors
- Terms of the deal

An entrepreneur can expedite the process by creating a concise, accurate, and compelling executive summary, or 2- to 3-page investment brief that addresses an investor's key concerns. The entrepreneur's ability to communicate her ideas effectively and succinctly through a written, oral, or, in some instances, video format is critical to receiving funding for the project.

Once a deal passes the first screen by meeting a majority of the initial criteria, a private equity firm begins an exhaustive investigation of the industry, the managers, and the financial projections for the potential investment. Due diligence may include hiring consultants to investigate the feasibility of a new product; doing extensive reference checking on management, including background checks; and undertaking detailed financial modeling to check the legitimacy of projections. The entire due diligence process takes from 30 to 90 days in a deal that receives funding.

Management

Most GPs list management as their most important criterion for the success of an investment. The management team is evaluated based on attributes that define its leadership ability, experience, and reputation, including:

- Recognized achievement
- Teamwork
- Work ethic
- Operating experience
- Commitment
- Integrity
- Reputation
- Entrepreneurial experience

GPs use a variety of methods to confirm the information provided by an entrepreneur, including extensive interviews, private detectives, background checks, and reference checks. During the interview process, the entrepreneur must provide compelling evidence of the merits of the business model and of the management team's ability to execute it. Therefore, the management team must clearly and concisely articulate the product or service concept and be prepared to answer a series of in-depth questions about it. In addition, the interview process provides an indication to both sides of the fit between the venture capitalist and the entrepreneur. A good fit is critical to the potential success of the investment because of the difficult decisions that will inevitably need to be made during the life of the relationship.

Some firms believe in the strength of management so much that they invest in a management team or a manager before a company exists. Often, these entrepreneurs have successfully brought a company to a lucrative exit and are looking for the next opportunity. Some venture firms give these seasoned veterans the title "entrepreneur in residence" and fund the search for their next opportunity.

Ideal Candidate

Again, private equity from institutional investors is ideal for entrepreneurial firms with excellent management teams. These companies should be predicted to experience or be experiencing rapid annual growth of at least 20%. The industry should be large enough to sustain two large, successful competitors. And the product should have:

- Limited technical and operational risks
- Proprietary and differentiating features
- Above-average gross margins
- Short sales cycles
- Repeat sales opportunities

Finally, the company must have the potential to increase in value sufficiently in 5 to 7 years for the investor to realize her minimum targeted return. Coupled with this growth potential must be at least 2 explicit discernible exit opportunities (sell the company or take it public) for the investor. The entrepreneur and the investor must agree in advance on the timing of this potential exit and the strategy. For example, an ideal entrepreneurial financing candidate is one who knows that he wants to raise $10 million in equity capital for 10% of his company and expects to sell the company to a Fortune 500 corporation in 5 years for 7 times the company's present value. This tells the investor that she can exit the deal in Year 5 and receive $70 million for her investment.

TABLE 8-3 Targeted IRR for Private Equity Investors

Private Equity Investor Type	Targeted IRR
Corporate finance	20–40%
Mezzanine funds	15–25%
Venture capital funds	38–50%

When an entrepreneur goes after private equity funding, he should know what kind of returns are expected. The targeted minimum internal rates of return for the institutional private equity industry are noted in Table 8-3.

Again, private equity investors make their "real" money when a portfolio company has a liquidation event: the company goes public, merges, is recapitalized, or gets acquired. Depending on the equity firm and its investment life cycle, the fund's investors typically plan to exit anywhere between 3 and 10 years after the initial investment. Among other things, investors consider the time value of money—the concept that a million dollars today is worth more than a million dollars 5 years from now—when determining what kind of returns or IRR they expect over time. Table 8-4 provides an approximate cheat sheet for the entrepreneur. As the table shows, an investor who walks away with 5 times her initial investment in 5 years has earned a 38% IRR.

During the 1990s, there was an explosion in the number of private equity funds formed. According to the National Venture Capital Association, the total

TABLE 8-4 Time Value of Money—IRR on a Multiple of Original Investment over a Period of Time

	2×	3×	4×	5×	6×	7×	8×	9×	10×
2 years	41	73	100	124	145	165	183	200	216
3 years	26	44	59	71	82	91	100	108	115
4 years	19	32	41	50	57	63	68	73	78
5 years	15	25	32	38	43	48	52	55	58
6 years	12	20	26	31	35	38	41	44	47
7 years	10	17	22	26	29	32	35	37	39

number of private equity funds (venture capital, mezzanine, and buyout) in the United States increased substantially, going from 150 in 1990 to 805 in 2000. Why? You know the answer: returns! In 2003, after the dot-com crash, this number had fallen to only 282. As private equity fund-raising returned in the mid-2000s, the number of funds climbed back to 499 in 2007, then fell again to 400 in 2012. Of those, the National Venture Capital Association reports that 183 are venture capitalists. Table 8-5 shows venture capital fund-raising from 1990 to 2012.[18]

TABLE 8-5 **Commitments to Venture Capital Funds**

Year	Funds Raised (Billions of Dollars)
1990	3.2
1991	1.9
1992	5.2
1993	4.5
1994	7.6
1995	9.4
1996	11.6
1997	17.7
1998	30.6
1999	53.6
2000	101.4
2001	38.9
2002	11.9
2003	10.6
2004	18.1
2005	30.6
2006	31.4
2007	29.4
2008	25.6
2009	16.2
2010	13.5
2011	19.3
2012	20.1

Latin America	Europe	Asia
Exxel Capital Partners	Merlin Ventures	SOFTBANK Capital
GP Capital Partners	Early Bird Ventures	Attractor Investors
CVC/Opportunity Equity Partners	3i	Vertex Management

Figure 8-2 **Various International Private Equity Firms**

INTERNATIONAL PRIVATE EQUITY

Over the last decade, private equity has exploded around the globe. While North America still represents 41% of all private equity dollars, other regions are catching up, and fund-raising is increasing around the world. While much of the capital comes from U.S. investors, foreign investors, including governments such as those of China and Kuwait, have allocated assets to private equity investing. Within the venture capital world, the United States is still dominant. With a staggering 71% of the venture capital raised by G7 nations, the United States remains the center of entrepreneurial activity.

Both the number of funds and the amount of capital that has been raised in Europe, Latin America, and Asia have dramatically increased each year. Most of the money, estimated to be 60 to 70%, has come from investors in the United States, including pension funds, insurance companies, endowments, and wealthy individuals. Several of the international funds are highlighted in Figure 8-2. The amount of capital raised in 2012 was $31.2 billion in Europe,[19] $64.9 billion in Asia,[20] and (in 2011) $8.4 billion in Latin America and the Caribbean.[21]

ADVICE FOR RAISING PRIVATE EQUITY

Derrick Collins, a former general partner at Polestar Capital and currently dean of the School of Business at Chicago State University, gives the following advice to entrepreneurs who are interested in obtaining equity capital:

- Do your homework. Seek investors who have a proclivity for your type of deal. Approach only those who are buying what you are selling. Pursue capital from firms that explicitly state in their description an interest in your industry, the size of the investment you want, and the entrepreneurial stage of your company.

- Get an introduction to the investors prior to submitting the business plan. Find someone who knows one of the general partners, limited partners, or associates of the firm. Ask that person to call on your behalf to give you an introduction and endorsement. This action will maximize the attention given to your plan and shorten the response time.

If these steps result in a meeting with a private equity investor, Tom Cox, a general partner of Cascade Partners, puts it this way:

> Be alert to the behavior of a venture capitalist who "SITS" on your presentation, which means they "Show Interest Then Stall." This will be obvious from the pattern of calls you make to them, and whether those calls are returned in a timely manner, as well as to the detailed content of the conversations. A slow "maybe" feels much worse, but is more common than a fast "no."

Increasing Specialization of Private Equity Firms

There has been an increasing trend toward private equity firms specializing in a particular industry or stage of development. Firms can be categorized as either generalists or specialists. Generalists are more opportunistic and look at a variety of opportunities, from high-tech to high-growth retail. Specialized firms tend to focus on an industry segment or two, for instance, software and communications. Notice that these are still very broad industries.

Specialization has increased for several reasons. First, in an increasingly competitive industry, venture capitalists are competing for deal flow. If a firm is the recognized expert in a certain industry area, then it is more likely that this firm will be exposed to deals in this area. Additionally, the firm will be better able to assess and value the deal because of its expertise in the industry. Finally, some specialized firms are able to negotiate lower valuations and better terms because the entrepreneur values the industry knowledge and contacts that a specialized firm can provide. Entrepreneurs should keep this in mind when raising funds. As important as it is for them to target the correct investment stage of a prospective venture capital firm, it is equally important that they consider the firm's industry specialization.

Identifying Private Equity Firms

One of the best resources for finding the appropriate private equity firm is *Pratt's Guide to Private Equity and Venture Capital Sources*, which lists companies by state, preferred size of investment, and industry interests. Several additional resources are available online:

1. The National Venture Capital Association at www.nvca.org or 703–351–5269
2. Venture One at ventureone.com
3. University of New Hampshire, Peter T. Paul College of Business and Economics Center for Venture Research Capital Locator at https://paulcollege.unh.edu/research/center-venture-research/capital-locator
4. CrunchBase at http://www.crunchbase.com/financial-organizations

The final suggestion is to pursue the opportunity to make a presentation at a venture capital forum such as the Springboard Conference for female entrepreneurs or the Mid-Atlantic Venture Fair, which is open to entrepreneurs in all industries and at all stages of the business cycle. These are usually 2-day events in which entrepreneurs get a chance to present to and meet local and national private equity providers. Typically the entrepreneur must submit an application with a fee of approximately $200. If the investor is selected to make an 8- to 15-minute presentation, an additional fee of $500 or so may be required. The National Venture Capital Association should be contacted to find out about forums and their locations, times, and dates.

SMALL-BUSINESS INVESTMENT COMPANIES

The federal government, through the Small Business Administration (SBA), also provides equity capital to entrepreneurs. Small-business investment companies (SBICs) are privately owned, for-profit equity firms that are licensed and regulated by the SBA. SBICs invest in businesses employing fewer than 500 people and showing a net worth not greater than $18 million and an after-tax income not exceeding $6 million over the 2 most recent years. There are more than 300 licensed SBICs in the country with more than $18 billion nationwide. In 2012, the SBIC program firms invested $3.1 billion in equity and debt capital. The firms invested in 937 different small businesses.[22] Investments ranged from $250,000 to $5 million.

SBICs were created in 1958 for the purpose of expanding the availability of risk capital to entrepreneurs. Many of the first private equity firms were SBICs. And many of the country's successful companies received financing from an SBIC. These include Intel, Apple, Whole Foods Market, Costco, and Outback Steakhouse. They also include some notable debacles like the venture begun by Susan MacDougal, who used her $300,000 to invest in a little real estate project called the Whitewater Development Corporation.

In most ways, SBICs are similar to traditional private equity firms. The primary differences between the two are their origination and their financing. Anyone can start a traditional private equity firm as long as he can raise the capital. But someone who is interested in starting an SBIC firm must first get a license from the SBA. Interest in creating a Standard Debenture SBIC comes from the attractive financing arrangement: for every dollar the general partners raise for the fund, the SBA will invest $2 at a very low interest rate, with no payments due for either 5 or 10 years. Therefore, if the general partners obtain $25 million in commitments from private sources, the SBA will invest $50 million, making it a $75 million fund. Standard Debenture SBICs tend to focus on growth-stage companies rather than pure start-ups. The Early Stage Small Business Investment Company (SBIC) Initiative was created under the Standard Debenture model to commit up to $1 billion in SBA-guaranteed leverage over a 5-year period (2012–2016) to selected early-stage venture funds. The difference is that the match is 1-1 (not 2-1) up to $50 million.[23]

Also included under the SBIC program are Impact Investment SBICs. They are similar to SBICs in every way, except that they tend to make smaller investments and, most important, they are created specifically to provide investments in companies owned by socially and economically disadvantaged entrepreneurs.

Although they are not technically part of the SBIC program, the New Markets Venture Capital Program and the Rural Business Investment Program are modeled on the SBIC program. The two programs combined provide equity capital to entrepreneurs with companies in rural, urban, and specially designated low- and moderate-income (LMI) areas.[24]

Overall, the SBIC program has clearly been a strong contributor to the emergence and success of entrepreneurship in America. It has increased the pool of equity capital available for entrepreneurs, and also made this capital obtainable by underserved entrepreneurs. The general private equity industry has a reputation for being interested only in investments in technology entrepreneurs. In contrast, SBICs have a reputation for doing "low-tech" and "no-tech" deals. Both reputations are unfounded. Traditional private firms such as Thoma Cressey Equity Partners invest in later-stage "no-tech" companies, and SBICs such as Chicago Venture Partners invest in technology companies. In fact, 11 of the top 100 companies on the 2005 Inc. 500 list of America's fastest-growing companies received SBIC financing, as did 8 of the top 100 "Hot Growth Companies for 2005" featured in *BusinessWeek*.[25] Figure 8-3 lists a sample of successful SBIC-backed companies.

America Online	Leap Into Learning, Inc.
Amgen, Inc.	Metrolina Outreach
Apple Computer	Octel Communications
	Outback Steakhouse
Compaq Computer	PeopleSoft
Costco Wholesale Corp.	Potomac Group, Inc.
Datastream	Radio One
Federal Express	
Gymboree	Restoration Hardware, Inc.
Harman International	Sports Authority
Healthcare Services of America	Staples
Intel	Sun Microsystems
Jenny Craig Inc.	Telesis
La Madeleine Inc.	Vertex Communications Co.

Source: Small Business Administration, www.sba.gov/aboutsba/sbaprograms/inv/INV_SUCCESS_STORIES.html.

Figure 8-3 **SBIC-Backed Companies**

A free directory of operating SBICs can be obtained by calling the SBA Office of Investments at 800-827-5722 or going online at http://www.sba.gov/content/sbic-directory. There is also a national SBIC trade association at www.sbia.org.

INITIAL PUBLIC OFFERINGS

Every year, hundreds of entrepreneurs raise equity capital by selling their company's stock in the public market. This process of selling a typical minimum of $5 million of stock to institutions and individuals is called an *initial public offering (IPO)* and is strictly regulated by the SEC. The result is a company that is "publicly owned." For many entrepreneurs, taking a company public is the ultimate statement of entrepreneurial success. They believe that entrepreneurs get recognized for one of two reasons: having a company that went bankrupt or having one that had an IPO. Timing is everything with an IPO issue. The late 1990s were record-breaking days of glory, the early 2000s were miserable, and IPOs then began to rebound through 2007. Beginning in 2008, IPOs bottomed at 21 and stumbled to recover even to modest levels compared to historical IPO rates.

When a company "goes public" in the United States, it must meet a new standard of financial reporting, regulated by the Securities and Exchange Commission. All the financial information of such a company must be published quarterly and distributed to the company's shareholders. Therefore, because of the SEC's public disclosure rules, everything about a publicly owned company is open to potential and present shareholders. Information such as the president's salary and bonus, the company's number of employees, and the company's profits are open to the public, including competitors.

Going public was extraordinarily popular during the 1990s. From 1970 to 1997, entrepreneurs raised $297 billion through IPOs. More than 58% of this capital was raised between 1993 and 1997.[26] In 1999 and 2000, entrepreneurs were the highly sought-after guests of honor at a record private equity feast. The money flowed, and entrepreneurs could, in essence, auction off their business plans to the highest bidders. Average valuations of high-tech start-ups rose from about $11 million in 1996 to almost $30 million in 2000.[27] But by the summer of 2000, as the Nasdaq began to crash, venture capital investments began to slow dramatically. As Table 8-6 shows, the boom began to end in 2000

TABLE 8-6 **Number of Initial Public Offerings**

	Number of IPOs	Amount Raised, in Billions
1990	115	$ 4.3
1991	294	$ 16.4
1992	415	$ 22.6
1993	526	$ 31.5
1994	411	$ 17.5
1995	460	$ 28.9
1996	688	$ 42.4
1997	485	$ 32.4
1998	316	$ 34.3
1999	485	$ 64.9
2000	382	$ 64.9
2001	79	$ 34.2
2002	70	$ 22.1
2003	67	$ 10.1
2004	183	$ 31.9
2005	168	$ 28.6
2006	162	$ 30.6
2007	162	$ 35.8
2008	21	$ 22.8
2009	43	$ 13.3
2010	101	$ 30.6
2011	82	$ 27.8
2012	103	$ 31.8

Source: Jay R. Ritter, "Initial Public Offerings: Updated Statistics," June 30, 2013, http://bear.warrington.ufl.edu/ritter/IPOs2012Statistics.pdf; based on data from Dealogic and Thomson Financial.

when the public markets became less interested in hyped technology companies that had no foreseeable chance of making profits. According to research by PricewaterhouseCoopers, in the first three months of 2001, venture capitalists reduced their investments in high-tech start-ups by $6.7 billion—a 40% drop from the previous quarter. In the first quarter of 2001, only 21 companies went public compared with 123 in the same quarter a year earlier. And by late 2001, the IPO market was down dramatically.

For firms that are still committed to going public with an IPO issue during sluggish times, patience had better be a core competency. Venture Economics, a research firm that follows the venture capital industry, studied the time it takes a company to go from its first round of financing to its initial public offering. In 1999, a company took an average of 140 days; 2 years later, that average had surged to 487 days—a jump of 247%.

1990s IPO Boom

The stock market boom of the 1990s was historic. In 1995, Netscape went public despite the fact that it had never made a profit. This was the beginning of the craze for companies going public even though they had no profits. In the history of the United States, there has never been another decade that had as many IPOs or raised as much capital. *Barron's* called it one of the greatest gold rushes of American capitalism.[28] Another writer called it "one of the greatest speculative manias in history."[29]

The frothy IPO market was not limited to technology companies. On October 19, 1999, Martha Stewart took her company public, and the stock price doubled before the end of the day. Vince McMahon, the onetime owner of the World Wrestling Federation, took his company public the same day. Disappointingly, the results were not as good as Martha's. The stock increased only a puny 48.5% by the day's end! In 2000, when many Internet companies were canceling their initial public offerings, Krispy Kreme was the second best-performing IPO of the year.[30]

Because the public markets were responding so positively to IPOs in the 1990s, companies began racing to go public. Before 1995, it was customary for a company to have been in business for at least 3 years and have shown four consecutive quarters of increasing profits before it could do an IPO. The perfect example was Microsoft. Bill Gates took it public in 1986, more than a decade after he had founded it. By the time Microsoft went public, it had recorded several consecutive years of profitability.

But as stated earlier, the Netscape IPO in August 1995 changed things for the next 5 years. In addition to having no profit, Netscape was very young, having been in business for only 16 months. By the end of 1999, the Netscape story was very common.[31] The absurdity was best described by a Wall Street analyst, who said, "Major Wall Street firms used to require four quarters of profits before an IPO. Then it went to four quarters of revenue, and now it's four quarters of breathing."[32]

This IPO euphoria created unparalleled wealth for entrepreneurs, especially those in Silicon Valley's technology industry. At the height of the boom in 1999, it was reported that Silicon Valley executives held $112 billion in stock and options. This was slightly more than Portugal's entire gross domestic product of $109 million.[33]

As all this information shows, entrepreneurs were using IPOs to raise capital for the company's operations as well as to gain personal wealth.

Public Equity Markets

After a company goes public, it is listed and traded on one of several markets in the United States. More than 13,000 companies are listed on these markets. The 3 major and most popular markets are the New York Stock Exchange (NYSE), the NYSE MKT LLC (formerly known as AMEX/American Stock Exchange), and the National Association of Securities Dealers Automated Quotations (Nasdaq). Let's look at each in greater detail.

NYSE

With its start in 1792, the New York Stock Exchange is the oldest trading market in the world. It also has the largest valuation. These 2 facts are the reason that the NYSE is called the "Cadillac of securities markets." Companies listed on this market are considered the strongest financially of the companies on the 3 markets. In order to be listed on the NYSE, the value of the company's outstanding shares must be at least $40 million, and its annual earnings before taxes (EBT) in the most recent year must be at least $5 million.[34] Companies listed on this market are the older, more venerable companies, such as General Electric, Sears, and McDonald's. In the fall of 2013, the total market value of all 1,867 companies listed on the NYSE was $16.6 trillion.[35]

NYSE MKT LLC

The NYSE MKT LLC Exchange is the world's largest market for foreign stocks and the second-largest trading market. The market value of a listed company must be at least $3 million, with an annual EBT of $750,000. Formerly known as the AMEX, the NYSE MKT exchange trades in both a human and an electronic format. The companies whose securities trade on the NYSE MKT are primarily those with smaller market capitalization.

Nasdaq

The Nasdaq market opened in 1971 and was the first electronic stock market. More shares (an average of 831 million per trading day)[36] are traded over this market than over any other in the world.[37]

The minimum market value for companies listed on this market is $1 million. There is no minimum EBT requirement. That is why this market, with more than 5,000 listings, is the largest in the world. The Nasdaq is heavily filled with tech, biotech, and small-company stocks. Trading on this market is done electronically. All the technology companies that have gone public since 1995 did so on the Nasdaq market.

Reasons for Going Public

Entrepreneurs take their companies public for several reasons. The first is to raise capital for the operations of the company. Because the money is to be used to grow the company rapidly, the equity capital provided through an IPO may be preferred over debt. In the cases of the tech companies of the 1990s that had negative cash flow, they could not raise debt capital. Only equity financing was available to them.

Even if a company can afford debt capital, some entrepreneurs prefer capital from an IPO when it is relatively cheap. Historically, the cost of IPO capital has been lower than the cost of debt. (Recently, however, debt capital has been less expensive.) Let's look at the math. Over the history of the Dow Jones Industrial Average, the average P/E ratio has been 15.5.[38] This means that investors have been willing to pay $15.50 for every $1 of earnings. Therefore, the cost of this capital has been 6.5% ($1/$15.50). The cost of debt to an operating company in the U.S. has been during the period 1947-2014 has been 9.84%,[39] indicated by the U.S. Prime Rate, an index of the most common interest rates offered at a given time by U.S. banks to its commercial clients. Since December 2008, the Prime Rate has remained constant at 3.25%.

Another reason for going public is that it can be easier to recruit and retain excellent employees by giving them publicly traded stock as part of their salaries. This allows employees to benefit personally when the value of the company increases as a result of their hard work.

Still another good reason is that an IPO provides the entrepreneur with another form of currency that can be used to grow the company. In the 1990s, companies' stock was being widely used as currency. Instead of buying other companies with cash, many buyers paid the sellers with their stock. The seller would then hold the stock and benefit from any future increases in its value. In fact, many deals did not close or were delayed in closing because the seller wanted the buyer's stock instead of cash. This was the case when Disney purchased the ABC network. Disney wanted to pay cash, but the members of the ABC team held out until they received Disney stock. Their reasoning was that $1 worth of Disney's stock was more valuable than $1 cash. They were willing to make the assumption that, unlike cash, which depreciates as a result of inflation, the stock would appreciate.

The final reason for going public is to provide a liquidity exit for the stockholders, including employees, management, and investors.

Reasons for Not Going Public

Taking a company public is extremely difficult. In fact, less than 20% of the entrepreneurs who attempt to take a company public are successful.[40] And the process can take a long time—as long as 2 years. Also, completing an IPO is very expensive. The typical cost is approximately $500,000. Then there are additional annual costs that must be incurred to meet SEC regulations regarding public disclosure, including the publication of the quarterly financial statements.

By the time most companies go public, they have received financing from family and friends, from angels, and at least two rounds from institutional investors. As a result, most founders will be lucky if they retain 10% ownership. The exception to this rule is Jeff Bezos, who owns 19% of Amazon.com. In the fall of 2013, that stake was worth $25.7 billion.

One of the greatest problems with going public is that most of the stock is owned by large institutional investors, which have a short-term focus. They exert continual pressure on the CEO to deliver increasing earnings every quarter.

The final reason for not going public is that while funds that the company receives when stock is sold can be used for operations right away, stock owned by the key management team cannot be sold immediately. SEC Rule 144 says that all key members of the company (officers, directors, and inside shareholders, including venture capitalists) cannot sell any of their stock. These key members own "restricted stock," or stock that was not registered with the SEC. This is in contrast to the shares of stock issued to the public at the IPO, which are unrestricted.

The holding period for restricted stock is 2 years from the date of purchase. After that period, the restricted stockholders may sell their stock as long as they do not sell more than 1% of the total number of shares outstanding in any 3-month period.[41] For example, if the entrepreneur owns 1 million of the 90 million shares of outstanding common stock, she may not sell more than 900,000 shares of the stock in a 3-month period.

Control

One negative myth about going public is that if the entrepreneur owns less than 51% of the company, he loses control. This is not true. Founders including Sergey Brin, Larry Page, Bill Gates, Jeff Bezos, and Michael Dell own less than 51% of their companies, but they still have control. The same is true of the Ford family, which owns only 2% of Ford Motor Company. However, this ownership is in the form of Class B shares, which provide them with 40% of the voting power. Bill Ford, the current executive chairman, now holds close to 11.5% of the nearly 71 million Class B shares held by the descendants of company founder Henry Ford.[42]

The key to having control is having influence on the majority of the voting stock. In some firms, some of the stock may be nonvoting stock, also known as capital stock. The entrepreneur, his family, and board members may own virtually none of the nonvoting stock but a majority of the voting stock. This fact, along with the entrepreneur's being in a management position and being the one who determines who sits on the board of directors, keeps him in control.

The IPO Process

As has been stated earlier, taking a company public can be expensive and time-consuming for the entrepreneur. But when it is done right and for the correct reasons, it can be very rewarding.

While it can take up to 24 months to complete an IPO, investment banking firm William Blair & Company said that 52 to 59 weeks is the norm.

Bessemer Venture Partners, a leading venture capital firm, accurately described a simplified step-by-step IPO process:

1. The entrepreneur decides to take the company public to raise money for future acquisitions.
2. He interviews and selects investment banks (IBs).
3. He meets with the IBs that will underwrite the offering.
4. He files the IPO registration with the SEC.
5. The SEC reviews and approves the registration.
6. The IBs and the entrepreneur go on a "road show."
7. The IBs take tentative commitments.
8. IPO.

Let's discuss these steps in more detail.

The IPO Decision

The entrepreneur's decision to do an IPO can be made almost the day she decides to go into business. Some entrepreneurs articulate their plans for going public in their original business plan. In starting the business, one of their future objectives is to own a public company. Others may decide to go public when they get institutional financing. For example, a venture capitalist may provide them with financing only if they agree to go public in 3 to 5 years. In such a case, the entrepreneur and the investor may make the decision jointly.

Other entrepreneurs may decide to go public when they review their 3- to 5-year business plan and realize that their ability to grow as fast as they would like will be determined by the availability of outside equity capital—more than they can get from institutional investors.

Interviews with and Selection of Investment Banks

Once the decision to go public has been made, the entrepreneur must hire one or more investment banks to underwrite the offering. This process of selecting an IB is called the "bake-off." Ideally, several IBs that are contacted by the entrepreneur will quickly study the company's business and then solicit, via presentations and meetings, the entrepreneur's selection of their firms. The IB's compensation is typically no more than 7% of the capital raised.

Underwriter(s) Meetings

After the IBs are selected, the entrepreneur will meet with them to plan the IPO. This process includes determining the company's value, the number of shares that will be issued, the selling price of the shares, and the timing of the road show and the IPO.

In typical public offerings, the underwriters buy all of the company's shares at the initial offer price and then sell them at the IPO. When underwriters make this type of agreement with the entrepreneur, this is called a firm commitment.

There are also underwriters that make "best-efforts" agreements. In this case, they will not purchase the stock, but will make every effort to sell it to a third party.

IPO Registration

The entrepreneur's attorney must file the registration statement with the SEC. This is a 2-part document. The first part is called a prospectus and discloses all the information about the company, including the planned use of the money, the valuation, a description of management, and financial statements. The prospectus is the document given to potential investors.

The first printing of this prospectus is called a *red herring* because it contains warnings to the reader that certain things in the document might change. These warnings are printed in red ink.

The second part of the document is the actual registration statement. The 4 items disclosed are:

- Expenses of distribution
- Indemnification of directors and officers
- Recent sales of unregistered securities
- Exhibits and financial statement schedules[43]

SEC Approval

The SEC reviews the registration statement in detail to determine that all disclosures have been made and that the information is correct and easy to comprehend. The reviewer can approve the statement, allowing the next step in the IPO process to commence; delay the review until changes are made to the statement that satisfy the reviewer; or issue a "stop order," which terminates the statement registration process with a disapproval decision.

The Road Show

Once approval of the registration statement has been obtained, the entrepreneur and the IB are free to begin the process of marketing the IPO to potential investors. This is called the *road show*, where the entrepreneur makes presentations about the company to the potential investors that the IB has identified.

Investment Commitments

During the road show, the entrepreneur makes a pitch for why the investors should buy the company's stock. After each presentation, the IBs will meet with the potential investors to determine their interest. The investors' tentative commitments for an actual number of shares are recorded in the "book" that the IB takes to each road show presentation.

The IB wants to accumulate a minimum number of tentative commitments before proceeding to the IPO. IBs like to have three tentative commitments for every share of stock that will be offered.[44]

The IPO

On the day when the IPO will occur, the investment bank and the entrepreneur determine the official stock selling price and the number of shares to be sold. The price may change between the time the road show began and the day of the IPO, as a result of interest in the stock. If the tentative commitments were greater than a 3-to-1 ratio, then the offering price may be increased. It may be lowered if the opposite occurred. That is exactly what happened to the stock of Wired Ventures, which attempted to go public in 1996. Originally the company wanted to sell 4.75 million shares at $14 each. By the date of the IPO, it made the decision with its IB, Goldman Sachs, to reduce the offering to 3 million shares at a price of $10 per share. One of the reasons for this change was the fact that hours before the stock had to be officially priced for sale, the offer was still undersubscribed by 50%. Even at this lower price, though, the IPO never took place. Wired Ventures was not able to raise the $60 million it sought, and it incurred expenses of approximately $1.3 million in its attempt to go public.

Choosing the Right Investment Banker

As the preceding information shows, the ability to have a successful IPO is significantly dependent on the IB. The most critical features of an IB are its ability to value the company properly, assist the attorney and the entrepreneur in developing the registration statement, help the entrepreneur develop an excellent presentation for the road show, access its database to reach the proper potential investors and invite them to the presentation, and sell the stock. Therefore, the entrepreneur must do as much as possible to select the best IB for his IPO. Here are a few suggestions:

- Identify the firms that have successfully taken companies public that are similar to yours in size, industry, and amount to be raised.
- Select experienced firms. At a minimum, the ideal firm has underwritten 2 deals annually for the past 3 years. The firms that are underwriting 8 deals per year, or 2 each quarter, may be too busy to give your deal the attention it needs. Also eliminate those whose deals consistently take more than 90 days to get registration approval.

- Select underwriters that price their deals close to the stock's first-day closing. If an underwriter prices the stock too low, so that the stock increases dramatically in price by the end of the first day, then the entrepreneur sold more equity than she needed to. For example, if the initial offering was 1 million shares at $5 per share and the stock closed the first day at $10 per share, then the stock was underpriced. Instead of raising $5 million for 1 million shares, the entrepreneur could have raised the same amount for 500,000 shares had the underwriter priced the stock better.
- Select underwriters that file planned selling prices that are close to the actual price at the initial offering. Some underwriters file at one price, then try to force the entrepreneur to open at a lower price so that they can sell the stock and their investors can reap the benefits of the increase. This maneuver, when it is done, usually takes place a day or so prior to the IPO, with the underwriter threatening to terminate the offering if the price is not reduced. To minimize the chances of this happening, the entrepreneur should select only underwriters that have a consistent pattern of filing and bringing the stock to the market at similar prices.
- Select underwriters that have virtually no experience with failing to complete the offering. Companies that file for an IPO but do not make it are considered "damaged goods" by investors.
- Get an introduction to the investment banker. Never cold-call the banker. The company's attorney or accountant should make the introduction.[45]

DIRECT PUBLIC OFFERINGS

In 1989, the SEC made it possible for companies that are seeking less than $5 million to raise it directly from the public without going through the expensive and time-consuming IPO process described earlier. This direct process is aptly called a *direct public offering*, or DPO. In a DPO, shares are usually sold for $1 to $10 each without an underwriter, and the investors do not face the sophisticated investor requirements. Forty-five states allow DPOs, and the usual legal, accounting, and marketing fees are less than $50,000.

There are three DPO programs that have been used by thousands of entrepreneurs. The programs are:

1. Regulation D, Rule 504, which is also called the Small Corporate Offering Registration, or SCOR
2. Regulation A
3. Intrastate

The SEC has a free pamphlet entitled "Q & A: Small Business and the SEC—Help Your Company Go Public" available on its website at www.sec.gov. Let's discuss each DPO program in more detail.

- *Small Corporate Offering Registration.* In the Small Corporate Offering Registration, or SCOR, program, the entrepreneur has 12 months to raise a maximum of $1 million. Shares can be sold to an unlimited number of investors throughout the country via general solicitation and even advertising. One entrepreneur who accessed capital via a DPO was Rick Moon, the founder of Thanksgiving Coffee Co. Rick raised $1.25 million in 1996 for 20% of his coffee and tea wholesaling company, which had annual revenues of $4.6 million. He aggressively advertised the offering to his suppliers and customers on his website, in his catalog, on his coffee-bean bags, and on the bean dispensers in stores.[46]
- *Regulation A offering.* Under the Regulation A program, an entrepreneur can raise a maximum of $5 million in 12 months. Unlike offerings under SCOR, where no SEC filings are required, offerings under Regulation A must be filed with the SEC. Otherwise, all the attributes of SCOR are applicable to Regulation A. Dorothy Pittman Hughes, the founder of Harlem Copy Center, with $300,000 in annual revenues in 1998, began raising $2 million under this program by offering stock for $1 per share. The minimum number of shares that adults could buy was 50; for children, the minimum was 25.[47]
- *Intrastate program.* The intrastate program requires companies to limit the sale of their stock to investors in one state. This program

> has other significant differences from SCOR and Regulation A. First, there are no federal laws limiting the maximum that can be raised or the time allowed. These two items vary by state. The other difference is that the stock cannot be resold outside the state for 9 months.

DPOs are best suited for historically profitable companies with audited financial statements and a well-written business plan. Shareholders are typically affinity groups that are somehow tied to the company, such as customers, employees, suppliers, distributors, and friends. After completing a DPO, the company can still do a traditional IPO at a later date. Real Goods Trading Company did just that. In 1991, it raised $1 million under SCOR. Two years later, it raised an additional $3.6 million under Regulation A. Today, its stock is traded on the Nasdaq market.

DPOs have a few negative aspects. First, it is estimated that more than 70% of those companies that register for a DPO fail, for various reasons. But the greatest drawback is the fact that there is no public market, like the NYSE, for DPO stock. Such an exchange brings sellers and buyers together, and that does not exist for DPOs. Therefore, the ability to raise capital is negatively affected by the potential investors' legitimate concerns that their investment cannot be made liquid easily. Another problem is that the absence of a market leaves the market appreciation of the stock in question. One critic of DPOs said, "There is no liquidity in these offerings. Investors are stepping into a leg-hold trap."[48] As a result, DPO investors tend to be long-term-focused. Trading in the stock is usually arranged by the company or made through an order-matching service that the company manages. The shareholders can also get liquid if the company is sold, the owners buy back the stock, or the company does a traditional IPO.

Because this is a book about finance, not about law, we have intentionally avoided a long discussion of the legal aspects of entrepreneurship. That doesn't mean that you should ignore the legal ins and outs of running a business or getting one started. One great resource that comes highly recommended from my students is the book *The Entrepreneur's Guide to Business Law* by Constance Bagley and Craig Dauchy.

THE FINANCING SPECTRUM

There's an old dog food commercial that features a frolicking puppy changing into a mature dog before our eyes. The commercial reminds pet owners that as their dogs grow, the food that fuels them needs to change too. Businesses are the same way with equity financing. As a business evolves from an idea into a mature company, the type of financing it requires changes. At the end of Chapter 6, the steps through which many successful high-growth entrepreneurs raised their equity capital were highlighted in the financing spectrum.

An actual entrepreneur who raised money from almost all the sources of capital on that spectrum was Jeff Bezos. Figure 8-4 shows when Bezos raised capital and from whom.

July 1994	October 1994 and February 1995	December 1995	1996	May 1997
Amazon.com	Amazon.com	Amazon.com	Amazon.com	Amazon.com
concept	incorporation and launch	operating	growing	exponential growth
↓	↓	↓	↓	↓
Capital from personal savings	Capital from mother and father	Capital from angels	Capital from venture capitalist	Capital from IPO
• $15,000 interest-free loan	• 582,528 shares of common stock sold to father for $100,000	• Raised $981,000 at a $5 million premoney valuation	• $8 million from KPCB at a $52 million premoney valuation	• Raised $54 million
• $10,000 equity investment for 10 million shares of common stock	• 847,716 shares of common stock sold to mother for $144,000			

Figure 8-4 **Jeff Bezos's Financing Spectrum**

9

Financing for Minorities and Women

INTRODUCTION

Minority- and women-owned firms are powerful economic forces in the small-business world. Minority-owned businesses grew more than twice as fast as U.S. firms overall between 2002 and 2007, increasing from 4.0 million to 5.8 million firms.[1] The following statistics are from the most recent Survey of Business Owners, completed by the U.S. Census Bureau in 2010 (which reports on 2007 data)[2]:

- Minority-owned firms generated $1.03 trillion in annual revenue, of which 84% was generated by firms with employees.
- While Hispanics controlled the largest share of firms owned by minorities and constituted the largest minority business community, Asian-owned firms had the largest share of minority-owned business revenues—50%.
- Black-owned firms experienced explosive growth. The total number of black-owned firms grew 60%, while their total receipts grew 55.1%.

- Women who owned 51% or more of a company owned 17.5% of all private firms with employees in the United States; women who owned 30% or more of a company owned 18.8% of all private firms with employees.[3]
- Native American businesses generated $34.4 billion in revenues, which was an increase from $26.9 billion.

My mother, Ollie Mae Rogers, was the first entrepreneur I ever met, and accordingly, I have a tremendous amount of respect for women entrepreneurs. Women-owned businesses in 2012 generated an estimated $1.3 trillion in annual sales, employing 7.7 million.[4] Between 2002 and 2012, the number of women-owned firms increased from 6.5 million to an estimated 8.3 million, an increase of 28.6%, exceeding the growth during the same period in the number of all privately held firms in the United States by 5.5%.[5] Between 1997 and 2007 (the most recent accurate data available), the number of privately held firms that were more than 50% owned by women of color grew 191.4%, while revenues increased 78.1% from 2002 to a total of $36.8 billion.[6]

Needless to say, minority and women entrepreneurs have played the game of catch-up brilliantly, and they have forced the traditional small-business infrastructure to change. Thank God we are past the era when a woman could not get a loan without her husband's signature and it was legal to reject a loan application from a person simply because of his ethnicity or race! The laws that made such gender and racial discrimination legal had a profound effect on minority and women entrepreneurship. The inability to access capital other than from personal savings, family, friends, and angels retarded the growth of most entrepreneurs from these two sectors. Given the absence of growth capital from financial institutions, these entrepreneurs, in essence, were involuntarily relegated to a life as mom-and-pop, or lifestyle, entrepreneurs. The result is that we have virtually no major corporations that were founded by minorities or women.

Recent research from the SBA also indicates that race is a significant predictor of the likelihood of opening a business and that the odds of a minority person opening a business are 55% lower than those for a nonminority. The data in Table 9-1 show the composition of the total U.S. population side by side with a breakdown of U.S. business receipts by race. While the situation continues to improve, these data clearly indicate that the process is still ongoing.

TABLE 9-1 **Composition of U.S. Population Versus Share of Business Receipts**

Group	Share of Population[7]	Number of firms (with or without paid employees)[8]	Share of Business Receipts[9]
White	62.8%	77.3%	90.0%
Hispanic	16.9%	8.6%	3.2%
Black	12.3%	6.7%	1.1%
Asian/Pacific Islander	5.1%	5.8%	4.6%
Native American/ Other	3.0%	1.6%	1.1%
Female	50.8%	29.6%	10.9%

And while there are federal laws that prohibit gender and racial discrimination in debt and equity financing, it is sad to report that even today, minority and women entrepreneurs are receiving a pittance of all the capital provided to entrepreneurs.

Still, there are an increasing number of investment firms that are focusing on all kinds of niches, and these firms are an important resource. For example, there are specialized firms that target entrepreneurs who are female, are minorities, or are in industries such as consumer goods, food products, banking, and sports. There are even firms that will invest only in companies in certain geographic regions, such as the New England region or rural areas. A few of these specialized firms are listed in Figure 9-1.

Name	Targeted Investments
Buckhead Investments	Atlanta, Georgia
Lipman Brand Investments	Sports-related companies
Hispania	Hispanic entrepreneurs
Venture Fund	Women-owned businesses
Ceres	

Figure 9-1 **Niche Equity Investment Firms**

MINORITIES—DEBT FINANCING

Historically, the success rate of minority entrepreneurs in raising debt capital is low. Research commissioned by the Small Business Administration showed that minorities face significantly lower approval rates for credit than firms owned by white owners. The data in Table 9-2 show approval rates for minority-owned firms.

Low approval rates inhibit minorities from initiating loan applications out of fear of having the loan application rejected. Minority-owners are more than two and a half times more likely to not apply for a loan than white owners.

The result is that minority-owned companies use personal financing more than white-owned companies do. SBA data suggest that only 9.5% of white-owned businesses use a credit card in their business, whereas 20.6% of Islander-owned, 15% of black-owned, and 13% of Hispanic-owned businesses do.

Minority entrepreneurs who are seeking debt capital should approach those institutions that are friends to minorities. Where better to turn than the U.S. Department of the Treasury, which as a result of Section 4112 of the Small Business Jobs Act of 2010 created the Small Business Lending Fund (SBLF) with a specific charter to increase lending to small businesses, including minority-owned businesses. Treasury provided $4.0 billion to 332 community banks and community development loan funds (CDLFs) in September 2011, with the potential to impact $9.3 billion in lending. A list of the participating community banks and CDLFs is in the Appendix of the Treasury's inaugural report on its activities.[11]

The Business Consortium Fund, Inc. (BCF) is a business development and financing organization created by the National Minority Supplier Development Council (NMSDC) to exclusively support the ethnic minority-owned business community. The BCF can provide direct loans to NMSDC

TABLE 9-2 **Loan Approval Rates for Business Owners**[10]

Black/Hispanic	28%
White	67%
All firms	61%

certified Minority-owned Business Enterprises (MBEs) in either a term loan (of a maximum 7 years) or line of credit up to a maximum of $500,000 and a minimum of $75,000.[12] The list of 73 BCF lenders covers 26 states.[13]

Another source of debt financing is SBA lenders. The number of SBA loans has fluctuated, rising from 37,528 in 2001 to 88,912 in 2005, and declining to 44,377 in 2012.[14] During this period, the share of total loans to minorities has also varied similarly, rising from 25% to 29% and then declining to 23%. Large financial institutions that lend to minority firms include Wells Fargo and Accion USA, the largest business lender of its kind in the United States, make loans from $500 to $25,000.

Internet-based portals (a.k.a. "online marketplaces") offering efficient loan application processes to the business owner have proliferated as business owners, lenders and technology entrepreneurs have worked together. Of course, many banks today offer "online application" services to prospective borrowers, which are no more than digital substitutes for completing what used to be a paper-based loan application at a bank branch. More interesting to consider are third-party websites, essentially digital two-sided marketplaces organized by technology entrepreneurs who aggregate hundreds of lenders to bid for or look at loan applications made by business owners. It has only been in the recent couple years that such lending activity was socially acceptable online, although similar websites had been available for personal loans. And only recently have business owners become comfortable with submitting their information through this impersonal process.

While there are too many such business loan marketplaces to mention, consider Intuit Quickbooks Financing[15] or Biz2Credit[16] as options. The technology behing Intuit's Quickbooks Financing was developed by Brandon Hinkle, a former commercial loan officer who earned his MBA while starting a new venture, Plura Financial Solutions, which utilized sophisticated algorithms (i.e., interconnected rules) that interpreted loan application inputs to determine the fit of an applicant to several lending instiutions. Intuit purchased Hinkle's company in 2012 and hired him to adapt his system to their community of millions of Quickbooks users. After just a few short months Hinkle generated thousands of loan applications and loans for Intuit's community of business owners, all made possible through the convenience and comfort of a Quickbooks account.[17]

MINORITIES—EQUITY FINANCING

Less than 1% of all equity capital provided by institutional investors has gone to minority entrepreneurs. Part of the problem is participation rates. For example, only 6.9% of entrepreneurs who presented their business concepts to angels were minority entrepreneurs. Strong evidence suggests that the problem is a lack of opportunity. The yield, or percentage of approved investments, for minority-owned firms was 7.1%, or close to two-thirds the general yield rate. This makes no sense in light of the fact that from 1998 to 2011, investment firms targeting minorities returned an average of 20.9% compared to 11.8% for all private equity firms.[18]

Virtually all of that capital has come from firms that are associated with the National Association of Investment Companies (NAIC). These NAIC-related firms explicitly target investments in minority-owned companies and work together extensively to find minority investments. As proof, a survey of these firms indicated that 100% of them had participated in syndicated deals. Some also invest proactively in women entrepreneurs. There are more than 50 NAIC firms in the United States that have invested more than $2.5 billion in approximately 20,000 ethnically diverse businesses. By 2011, these firms had a collective $14 billion of capital under management.[19]

Almost every high-growth, successful, minority-owned company has received financing from an NAIC-affiliated firm. A few of the equity capital recipients are listed in Figure 9-2.

Equity capital has also been made available to minority entrepreneurs by angel investors. Check for a local angel group in your area. The National Minority Angel Network (NMAN) was founded in 2012 to identify diverse and otherwise unseen deal flow from primarily minority, woman, and veteran entrepreneurs and link them with investors and corporations that seek to invest in them or utilize their products or services. Entrepreneurs can be early-stage to late-stage and from any type of company (for-profit or not-for-profit) or industry. NMAN attempts to overcome geographical limitations by using technology services and a web-based portal for deal flow, document management, communications, and calendaring. See its website at www.nmanetwork.com.

Company	Minority	Description	NAIC Member
Radio One	Black	Public company (Nasdaq: ROIA). Largest station targeting African Americans	TSG Capital
Black Entertainment Television	Black	Former public company (NYSE: BTV). Acquired by Viacom	Syncom
Z-Spanish Media	Hispanic	Largest Spanish-language media network	TSG Capital
Watson Pharmaceuticals	Asian	Public company (NYSE: WPI)	Polestar Capital
BioGenex Laboratories	Indian		Pacesetter

Figure 9-2 **Various Equity Investments from NAIC Member Firms**

Minority entrepreneurs who are seeking equity capital should contact the NAIC at www.naicpe.com to get a complete list of the member funds. A few are presented in Figure 9-3.

NAIC Member	Location	Phone
Black Enterprise/Greenwich	New York	212-816-1189
Altos Ventures	Menlo Park, Calif	650-234-9771
Syncom Venture Partners	Bethesda, Maryland	301-608-3203
ACON Investments	Washington, DC	202-454-1100

Figure 9-3 **Various NAIC Members**

Equity investments into minority entrepreneur firms often are combined with advice and coaching through organizations dedicated to their success. Together, as entrepreneurs become successful financially, the equity capital has a better chance of being returned to investors, at a multiple! Below is a list of several organizations which support minority entrepreneurs across the United States:

- ALPFA: Association of Latino Professionals in Finance and Accounting
- NBMBAA: National Black MBA Association
- NUL: National Urban League - Entrepreneurship Centers
- NSBE: National Society of Black Engineers
- NMSDC: National Minority Supplier Development Council
- NSHMBA: National Society of Hispanic MBAs
- SCORE-Minority Entrepreneurs
- The Latino Coalition
- UFSC: Urban Financial Services Coalition

WOMEN—DEBT FINANCING

Women have historically had a tougher time getting debt capital from institutions such as banks, but as that situation has become more visible, more organizations and programs have been developed to understand the issues and address them. Biz2Credit, an online marketplace for loan applications, mentioned earlier, analyzed 14,000 loan applications made on its platform by U.S. applicants in 2012. While this was not a government-sponsored study, it reflected so many applications that the data can be educational. Several important findings emerged[20]:

- Fewer women than men registered on the site to begin the loan application process (29% women vs 71% men)
- Women-owned companies experienced 15%–20% lower loan approval rates than male-owned firms
- Credit scores for women-owned businesses were on average 40 points lower than male-owned businesses

This analysis shows there is still considerable advancement to make for women entrepreneurs. In the SBA-commissioned study mentioned before, researcher Alicia Robb found that in 2010, 8% of experienced female entrepreneurs versus 12% of experienced male entrepreneurs applied for a loan in that year.[21] Among women, 21% cited "fear of rejection" as their reason for not applying for a loan, while 18% of men cited the same reason in that year.[22]

This study was insightful in that it distinguished that over a 4-year period (2007–2010), female-owned firms sought out and secured half the amount of outside debt capital ($106,000) as male-owned firms ($215,000).[23] Women-owned firms used their personal credit to support their venture with 14% more capital than men did.[24] Male-owned firms generated debt capital from friends and family sources over 4 years at nearly double the amount ($23,000) than female-owned firms ($12,000), which is a result of several factors including loan application rates, loan acceptances, and the amount requested.[25] While the amounts shown are relatively small, the disparate differences demonstrate the point that women entrepreneurs have a different experience of debt capital than men.

Women who are seeking debt financing should approach institutions that want to do business with women. Those firms include SBA lenders and banks such as Wells Fargo, which in 1994 made a commitment to lend $1 billion to women entrepreneurs. A year later, Wells Fargo became so convinced that financing women entrepreneurs was a great strategy that it increased its commitment to $10 billion, to be invested over a 10-year period. In the following 10 years, Wells Fargo lent more than $25 billion through 600,000 loans to women business owners, and continues to be a leading lender to women.[26] This additional commitment came after the National Foundation for Women Business Owners published research showing that investing in women entrepreneurs was sound business because they had a better chance of repaying business loans. This fact was proved by information showing that, on average, women-owned companies stay in business longer. Specifically, nearly 75% of women-owned firms founded in 1991 were still in business three years later, compared with 66% of all U.S. firms.[27] Other banks that have actively targeted women-owned businesses include KeyBank, through its Key4Women program, and Citi, which actively curates a women-focused site at womenandco.com. Both banks have successfully provided more than $1 billion in loans to women.[28]

While the SBA has supported women's businesses, the percentage of guaranteed loans going to women fell from 22% in 2004 to 17% for the years 2011 to 2013.[29] A few other institutional sources of debt capital for women entrepreneurs are listed in Figure 9-4.

Source	Description/Contact
Accion U.S. Network	Microlending us.accion.org
Count Me In for Women's Economic Independence	countmein.org
Opportunity Fund	Opportunity Fund. org
SBA, Office of Women's Business Ownership	202-205-6673
Wells Fargo Bank	800-359-3557
Women & Co. by Citi	womenandco.com 1-800-846-5200

Figure 9-4 **Various Women-Focused Institutional Debt Sources**

WOMEN—EQUITY FINANCING

The year 2000 was the first year in which women received more than 2% of institutional equity capital. In 2000, they received 4.4%.[30] According to the Robb study of firms from 2007–2010, women business owners generated only one-sixth of the outside equity capital compared to male business owners.[31] According to a study commissioned by the Center for Women's Business Research (formerly the National Foundation for Women Business Owners), women entrepreneurs who are seeking or have obtained equity capital find their sources of funding in three ways: word of mouth (60% of recipients, 49% of seekers), their own networks of business consultants (50% of recipients, 42% of seekers), and investors who have sought them out (38% of recipients, 39% of seekers).[32]

My advice would be the same as with the debt capital sources: go to sources that are interested in doing business with women. Figure 9-5 lists equity funds that target women entrepreneurs. Another great source of equity capital is angel investors. Figure 9-6 lists those investors who are interested in financing women entrepreneurs.

A leader in the campaign to accelerate women's access to equity markets is Springboard Enterprises. Springboard states that it has assisted 537 women-led companies that participated in Springboard's accelerator programs and subsequently have raised $6.2 billion. Overall, 83% of Springboard companies are still in business as independent or merged entities, including 10 IPOs. Springboard's

Source	Location	Information
Three Guineas Fund	San Francisco, California	3gf.org
Ceres Venture Fund	Evanston, Illinois	ceresventurefund.com
Illuminate Ventures	Oakland, California	illuminate.com
Texas Women Ventures	Dallas, Texas	texaswomenventures.com

Figure 9-5 **Women-Focused Private Equity Firms**

website (www.sb.co) has a Learning Center (sb.co/learning) that is a good resource for women entrepreneurs.

In addition to Springboard, there are several other resources and organizations devoted to helping women entrepreneurs. Some of these include:

- The Center for Women in Business (CWB), a program of the U.S. Chamber of Commerce Foundation, promotes and empowers women business leaders to achieve their personal and professional goals (http://cwb.uschamber.com/).
- The SBA's Online Women's Business Center. The SBA's Office of Women Owned Small Businesses (WOSB) and economically disadvantaged women-owned small business (EDWOSB) promotes the growth of women-owned businesses through various programs that address business training and technical assistance and provide access to credit and capital, federal contracts, and international trade opportunities. Every SBA district office has a women's business ownership representative, providing a national network of resources for women entrepreneurs (http://www.sba.gov/wosb).

Source	Location	Information
Astia Angels Network	San Francisco, California	astia.org
Seraph Capital Forum	Seattle, Washington	seraphcapital.com
Golden Seeds	New York, New York	goldenseeds.com
Phenomenelle Angels	Madison, Wisconsin	phenomenelleangels.com

Figure 9-6 **Women-Focused Angel Investors**

- National Association of Women Business Owners. The National Association of Women Business Owners (NAWBO.org), headquartered in the Washington, DC, metropolitan area, is the only dues-based national organization representing the interests of 10 million women entrepreneurs in all types of businesses. The organization currently has more than 80 chapters and is represented in 60 countries through its affiliation with the World Association of Women Entrepreneurs.
- Center for Women & Enterprise. CWE is the largest regional entrepreneurial training organization in Boston and Worcester, Massachusetts, and Providence, Rhode Island. Its mission is to empower women to become economically self-sufficient and prosperous through entrepreneurship (www.cweonline.org)
- Women's Business Enterprise National Council (WBENC). WBENC, founded in 1997, is the largest third-party certifier of businesses owned, controlled, and operated by women in the United States. WBENC, a national 501(c)(3) nonprofit, partners with 14 Regional Partner Organizations to provide its world-class standard of certification to women-owned businesses throughout the country. WBENC is also the nation's leading advocate of women-owned businesses as suppliers to America's corporations (www.wbenc.org)
- Women's Business Development Center (WBDC). The WBDC, with headquarters in Chicago, offers a full-service approach to launching emerging businesses and strengthening existing businesses owned by women in a 9-state midwestern area. Services of the WBDC include online e-learning, in-person workshops, and one-on-one counseling on all aspects of business development, including marketing, finance, business management, technology integration, and more. The WBDC has consulted with more than 66,000 women entrepreneurs, helping them to start and grow their businesses, and facilitated the receipt of more than $81 million in loans and $900 million in government and corporate contracts to women business owners (www.wbdc.org)

While things are improving for both women and minorities, it is not happening fast enough. Poor access to capital for these 2 groups is hurting America. Former SBA chief Aida Alvarez stated it beautifully when she said: "Businesses owned by women and minorities are multiplying at a faster rate than all other U.S. businesses. If we don't start investing now in the potential of the businesses, we will not have a successful economy in the new millennium."[33] Perhaps the new incoming SBA Administrator (nominated in January 2014), Ms. Contreras-Sweet, who is a first-generation American and Latina from California, and founder and executive chair of ProAmerica Bank, the first Latino-owned bank in California,[34] will be a step in the right direction for women and entrepreneurs of color.

10

Taking a Job with an Entrepreneurial Firm

INTRODUCTION

One of the unexpected discoveries resulting from staying in touch with students several years after they graduate has been that a large percentage of those who indicate that they are involved in entrepreneurship are employees in, not cofounders of, an entrepreneurial firm. They had resigned from their safe job with a successful investment banking, consulting, or manufacturing company and had taken a job with a start-up firm. How does a person make such a decision to leave the security of a well-established, in many instances Fortune 500, company to work for a high-risk venture in its embryonic stages of development?

The following case study, followed by an analysis of the situation, should be used as a template for answering these questions: Should I leave my job to take a job with a start-up? How should I do a financial analysis of the decision?

CASE STUDY: CONSIDERING A JOB OFFER FROM AN EARLY-STAGE COMPANY

In her Chicago home on a warm Friday afternoon in June, Nailah Johnson, who was graduating from her weekend Executive MBA (EMBA) program in 2 weeks, hung up the phone. She was happy. John Paul, founder of AKAR and Johnson's potential future employer, had said as their conversation ended: "Tell me what it would take to get you on board."

For many reasons, Johnson was excited about joining an entrepreneurial firm and possibly much later even buying her own business. She recalled including this goal in the essays that had helped her gain admission to her EMBA program 2 years earlier. The role that Paul wanted Johnson to have at AKAR was appealing: a director of sales and marketing position with significantly more responsibility than she currently had, and with a possible promotion to vice president in less than 12 months. Johnson had heard about the many downsides and upsides of positions with an early-stage company. If the company failed, she could face a direct financial loss because employees at start-ups were paid low salaries. On the other hand, the financial rewards could be lucrative if the employees owned part of the company and its value increased.

Johnson had joined Motorola Solutions in 2010 as a director of operations. Recently, based largely on her EMBA training and her desire to broaden her on-the-job skills, she had successfully moved to a senior director of sales role. She and her husband enjoyed comfortable professional and social lives in Chicago. Just 2 days earlier, Johnson had informed her husband that she was pregnant with their first child. They expected this new addition to their family to increase their annual budget by $19,000. Early in their marriage, they had envisioned her becoming a full-time mother when the time came.

Still giddy from Paul's call, Johnson sat at her kitchen table, thinking about what he had said: "The sooner we can start you, the better." Until that moment, Johnson would have predicted that she would accept the position with AKAR on the spot, on almost any terms that sounded reasonable; after all, she had invested many months and a great deal of energy in making the offer happen. But now, as the costs and benefits of the position swirled through her mind, she felt unsure about what terms to request. Johnson owed Paul an answer in 5 days, but she was not sure that she could determine what she wanted even if she had three months. She also considered rejecting this opportunity because the risk was too high and the timing was poor. Finally, she wondered, if she took this or any other job, would she ever become an actual entrepreneur, or would she always be simply someone's employee? Should she pursue acquiring her own company instead?

In many ways, Johnson's career was typical for an MBA student. Thus, despite her interest in entrepreneurship, seriously considering an offer from an early-stage company was new territory for her. As Johnson reflected on the offer's pros and cons, she thought back to the path that had led her here.

Walking the Straight and Narrow

Johnson had attended Williams College, graduating near the top of her class (see Figure 10-1 for Johnson's résumé). Immediately after college, she began her career at Sun Microsystems and later moved to Motorola Solutions. Although she enjoyed working on mobile solutions, she found the business issues related to them even more interesting: Who were their target segments? What were the best ways of distributing and marketing the products? What kinds of new products were most likely to survive?

These interests led to Johnson's application to the EMBA program. Because she had always had an interest in start-ups, she took several courses in entrepreneurship and joined the entrepreneurship club. As part of these student activities, Johnson enjoyed discussing entrepreneurship, especially the potential for new high-tech products, but her career goals remained focused on larger-company opportunities. In line with this, she pursued a marketing manager position at Motorola and was pleasantly surprised to receive an offer. The new position came with a salary of $115,000 (a 30% raise that put her in the 28% tax bracket), bonus potential of approximately 25% of her salary, and responsibilities for marketing a next-generation mobile video device. Johnson loved the work, and was already in line for a promotion to business development manager.

Taking on the new position a year ago had not been the only change in her life: she had married Naeem, her classmate, soon afterward. They had purchased a $400,000 two-bedroom condo in Chicago. The Johnsons made a 20% down payment (their entire savings) and secured a 30-year fixed-rate mortgage

Nailah Johnson

EDUCATION:

2011–present KELLOGG SCHOOL OF MANAGEMENT, Evanston, IL
Executive Master of Business Administration, GMAT 770

- Majors in Management & Strategy, Finance, and Marketing
- Member of NBI team that created a strategic marketing plan for Handi-Ramp Foundation; member of Kellogg team that reached the school finals for AT Kearney Global Prize competition
- Entrepreneurship Club Member; GIM-China participant; logistics director for India Business Conference

2002–2006 WILLIAMS COLLEGE, Williamstown, MA
BACHELOR OF SCIENCE IN COMMUNICATIONS, GPA: 3.92/4.0

- Financed 100% of education through assistantships
- Selected as key instructor for freshman-level mathematics courses. Taught classes of 40 students, consistently receiving high ratings (4.5/5). Selected to teach remedial courses
- Member of school's 5-person badminton team. Won the zonal championship in 2004

EXPERIENCE:

2010–present MOTOROLA SOLUTIONS, Chicago, IL
Senior Director of Sales (2012–present)

- Manage marketing for next-generation mobile video service with expected commercial value of $48 million over 5 years
- Coordinated cross-functional team, including 8 experts from different divisions of Motorola, to develop marketing plan for mobile video system
- Independently led research initiative to explore new distribution channel for music and talk shows on cell phones. Market estimated at $2 billion

Director of Global Product Marketing and Director of Operations (2010–2012)

- Selected technical consultant on an 8-month-long project valued at $2 million. The project cemented Motorola's relationship with a major external customer
- Collaborated with 6 other research experts to develop differentiating technology for the $13 billion home networking market. Technology is showcased in Motorola Solutions' Horsham (PA) innovation center
- Selected into Motorola Solutions' Applications Research patent committee of 10 senior researchers among 800 to evaluate the technical and business viability of innovation ideas; authored 8 Motorola patent applications and five external publications

Figure 10-1 **Nailah Johnson's Résumé**

2006–2010 SUN MICROSYSTEMS, Oak Brook, IL

Senior Product Manager (2008–2010)

- Led eight-person, $2 million platform integration project for new SPARC station products
- Presented major Sun engineering initiatives to more than 100 client managers at annual customer meeting
- Selected from more than 60 other project leaders to demonstrate research prototype at WIRED NextFest 2008. More than 20,000 members of the public attended the exposition

Product Manager (2006–2008)

- Presented research to senior Sun executives. Presentation was subsequently broadcast to more than 30,000 Motorola engineers
- Awarded "Significant Achievement Award" for integrating third-party location detection system 1 month ahead of schedule

ADDITIONAL INFORMATION:

- Robot inspector for Midwest regional championship. USFIRST, an organization that aims to increase interest in science and engineering among children, hosted the event
- College lacrosse enthusiast (fanatical supporter of Williams College). Enjoy playing golf and traveling

Figure 10-1 (***Continued***)

at 6% interest. The mortgage and their school loans were their only debts. Their monthly assessment, taxes, and insurance were approximately 40% of the mortgage. All other household expenses, including telephone, electricity, cable, gas, and groceries, were approximately 35% of the monthly mortgage. They owned 2 cars, which were paid in full.

By the time Johnson was considering a position with AKAR, Naeem had also been promoted at Kraft; his salary was $105,000, with a bonus of approximately 20%. His company's health, medical, dental, and vision care insurance were all free. Together, the couple led a busy but enjoyable life, building their career experience, earning their MBAs, and taking vacations. They spent approximately 25% of Naeem's monthly salary on recreational activities. Despite some tuition reimbursement from their companies, they had amassed significant student debt.

Figure 10-2 is a summary of all of Nailah's loans processed by the financial aid office as of June 14, 2013. The principal amounts listed are the original principal balances. These amounts do not reflect any payments made on these loans. Loans from other institutions are not included on this form.

The Search for More

While she had been successful in her career path to date, for the last several months, Johnson had found that several questions were frequently on her mind: Is this all there is, careerwise? How can I keep more of the value that I am creating for myself? How can I become a millionaire without risking everything? These questions also arose when she recalled how much she had enjoyed her entrepreneurship classes or heard news of others' entrepreneurial accomplishments.

According to her alumni magazine, Deniece Grant, a recent alumna from the part-time evening program, had raised $4 million in angel and early-stage venture capital for the company she founded, which provided software that allowed computers to search automatically for information related to documents that the user was working on. Grant gave "put rights" to some of her managers who owned stock in the company. She had originally given these employees restricted stock units (RSUs) when they were hired.

Raymond Robinson, a friend of Johnson's in Chicago who had graduated from the full-time day program 2 years earlier, was already a vice president with a 2% ownership stake after exercising the stock options given to him when he was hired by a wireless technology company that had just completed a successful initial public offering (IPO). Robinson was now a multimillionaire. His stock options had originally been scheduled to vest 20% annually after his second year of employment. However, the IPO triggered the "change in control" clause, resulting in the immediate full vesting of 100% of his options. "That could be me," Johnson thought when she heard such stories.

Four months ago, after the completion of a very challenging project at work, Johnson had decided to stop sitting on the sidelines of entrepreneurship.

Lender	Guarantor	Interest	Loan Type	Amount Borrowed
Kellogg 555 Clark St. Third Floor Evanston, IL 60208	Illinois Student Assistance Co. 500 W. Monroe 3rd Floor Springfield, IL 62704–1876	6.8%	Subsidized Stafford	$17,000.00
Kellogg 555 Clark St. Third Floor Evanston, IL 60208	Illinois Student Assistance Co. 500 W. Monroe 3rd Floor Springfield, IL 62704–1876	6.8%	Unsubsidized Stafford	$22,000.00
Kellogg 555 Clark St. Third Floor Evanston, IL 60208	Kellogg 555 Clark St. Third Floor Evanston, IL 60208	5.0%	Perkins	$12,000.00
Total				**$51,000.00**

Figure 10-2 **Loan Summary**

Kellogg School of Management
Office of Financial Aid
June 14, 2013
Nailah Johnson
652 W. Evans Dr.
Chicago, IL 60601
Separation Date: 14-JUNE-2013
School: Kellogg School of Management

She began reading entrepreneurship magazines and books, reaching out to friends who she thought would know of opportunities with early-stage companies, scouring the business school's alumni database for people in small firms, and setting up as many informational interviews as she could. Johnson also connected with a recruiter who specialized in placements at early-stage firms and a business broker who could show her businesses for sale. The time she spent on the search, on top of her responsibilities at work and at school, left Johnson with almost no space in her weekly schedule for fitness, social activities, or spending time with Naeem. But it felt like the right thing to do.

Despite Johnson's enthusiasm for the search, months passed without major progress. If anything, like a corporate Goldilocks, she discovered many of the things she was not seeking in a new opportunity: she rejected several positions that had initially appeared to be promising—they were too risky (a 5-person software company in the initial fund-raising stage), not exciting enough (a firm that provided marketing solutions to the paper industry), or too strange (a venture that developed software so proprietary that the founders asked all employees to sign nondisclosure agreements—daily).

But 2 months earlier, Johnson's luck had changed when she met John Paul. Johnson had signed up to meet him through the entrepreneurship center's Entrepreneur-in-Residence program (EIR), through which entrepreneurs and principal investors spent a full day meeting in 30-minute sessions with individual students to answer questions and provide experience-based insights.

AKAR: The Opportunity

John Paul was only 46 years old, but he had already sold 2 companies. According to an article Johnson had read, AKAR, Paul's most recent venture, was very promising and had received significant industry attention. The article also characterized Paul as a "gambler with great judgment—or maybe great luck."

After dropping out of Grambling University in 1989, Paul had worked as a computer programmer for a series of video game manufacturers before moving into roles in operations and database design. He prided himself on being self-taught in most aspects of business, from finance to marketing: "Best teachers I ever had? Trial and error," he often said. Paul had sold his first company, GamerParadize (launched out of his apartment 6 years earlier), one of the first online gaming portals, to Midway Games for $40 million (20 times its revenues) in its third year of operations. Paul owned 60% of the company, and the top 2 levels of management (vice presidents and managers), consisting of 9 people, owned 20%. At closing, the 4 vice presidents shared $4 million. The remaining 20% went to the investors, who had invested $2 million 5 years earlier.

Paul was much more ambitious for his second company: to fund X-Cell, an Internet design and security firm, he had obtained venture backing of $15 million. He had "call rights" agreements with all managers who owned stock in the company, giving him the option to buy back the stock at any time at 3 times the original price. Unfortunately, because of a patent-related lawsuit, X-Cell had to stop marketing its main security product, and Paul and the investors decided to sell off all the firm's assets in 2009, losing a portion of their investment.

AKAR was Paul's current company. Based in Chicago, the tech company had been built around a simple idea that Paul had developed with his chief technology officer (CTO), who had worked with Paul at X-Cell: distributing digital information across several geographically dispersed storage sites to store it more securely, reliably, and cost-effectively. AKAR was commercializing this idea as an online data storage service while offering commercial software for firms that were seeking to build their own storage capabilities. With this value proposition, AKAR was trying to capture a share of the $43 billion global data storage management services market, with an initial focus on the $3.3 billion U.S. market for automated data backup services.

At the time that Johnson met Paul, AKAR had just launched the commercial version of its backup services. With only a few loyal customers in place, the firm's revenues were minimal, but Paul—and many observers—was confident that that would change soon (see Figure 10-3 for AKAR's pro forma financials). Paul had self-funded much of AKAR, but he had also received Round A financing of $3.2 million from a venture capital group in return for 23% of AKAR.

In addition to CEO Paul, AKAR had 14 employees; most of these were engineers with hardware and/or software experience, and several of them had come to AKAR directly from college. None of them, including Paul, was paid a 6-figure salary. Paul believed that everyone should sacrifice salary for annual performance bonuses and company stock. The only other senior manager at

	Best-Case Scenario				
	Year 1	**Year 2**	**Year 3**	**Year 4**	**Year 5**
Revenue	$950,000	$5,000,000	$10,000,000	$20,000,000	$40,000,000
	Most-Likely-Case Scenario				
	Year 1	**Year 2**	**Year 3**	**Year 4**	**Year 5**
Revenue	$950,000	$2,500,000	$5,000,000	$7,500,000	$15,000,000
	Worst-Case Scenario				
	Year 1	**Year 2**	**Year 3**	**Year 4**	**Year 5**
Revenue	$950,000	$1,500,000	$2,500,000	$3,000,000	$3,500,000

Figure 10-3 **AKAR Financials (Pro Forma)**

AKAR was Mark Chin, the CTO. Chin had helped Paul build X-Cell. "My right- and left-hand man," Paul often called him.

From the moment Johnson met Paul, she described the recruiting process as "casual, but intense." For example, the day after the event where they first met, Paul called Johnson and told her how impressed he had been by her qualifications. "You'd make a heck of a marketing director," Paul said numerous times. In the weeks that followed, they kept in close contact: 3 phone calls that lasted late into the night, several strings of e-mail correspondence, and 2 dinners. During these interactions, they discussed technology trends, the fit between Johnson and AKAR, sports, and Paul's personal life. Johnson learned that Paul had been divorced and remarried ("Second time's the charm, so far") and had 2 elementary school–age stepchildren, a 132-foot yacht ("Want to sail her around the world—hopefully after selling this company"), and Type II diabetes ("For me, they're not doughnuts, they're dough-nots").

One month ago, Paul had invited Johnson to meet the CTO and tour AKAR's office, a hip loft space in the Bronzeville neighborhood of Chicago. The meeting with CTO Chin was similar to Johnson's encounters with Paul: casual but intense. For almost two and a half hours, Chin discussed AKAR's products, mission, and culture, rarely pausing to ask Johnson questions. When he did, it was typically to probe Johnson's level of commitment to AKAR's vision and mission. During the marathon interview, Chin used the phrase "John's way" often, endowing it with an almost mythical quality. After the interview, Paul and Chin introduced Johnson to several of the other employees and took her out to dinner with a customer. On her way home, an exhausted Johnson called Naeem. "It's like I already work there," she told him.

Four days after the meeting, Paul called Johnson with good news: the team wanted to make her an offer. "But first," Paul said, "it would mean a lot to us if you and Naeem came to 'Shut Up and Sing' in 2 weeks." Johnson thought she had misheard Paul, until he explained: Shut Up and Sing was a party for all AKAR employees and their spouses or partners that Paul threw twice a year at his house. The two main ingredients were homemade sangria and karaoke.

Two weeks later, Johnson and her husband attended the party. Paul stayed by Johnson's side most of the night, guiding her around his large lakefront home and introducing her as "guest of honor and future marketing director." For Johnson, the night was a blur of smiling faces, handshakes, and her singing "Girls Just Wanna Have Fun" in front of about 50 people she barely knew. She also could not help but feel that the party had been a final test for her, to see how well she would fit at AKAR.

Four days later, Paul called, as enthusiastic about Johnson as ever. Johnson had expected an offer from Paul, even if only verbal. Instead, Paul had said, "Tell me what it will take to get you on board."

Decisions, Decisions

As Johnson sat at her kitchen table, thinking about Paul's words and the position with AKAR, Naeem returned from work. She smiled at him. "They want to hire me," she said.

"Great news!" Naeem hugged her. "What's their offer?"

CASE STUDY ANALYSIS

The following questions illustrate key items for Nailah to consider as she evaluates the opportunity with AKAR.

Question 1: Should Nailah keep her job?

Yes	No
• She is expecting a new baby.	• The new job is an opportunity for entrepreneurial experiences.
• She has job security in her current position.	• There is limited financial upside in her current position.
• Her current company is stable and established.	

Question 2: Should Nailah pursue the AKAR employment opportunity?

Yes	No
• They want her	• Decrease in salary
• More responsibility	• Paul's quirky personality
• Promotion opportunities	• Company could fail
• Wealth opportunity	
• Nailah's passion for entrepreneurship	
• Paul's past success	
• Chance to experiment with entrepreneurship	

Question 3: What are Nailah's personal strengths and weaknesses?

Strengths	Weaknesses
• Smart	• Never been an entrepreneur
• Successful business career	• No finance experience
• Sincerely interested in entrepreneurship	
• Hired specialized recruiter	
• Worked with business broker	
• Participated in Entrepreneur-in-Residence program	

Question 4: What are John Paul's strengths and weaknesses?

Strengths	Weaknesses
• Founded two companies	• X-Cell failure
• Wealthy	• Quirky personality
• Willing to share wealth with employees	
• Made other people rich (GamerParadize), including:	
• Investors	
• Managers	

Question 5: What was the value of GamerParadize to each stakeholder?

Stakeholder	Total Financial Return
• Paul	• $24 million (60% of $40 million)
• Investors	• $8 million (20% of $40 million)
	• Original investment: $2 million
	• Time: 5 years
	• Cash-on-cash return: 4x
	• ROI: 300%
	• IRR: 32%
• Employees	• $8 million (20% of 40% million)
	• 4 V.P.s: $4 million, or $1 million each.
	• Managers: $4 million, or $800,000 each

Question 6: What is the Johnson family's current maximum income?

	Salary	Bonus	Total
Nailah (salary)	$115,000	$28,750	$143,750
		(25% of salary)	
Naeem (salary)	$105,000	$21,000	
		(20% of salary)	$126,000
Total	**$220,000**	**$49,750**	**$269,750**

Question 7: What is the Johnson family's after-tax cash flow?

	Worst-Case (Without Bonus)	Best-Case (with Bonus)
Nailah and Naeem	$220,000	$269,750
28% tax	-$61,600	-$75,530
Total	**$158,400**	**$194,220**

Question 8: What is the Johnson family's current budget?

Expense	Annual	Monthly
1. New baby	$19,000	$1,583.33
2. Household expenses (35% of monthly mortgage)	$8,058	$671.50
3. Assessments, taxes, and insurance (40% of monthly mortgage)	$9,209	$767.42
4. Recreational activities (25% of Naeem's monthly salary)	$26,250	$2,187.50
5. Five school loans (10-year amortization)	$6,913	$576.10
6. Mortgage (principal and interest)	$23,022	$1,918.56
Total	**$92,452**	**$7,704.56**

Question 9: What is the minimum amount of cash that Nailah needs to bring home if the Johnson family is to pay its expenses?

Naeem's salary (worst case, without bonus)	$105,000
Taxes	- $29,400
Naeem's after-tax cash	$75,600
Family budget	$92,452
Naeem's after-tax cash	- $75,600
Cash needed from Nailah	**$16,582**

Question 10: What should Nailah propose?

Key Terms to Propose

At least 4% raise annually
Put rights

2–3% ownership
Starting salary $95,000

Change of control clause with immediate vesting
6-week maternity leave with full pay

No termination without cause
3-year contract

Stock options or restricted stock units

Question 11: What is the difference between stock options and restricted stock units?

	Stock Options	**Restricted Stock Units**
Stock-based compensation?	Yes	Yes
Employers required to expense immediately?	Yes	Yes
Taxed when?	At exercise of option	At time of vesting
Employer required to withhold taxes?	No	Yes. Some options: 1. "Same-day sale" 2. "Sell to cover" (sell just enough to cover taxes) 3. "Cash transfer" (you give the employer cash to cover taxes and keep all the shares
Retains value?	Not always. Example: • Strike price: $10 • Stock price: $8 • Has no value • "Underwater" • Lost 100%	Yes. Example: • Given at $10 • Stock price at vesting: $8 • Lost 20%

Question 12: What is the potential future value of AKAR?

GamerParadize	20 x multiple of revenue
Best	20 x $40,000,000 = $800 million
Likely	20 x $15,000,000 = $300 million
Worst	20 x $3,500,000 = $70 million

Question 13: How much could Nailah make?

Nailah's potential ownership stake	2% x potential future value of AKAR
Best	2% x $800 million = $16 million
Likely	2% x $300 million = $6 million
Worst	2% x $70 million = $1.4 million

Question 14: Is she entitled to 2% of the company or 2% of the new value of the company?

She's entitled to 2% of the company.

Question 15: What is the starting point for Nailah's value?

Equity series	**A**
Investment	$3.2 million
Premoney valuation	$10,713,043
VC ownership stake	23%
Equation for postmoney valuation	23% × Y = $3,200,000
Postmoney valuation (Y)	$13,913,043

Question 15a: What is the worst case for Nailah?

Worst-case future value of AKAR	$70,000,000
VC ownership	$13,913,043
Remaining equity	$56,086,057
Nailah's ownership stake	2%
Nailah's potential return	$1,121,739

Question 15b: What is the financial difference between staying and going?

Scenario 1: Remain at job for 5 years with 4% increase annually

Year	Worst Case (Guaranteed Compensation)	Upside (Bonus)
0	$115,000	$0
1	$119,600	$29,900
2	$124,384	$31,096
3	$129,359	$32,339
4	$134,533	$33,663
5	$139,914	$39,978
Total	**$647,790**	**$161,946**
Total value of staying	**$809,736**	

Scenario 2: Take AKAR job with 4% annual increase

Year	Worst Case	Equity
0		
1	$95,000	
2	$98,800	
3	$103,740	
4	$107,889	
5	$112,204	$1,121,739
Total	**$517,633**	**$1,121,739**
Total value of taking job	**$1,639,372**	

Comparison of Staying Versus Going:	
Value of staying	$809,736
Value of going	$1,639,372
Difference	$829,636
Percent difference	102.26% better to take AKAR job

11

Intrapreneurship

INTRODUCTION

Joseph Alois Schumpeter, an Austrian-trained economist who taught at Harvard, is considered the chief proponent and popularizer of the word *entrepreneur* in 1911. During the next decade, he made the following statement in support of the idea that entrepreneurship was not limited to small start-up firms, but could also occur within big established firms: "Innovation within the shell of existing corporations offers a much more convenient access to the entrepreneurial functions than existed in the world of owner-managed firms. Many a would-be entrepreneur of today does not found a firm, not because he could not do so, but simply because he prefers the other method."[1]

Thus, the idea of corporate entrepreneurship was born almost 100 years ago. This activity is now commonly referred to as *intrapreneurship*. While I introduced intrapreneurship in Chapter 1 when I discussed the entrepreneurial spectrum, I chose not to discuss it in greater detail at that time because I believe that an entire chapter should be devoted to the subject. I also believe that to really understand intrapreneurship, one must thoroughly understand entrepreneurship, and therefore I wanted the reader to have fully digested all the lessons about entrepreneurship in the previous chapters before tackling this subject.

Intrapreneurship is the spirit and act of entrepreneurship in a corporate setting. I have done training sessions on the topic of intrapreneurship at Nike, Hearst Management Institute, S. C. Johnson, Allstate Insurance Company, the National Association of Broadcasters, and the American Press Institute. These are companies and organizations that know that we live in a world in which time is not what it used to be. This is the age of "Internet time," where compared to a decade ago, a year is 6 months, a month is a week, and a week is a day. Therefore, corporations must know that they cannot rest on yesterday's successes. They must also realize that growth can no longer come simply from increasing prices. Today, more than ever before, we live in a global world. Instead of accepting price increases on products or services, customers will go to the Internet to find the same products or services at a lower price. As a result, corporations must continue to remain hungry, with a sense of urgency, creativity, and, most important, vision.

Bob Morrison, the former CEO of Quaker Oats, is a great example of corporate leadership embracing the intrapreneurial spirit. At a company meeting, he announced to his employees, "We must change the mind-set and culture at Quaker. We must think and act like a small, entrepreneurial company."

THE INTRAPRENEURSHIP SPECTRUM

To give greater clarity to the subject of intrapreneurship, I have created the intrapreneurship spectrum in Figure 11-1.

Caretaker

While the caretaker is not an intrapreneur, this category is included on the spectrum simply as a point of reference. This is a corporate employee who is the

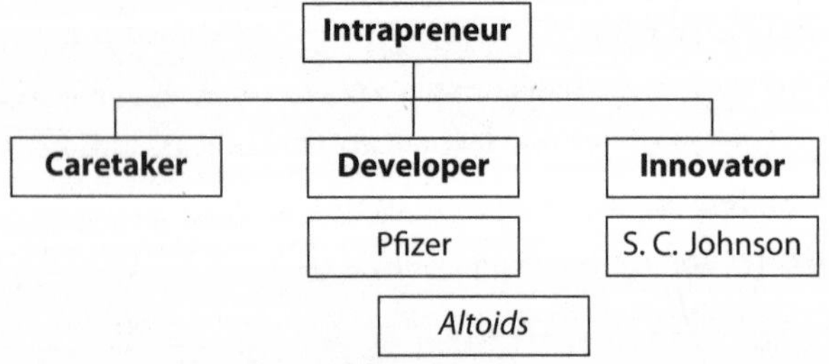

Figure 11-1 **Intrapreneurship Spectrum**

antithesis of the intrapreneur. All things entrepreneurial are anathema to him. He is most satisfied by inheriting an established product line that has a solid customer and employee base with moderate growth.

Developer

This is the intrapreneur who takes a company's existing products or services and pursues high growth by targeting new customers and markets. While the products or services are not new, they have no brand equity with the new targeted markets. For example, Altoids was a 200-year-old British product that was originally used to calm upset stomachs. It was owned by Kraft Foods, then by William Wrigley Jr. Company (now owned by Mars Corporation), and today it is one of the most popular breath mints, with more than 20% of the $300 million U.S. breath mint category.

Another great example is Pfizer's introduction of sildenafil, a drug that was initially studied for hypertension. It was patented in 1996. The story goes that when male patients used the drug, their wives complained to the doctors that their husbands were now chasing them around the house like they had done during their honeymoon decades earlier. With these data, in 1998, Pfizer decided to target a new market for the same drug, which we all know as Viagra.

Innovator

This is the intrapreneur who pursues high growth for her company through new products, services, and/or business models. The innovator is not a member of the company's R&D department, and therefore creating new products, services, or business models is not her official responsibility.

A great example of an intrapreneur in this category is Sam Johnson, the former CEO of S. C. Johnson. Several decades ago, Sam, the grandson of the company's founder, decided to pursue the development of a new product without the approval of his father, who was the CEO. The company, which now manufactures an entire spectrum of consumer products, including Glade air fresheners, Windex, Scrubbing Bubbles toilet cleaners, and Oust air sanitizer, was primarily a manufacturer of wax cleaners. Sam came to his father and informed him that he had developed a new product, outside of the research and development department. His father's reply was, "That's fine as long as it has wax in it." Sam responded, "No, it does not have wax among its ingredients, and if you included it, the product would be less effective." Sam's new product was a pesticide that we all know today as Raid.

INTRAPRENEURSHIP MODELS

Intrapreneurs, whether they are developers or innovators, use different formal or informal models to bring their innovative ideas to fruition. The best descriptions of these models were published in a recent research paper by corporate entrepreneurship expert Robert C. Wolcott, an outstanding scholar and adjunct professor in the Center for Research in Technology and Innovation at the Kellogg School of Management, and Michael Lippitz, a research fellow at Northwestern. These models are the Opportunist, the Enabler, and the Producer.[2]

The Opportunist

This model basically says to employees, "Do whatever you want to do, because the company does not have any formal systems related to corporate entrepreneurship." This is a model in which new services or products, like Raid, come from individual champions, not through systems. Ironically, being successful with this model typically leads an organization to implement a more formal model, such as the Producer or the Enabler.

The Enabler

This model says to employees, "Anybody in the company can come up with a new service or product, but here is the process for developing it." With this model, the company explicitly communicates to its employees the procedures for requesting development capital and the criteria that will be used to determine which projects receive funding. Google is a company that has had major success with this model. For example, its service Google Talk (now "GChat"), which is a free system for instant and voice messaging, came from an employee as part of the company's 10% program. This innovative program allows all employees to devote 10% of their daily working hours to the development of their own ideas. As one

Google employee stated, "We're an internal ecosystem for entrepreneurs . . . sort of like the Silicon Valley ecosystem, but inside one company."

The Producer

This model openly recognizes and proactively supports the importance of entrepreneurship in a corporate setting. The company creates a separate entity that has the specific task of creating new products or services outside of the present business. Several companies have embraced this model, including Xerox, with its New Enterprises Division; Coca-Cola's Innovation centers in 5 different locations throughout the world; and Cargill's Emerging Business Accelerator division.

TRAITS OF THE HIGH-GROWTH INTRAPRENEUR

Successful high-growth entrepreneurs and intrapreneurs share some but not all of the same traits. A few unique attributes of the intrapreneur include:

- Risk taker
- Hard worker
- Has a plan
- Good manager
- Visionary
- Profit focused
- Innovator
- Accepts being managed

Some of these traits are worth discussing in more detail.

Risk Taker

The successful intrapreneur is not a blind risk taker. He has a plan, especially if he works for a company that uses the developer or innovator model, and he executes that plan according to a defined timeline. This is called "planning the work and working the plan." Unlike the entrepreneur, who typically risks her personal assets, the intrapreneur's risk is much less. At worst, he could lose his job if his new ideas or innovations are not commercially successful. However, while the intrapreneur's risk may be less than the entrepreneur's, he certainly assumes greater risk than the average corporate employee.

Accepts Being Managed

One of the reasons why some people become entrepreneurs is that they want to be as independent as possible. Specifically, they loathe the idea of having a boss. In contrast, the intrapreneur, given her status as an employee, accepts the fact that she answers to a manager above her. She does not have carte blanche to do anything that she wants to do. She must usually seek and receive approval from a higher authority in the company's organization chart. The intrapreneur generally accepts being managed by others as a standard way of doing business.

ACTS OF INTRAPRENEURSHIP

Intrapreneurial activities include acquisitions of other companies and product lines, the introduction of new products outside of the traditional research and development process, the creation of new strategic partners, and changes in a company's business model. Let's review, through anecdotes, each of these activities in greater detail.

Acquisitions of Other Companies and Product Lines

In 1998, McDonald's purchased 90% of Chipotle Mexican Grill, a chain of 14 restaurants that was founded in 1993 by Steve Elis, a professional chef trained at the Culinary Institute of America. This acquisition was truly an intrapreneurial act of innovation on McDonald's part. Prior to this acquisition, the company had seemingly viewed innovation as simply putting the letters "Mc" on the beginning of any idea. For example, it unsuccessfully experimented with the McDiner, a restaurant serving traditional food, such as meat loaf and mashed potatoes, in a diner.

Introduction of New Products Outside of the Traditional R&D Process

A great example of the intrapreneurship model in which "products emerged from champions rather than systems," a phrase created by Bill Perez, occurred at S. C. Johnson with the development of its storage bag product line, which generates in excess of $150 million of annual revenues. The original idea and the development of the prototypes came not from the company's R&D department, but from 2 marketing department employees. The company had no plans to enter the storage bag category until these 2 intrapreneurs persuaded management that it was a business that could be grown fast. As Bill Perez, the former CEO of S. C. Johnson, said about the 2 employees, "Nobody asked them to do it."

Creation of New Strategic Partners

In 1994, Viacom, a $10 billion entertainment conglomerate that owned Madison Square Garden, MTV Networks, Showtime Networks, numerous theme parks, and dozens of television stations, purchased the 6,000-store Blockbuster video chain for $8 billion. Two years later, Blockbuster's cash flow had dropped 42%. Sumner Redstone, the 75-year-old chairman and founder of Viacom, knew that he had to make changes. Rather than simply cutting overhead, he got intrapreneurial.

Redstone knew that videos shown at home provided movie studios with nearly 3 times the revenue of showings in movie theaters. The studios charged Blockbuster a flat fee of $80 per video. In contrast, movie theaters usually did not pay a fixed price; instead, they split the revenues with the studios. Redstone decided that this partnership model between movie studios and theaters should also be applied to Blockbuster. The first studio that he approached with this partnership proposal was Warner Brothers, which rejected it. His next target was Disney, which he successfully convinced that it could make money if it treated Blockbuster as a partner, instead of as a customer. The agreement was that Blockbuster's fixed cost of $80 per video would be reduced to $8 and that Disney would receive 40% of the video's rental revenues for up to 26 weeks, at which time Blockbuster could sell the video, thereby recouping its original $8 investment.

The financial results were enormously positive for both parties because they reduced Blockbuster's outlay of capital while allowing it to increase its stock of the most popular videos. Six other studios followed Disney with a similar strategic partnership with Blockbuster, including Warner Brothers.

Changes in Business Model

Three of America's blue-chip companies, IBM, Best Buy, and Nike, have been wonderfully intrapreneurial by changing their business models. IBM, a company that was seemingly an antiquated, lumbering old has-been by the 1990s, was turned around by a great intrapreneur, Lou Gerstner, the CEO, who did not have a technology background when he came from RJR Nabisco. Gerstner successfully changed IBM from an equipment supplier, as it had been for its entire life, to a solution provider/consultant.

After Wal-Mart Stores, the world's largest retailer, began selling brand-name consumer electronics earlier this decade, it was assumed that Best Buy's revenues would decline dramatically. Instead of acting like a victim, however, Best Buy became intrapreneurial. Five years ago, it changed its model from being exclusively a retailer to being a solution provider, like IBM, by adding installation services and trained salespeople, which Wal-Mart did not offer. Best Buy's revenues increased 16%.

Phil Knight, the great entrepreneur who founded Nike in 1974 as an importer of running shoes, later changed its model to an athletic shoe and apparel manufacturer. Today it is also a successful retailer.

SIGNS OF INTRAPRENEURIAL SUCCESS

A company has successfully created an intrapreneurial spirit and program when it is unequivocally clear that it agrees to manage intrapreneurs differently from other employees by encouraging them and giving them the space and freedom to innovate.

Further evidence of intrapreneurship includes the company's acceptance of failure. Google is a great example. In response to an unsuccessful innovation that cost the company several million dollars, Larry Page, one of Google's founders, told the employee who had been in charge of the idea, "I'm so glad you made this mistake, because I want to run a company where we are moving too quickly and doing too much, not being too cautious and doing too little. If we don't have any of these mistakes, we're just not taking enough risk."[3]

The final sign of successful intrapreneurship is the company's proactively encouraging employees with creative ideas to step forward. An extreme example is Sealed Air Corporation, which has 25,000 employees. Its employees are encouraged to bring entrepreneurial ideas directly to its CEO.

STANDARD OPERATING PROCEDURES

The ideal intrapreneurship system should be made up of the following processes:

1. *The system should be simple and user-friendly.* The U.S. Forest Service Eastern Region changed its innovation suggestion process from a 4-page form to telling its employees, "If you have an idea, tell your supervisor or send an e-mail. If you do not get a response in 2 weeks, as long as the idea is not illegal, go ahead and implement it." Before the change, the 2,500 employees submitted, on average, 60 ideas annually. A year after the new procedures were implemented, 6,000 new ideas were submitted!
2. *Reward employees for successful ideas.* Share the wealth. Northwestern University has a results-oriented system that rewards anyone who develops an idea that gets commercialized. In 2007, chemistry professor Richard Silverman received his portion of the royalties that the university received from a pharmaceutical firm, Pfizer, which purchased Lyrica, a chronic pain relief drug that Silverman had created. The university received more than $700 million. Silverman's portion was not publicly disclosed, but it must have been many millions of dollars, given the fact that the Richard and Barbara Silverman Hall for Molecular Therapeutics and Diagnostics, a $100 million Northwestern University building that "brings together engineering, biology and chemistry for interdisciplinary research," was named for him and his wife.
3. *All ideas should be reviewed,* and the submitters should be informed of the decision as soon as possible.

4. *Every step in the review process should be transparent and well publicized*, as should the criteria used to approve ideas.
5. *The review and approval process should be managed by more than one person.*
6. *All intrapreneurial success stories should be publicized to all employees throughout the company.*
7. *Employee expectations should be proactively managed.*

Employees should be told that in the entrepreneurship world, most new companies do not succeed. And the same applies in the corporate intrapreneurship world, where most ideas will be rejected.

INTRAPRENEURSHIP BLUNDER

The implementation of the procedures just listed will almost guarantee that a company does not duplicate one of the greatest intrapreneurial blunders in corporate history. In the mid-1970s, Steve Wozniak, a college dropout and self-taught electronics engineer, worked at Hewlett-Packard (HP). He offered his employer the chance to develop the idea that he had for a user-friendly personal computer. Hewlett-Packard said no thank you. So with $1,300 derived from selling his van and other assets, he left HP at the age of 26 and, with the help of his friend Steven Jobs, developed the Apple I computer for their new entrepreneurial start-up, Apple Computer, Inc.

12

Crowdfunding

INTRODUCTION

One recent development that demands the attention of all entrepreneurs is the emergence of crowdfunding and crowdfund investing. A crowd is defined by the *Macmillan Dictionary* as "a large number of people in the same place." A crowd can, but does not necessarily, have a common purpose. Using the more sophisticated digital services available today that were not as easily accessible in the past, entrepreneurs can take advantage of the potential energy and resources of crowds.

For example, less than 24 hours after David Henneberry's boat had been ruined in Watertown, Massachusetts, a total stranger from Texas named Craig Dunlap started a campaign on Crowdtilt.com titled: "Let's Fix David Henneberry's Boat (That Got Ruined in the Boston Bomber's Standoff)!" Dunlap had written brief comments in the campaign in support of 66-year-old Henneberry, who was in Dunlap's mind an everyday American boating enthusiast whose boat had the misfortune of being used as Dzhokhar Tsarnaev's hideout. Dunlap started the campaign on April 20, 2013, with a goal of giving Henneberry $50,000 to purchase a new boat of his choosing.[1] A second complete stranger, Jeffrey Griffeth, saw the campaign on Crowdtilt.com and created a Facebook page to widen its exposure. In five days, the campaign had raised $13,662.26 from 430 contributors (strangers!) from 42 states and 8 countries when the Florida-based Boston Whaler company surprised everyone and donated $37,000 so that Dunlap's goal could be met. According to the campaign comments, a total of $50,597.50 was successfully given to Henneberry by Crowdtilt by May 12, 2013, only 22 days after the campaign began. The story was covered by *Time* magazine, *Bloomberg Businessweek*, and several other media outlets. Let's examine this phenomenon to see how it can be useful to you.

This chapter discusses (1) crowdfunding with pledge-based capital (i.e., financial commitments made by customers before they receive the item); (2) the steps in carrying out a crowdfunding campaign; and (3) crowdfund investing, the term for financing a venture by raising equity or debt capital from large crowds through licensed portals, which is made possible through the April 2012 JOBS Act (Jumpstart Our Business Startups Act).

CROWDFUNDING WITH PLEDGES

Crowdfunding refers to publicizing products or services while generating financial commitments through a web-based platform by creating an appealing website presentation and offering perks (rewards) for early orders of the product or premium add-ons that complement the order. On August 21, 2013, independent filmmaker Spike Lee of Brooklyn, New York, completed his first Kickstarter campaign for "The Newest Hottest Spike Lee Joint" movie by raising $1.42 million from 6,421 backers, which was $169,000 more than his $1.25 million goal.[2] His campaign generated 1,136 comments, most of which were supportive, but some of which raised concerns that his celebrity status detracted from the efforts of less-well-known independent filmmakers. Kickstarter answered these issues with statistics showing that Spike Lee in fact helped independent filmmakers by bringing his 30 years' worth of fans to the crowdfunding platform to support his effort, which led to their support of additional campaigns. Lee himself claimed that before there was a Kickstarter, he was performing many of the same crowdsourcing tasks, just without the benefit of technology. With this new platform, he plans to do more while promoting the platform to other artists. The same might be suitable for you.

There are more than 500 websites around the world listed on the website named "CrowdFunding Conference and Seminars,"[3] on which entrepreneurs create and run campaigns. The success rate of all campaigns on Kickstarter in August 2013, according to the site's statistics, was 44%, and of those, 76% were seeking pledge totals under $10,000.[4] Check each website to be sure that the industry you are in matches the type of crowd that favors that site, and keep your pledge goal modest! Pledge-based presales campaigns can be useful for individual projects, early start-ups, musician-entrepreneurs, and all sorts of creative offers. Indiegogo, for example, has helped creative types, change makers, and entrepreneurs to campaign for what matters most to them in each country in which the law allows this, and its system sends payments to locations in 75 to 100 countries each week.

One of the best parts of crowdfunding projects is that they involve generating revenue rather than involving either debt or equity; the entrepreneur's ownership remains intact.

CROWDFUNDING CAMPAIGNS

This could be a lot of work. Recently, new consulting firms such as Crowdfunding Planning.com are sprouting up that can assist in all phases of crowdfunding: setting goals, choosing the right platform, setting up the campaign, managing the campaign, and completing the effort. For some entrepreneurs, delegating this new type of work makes sense so that the core effort of the enterprise can remain the entrepreneurs' primary focus. For the "do-it-yourself" types, Figure 12-1 outlines the steps involved in launching the best possible campaign to raise either pledge-based, debt, or equity capital. Liz Wald, head of international and business development at Indiegogo.com, who provides encouragement and practical guides for each champion of a campaign, reviewed this list and provided several valuable additional steps. She provided an example of a student-run campaign and an example of an academic researcher's campaign from among the many that are available to consider.[5]

An entrepreneur who planned his campaign using the steps in Figure 12-1 is Hunter Hillenmeyer. Hillenmeyer, a former linebacker for the National Football League's Chicago Bears and one of my former MBA students, posted a campaign on Kickstarter featuring a mobile application ("app") produced by his venture,

1. Plan how a crowdfunding campaign fits into your overall goals.
    A. Remember that generating publicity is essential.
    B. The campaign attracts attention to the products and services being offered as well as to the financial aspects of the offer being made.
    C. Be prepared for feedback and comments, both favorable and unfavorable.
    D. Prepare how you wish to communicate your passion.
    E. Prepare the financial pro formas for the anticipated new orders or investment capital.
2. Plan the crowdfund campaign.
    A. Prepare the splash video or instruction videos that will run on your account on the crowdfunding platform.
    B. Prepare the rewards you will give to different levels of pledges. Think through them carefully, and be creative; for example, how can people participate beyond giving? For a significant donation, can they have some creative participation in the product or service?
    C. Prepare images, photos, and text.
    D. Sign up for additional social media, and also for tools that make posting to social media easier (e.g., Sprout Social or HubSpot).
    E. Prepare your initial e-mail, tweet, or Facebook post that will get your campaign started and give it momentum. These will be shared with your existing audience and should have a very specific call to action (e.g., donate on Tuesday at 10 a.m. and then share on Facebook).
    F. Build a team—more team members lead to more contributions. Divide and conquer, but be sure you are the leader who is organizing everything.
3. Plan how you plan to deliver on what you promised.
    A. In situations in which you will deliver products, line up manufacturing in advance and thoroughly understand costs and production time.
    B. Communicate the plan to return investors' capital after it has been raised.
    C. Utilize dividends or make plans for shipping products to people who made pledges.
    D. Consult with an attorney with expertise on securities regulations.

Figure 12-1 **Crowdfund Campaign Steps**

4. Choose a platform.
   A. Pledge based.
   B. Investment based.
      i. Equity.
      ii. Debt.
5. Choose a location.
   A. United States.
   B. Non–United States geographical.
   C. Digital/global/nongeographical.
6. Prepare your social media network and your public relations team.
   A. Start publicizing the upcoming campaign 3 months in advance.
      i. Add new platforms like Twitter, Facebook, and Pinterest.
      ii. Start posting the upcoming kickoff.
      iii. Generate buzz.
   B. Combine this with other marketing initiatives on your website and other places.
7. Prepare your existing digital network.
   A. Tell your Facebook friends about your upcoming campaign.
   B. Tell your Twitter followers the same.
   C. Update your primary website to provide current information—prepare cross-promotion text and links.
8. Prepare your nearby geographical network.
   A. Make fliers.
   B. Send promotional emails to friends and neighbors.
   C. Generate a specific call to action.
9. Launch your campaign.
   A. Run video.
   B. Update in real time.
   C. Be active on social media.
   D. Be bold and make the ask several times.
   E. Remain focused on operations during the campaign.
10. Fulfill on the legal requirements, both during and after the campaign.

Figure 12-1 (***Continued***)

11. Decide whether to accept the funds or not.
    A. Accept funds.
        i. New capital investors require communication, status updates, and treatment like any other investor.
        ii. Plan for returns early.
        iii. Share with investors upon exit.
    B. Do not accept funds.
        i. Convert investment interest into customer interest.
        ii. In writing, complete all documents in order and fairly so as to not upset the platform's rules and regulations
12. Publicize the results on social media.
    A. Continue to use the experience as a social marketing / content experience to draw attention to the venture.
    B. Develop social media relationships with others who have crowdfunded.

Figure 12-1 ***(Continued)***

OverDog, Inc. OverDog gives sports fans the chance to meet (digitally) with a professional athlete through this iPhone app, schedule a multiplayer game on Xbox or other platform, then record who won and by how much. For fans, it offers an opportunity to play a game with a celebrity. During the 29-day campaign, Hillenmeyer's pitch for OverDog's service raised pledges (offers by site visitors to prepay for his service) of $37,472 from 310 backers. That might seem like a lot or a little to you, but either way you look at it, this method of crowdfunding proved that it worked for him. In fact, Kickstarter published that it works for 4.76 million people who have pledged $778 million for more than 48,000 creative projects.[6]

If you look up Hillenmeyer's campaign on Kickstarter, you will see that it says, "Funding Unsuccessful." What? Well, at the outset, Hillenmeyer had set a pledge total goal of $100,000, so his campaign fell short by a whopping $62,528. On Kickstarter, if you do not reach your goal, you do not collect the pledges and your campaign is declared unsuccessful. On Indiegogo, by contrast, the entrepreneur can collect a pledge balance that is less than the goal. In Hillenmeyer's case, however, he believed that the campaign was successful, despite the fact that he did not collect the funds. He learned a lot about the process of putting up a crowdfunding campaign while also making sure that OverDog had enough fans involved so that the athletes always had somebody to play against.[7]

CROWDFUND INVESTING THROUGH THE JOBS ACT

Crowdfunding your start-up with pledges remains a fast-growing approach. In addition, for the community of entrepreneurs, investors, and investment bankers interested in raising high-growth capital in the form of equity or debt, a lot of work has been done recently by advocates and policy makers. Let's turn our attention to the April 5, 2012, legislation titled, Jumpstart Our Business Startups Act, or JOBS Act, which was passed into law as H.R. 3606 during the 112th Congress (2011–2012). This law stirred up passion, interest, and excitement within the entrepreneurship community from the time of its introduction in December 2011, and this continues today. Aren't entrepreneurs among the least interested in policy and legislation? What is in this law that has entrepreneurs so interested? What are the implications of the law for entrepreneurs now and into the future?

In a town hall event in June 2012 in Chicago by Sherwood Neiss, cofounder of the advocacy group Startup Exemption, which was the entity through which he and the other two cofounders, Jason Best and Zak Cassady-Dorion, pressed for the passing of the JOBS Act, he said that this congressional bill initiated an entire new financial asset class, similar to what happened when the money market fund and the exchange-traded fund (ETF) were invented. When an asset class is invented, so is an entire set of supporting trade organizations, financial firms, and products and services. Part of the excitement was for entrepreneurs to participate in the birth of a new industry whose goal was to help entrepreneurs gain access to additional sources of capital.

The JOBS Act includes seven sections, Titles I to VII. While the full text of the bill is available online,[8] the most significant sections to discuss are Titles I, II, and III.

Title I of the JOBS Act included a series of amendments to the Securities Act of 1933 (SA), the Securities Exchange Act of 1934 (SEA), the Sarbanes-Oxley Act of 2002, and the Investor Protection and Securities Reform Act of

2010 (Dodd-Frank). Each of these prior laws had a tremendous impact on the regulation of financial capital in the United States. Creating amendments to such lauded legislation was a powerful achievement. In Title I, the JOBS Act established a new category of company called an Emerging Growth Company, or ESG, and by so doing, added new features to the 1933, 1934, 2002, and 2010 acts. An ESG is an entity that generates less than $1 billion in revenues per year." and had not issued securities before December 8, 2011. Under the new legislation, ESGs were given special privileges and exemptions from each of the existing laws, relieving them from what would otherwise be a regulatory burden intended for larger companies. Table 12-1 summarizes the key exemptions.

Essentially, Title I lessens the regulatory burdens on small companies while they are raising funds.

Title II allows ESGs that are in the process of raising investment capital to advertise or make "general solicitations," something that is not allowed for larger companies. The implication of this section is that small companies can place advertisements on billboards, at transit stations, in magazines, or on websites promoting their intention to raise investment capital. Typically this type of advertisement is not allowed under Securities and Exchange Commission (SEC) rules for companies that are raising investment capital from qualified investors (e.g., accredited investors). Also, this section allows nonfinancial professionals (i.e., people other than brokers) to assist in soliciting funds, as long as they do not earn commissions and do not own shares in the company. Essentially, this gives advertising professionals the authority to do what they do best, as long as they do not participate in the proceeds of the transaction.

TABLE 12-1 **Title I ESG Exemptions**

Companies need to provide only 2 years of financial statements.
Accounting firms are exempt from attesting to (i.e., verifying the truth of) the company's internal controls.
Executive compensation and executive roles are reduced.
ESGs can be in communication with certain public institutions during the process of raising funds.

Title III is known in short as the "Crowdfund Act," and it establishes the rules under which an entrepreneurial firm can raise investment capital from the general public (i.e., nonaccredited investors). The bill requires that the securities of an ESG be offered through an intermediary, which could be a person registered as a broker or could be a new entity called a *funding portal* (essentially a professionally developed website dedicated to this specialized purpose). Human brokers are a fairly well understood element of the financial industry; however, this new entity, a funding portal, requires clearer definition. This section said that brokers and funding portals must be registered with the SEC and with a "self-governing authority" under the SEA of 1934, which, after the passage of the bill, was understood to be FINRA, the Financial Industry Regulatory Authority. Furthermore, the section declared that several efforts must be made in the name of protecting prospective investors: they can invest no more than 5% of their annual income or at most $2,000 if their income is less than $100,000, and no more than 10% of their annual income if their income is greater than $100,000. The funding portal has to verify income information in order to allow an investor to provide capital. Additional communications must be given to investors alerting them to the risks inherent in investing in the securities being offered and to the risk of fraud perpetrated by the ESG. Importantly for the entrepreneur of the ESG, a provision (302.4A.a.7) states that the intermediary can withhold all offering proceeds from the ESG until the target amount has been reached, and any investor can cancel his investment at any time before the proceeds are released to the ESG or the entrepreneur. It is possible that in one situation or another, an entrepreneur will not get the proceeds of his offering if communications with his hired intermediary were to become contentious for any reason. Also, this section requires intermediaries to communicate with one another in order to ensure that investors do not exceed their investment limit across all the investments they make. That will be difficult to manage—investors will be regulated through these offerings, which is not great. Among other items, the entrepreneur must disclose the names of all owners of the ESG/issuer who own more than 20% of the shares of the ESG. As a last item of note, once an investor owns the shares, she may not trade or sell them for 1 year unless that sale or trade is to an accredited investor, to a family member, part of another offering, or back to the issuer. Essentially, securities cannot be traded among nonaccredited investors.

Title III has several other detailed instructions that began the process of establishing the funding portals. To begin with, the section gave the SEC 270 days to formulate the rules. (Typically the SEC needs 90 days.) Even so, at the end of 270 days, the SEC requested and was given an extension of time, with the result that as of the writing of this book, the SEC had not yet established final rules on funding portals under Title III.

Title IV enables "small companies" to issue up to $50 million publicly and still be exempt from several regulations in the 1933 act. Title V limits an ESG to issuing no more than $10 million to 2,000 total investors, of which no more than 500 may be nonaccredited. Title VI applies those same limits to Bank Holding Companies (essentially allowing bank holding companies the same limits as other firms, up from the prior ceiling of 1,200 total investors) and 300 nonaccredited investors. And finally, Title VII directs the SEC to conduct marketing outreach on this act to the public, with an emphasis on small and medium-sized businesses and on women-, minority-, and veteran-owned businesses.

When Neiss spoke in Chicago, he emphasized that this mix of initiatives, even this entire funding portal industry that in principle created access to a wider set of investors, was not allowed to formally start or prosper until the administrative rules were determined and published by the ruling authority, in this case the SEC. Furthermore, no timeline for releasing its rules had been imposed on FINRA, Neiss mentioned. The effect of such a delay has been to dampen the excitement about funding portals. The domestic community of entrepreneurs awaits the issuance of the rules by the SEC and FINRA in order to launch this industry.

ALTERNATIVE CROWDFUND INVESTING APPROACHES

In the meantime, as anyone who knows entrepreneurs would suspect, several funding portal domain names have been purchased by entrepreneurs who are anticipating the release of the rules at any time. Some entrepreneurs with sufficient resources have been able to launch portals in advance by adhering to the rules, including Fundable.com and AngelList. Fundable.com organized its offerings to be consistent with the JOBS Act. To adhere to the waiting period on the SEC rules, all equity investments are processed manually rather than through the portal. Once the rules are announced, Fundable will be ready to process equity investments through an automated, digital process. AngelList, a widely popular platform (online at angel.co) on which founders list their new ventures and investors publicize their support, is actively preparing its stakeholders for the ability to advertise for investment capital. On the day of each SEC announcement, AngelList is a site to watch.

Another pair of entrepreneurs had the savvy insight to take advantage of the publicity of crowdfunding but remain within the historical SEC regulations for private offerings of securities (also known in part as Reg. D). Larry Baker and Charlie Tribbett, cofounders of Bolstr.com, organized their website to comply with all 50 state laws and U.S. law for private offerings of securities. With this approach, which is essentially digitizing a financial service that would otherwise be encumbered by differences in state laws, Baker and Tribbett can proceed to meet the needs of entrepreneurs without having to continue waiting for the SEC. Recently, Bolstr assisted Mr. Mike Connelly, co-owner of Rebell Conditioning, in raising $12,000 in under 48 hours from friends, family, and community members. This is crowdfunding at its finest.

Another important crowdfund investing platform for entrepreneurs, which is now quite a mature marketplace, is crowdfund investing with angel investors. As stated earlier, an angel investor is an individual or a small group of individuals who privately invest their own personal capital into entrepreneurial ventures. They are called "angels" because they personally and their investment capital can be a godsend to an entrepreneur at the right time. Contrast that genteel term with the names given to venture capitalists (professionals who invest primarily other people's money), and you can guess why it is sometimes better to be an angel. Substantial research and energy have been focused on angel networks for more than a decade now, and we cannot explore all that in detail here. Suffice it to say that one of their historical practices, hosting live, in-person pitch sessions, is nearly dead as a result of the power of crowdfund investing over the Internet. All the resources needed to organize people to get to a venue, assess a pitch, assess the entrepreneurs, wait for angels to ask questions (if they get to ask questions at all), evaluate the investment offer, and feel that relationships are forming pale in efficiency relative to the outcomes made possible by browsing the list of 1,000s of angels on Angel.co or Gust.com.

At this time, crowdfund investing with angel investors using the Internet is essentially an organized information exchange, and will remain so until Title III of the JOBS Act is put into effect. Actual monies do not change hands through the website (if money is exchanged, the site must register as a crowdfund investment portal, explained earlier). Rather, all the components of a pitch, including the investment offer, are shared between the entrepreneur and the prospective angel or angels. The online marketplace helps angels to see a variety of opportunities without using up much of their own time and resources during the search phase.

Most angel investments, as stated in Chapter 8, involve some form of equity. Occasionally investments by angels are arranged as convertible debt, which is a type of quasi-equity that is underwritten as a loan or liability to the entrepreneur until such time as a "professional" investment establishes customary terms. Even convertible debt is a type of equity, however, in the sense that the investment principal is not expected to be returned on an amortized basis, as it is with a typical loan agreement. Therefore, at some point in the discussions between the entrepreneur and the angel, a legal document needs to be written that explains the rights and benefits of each party. While communication between the entrepreneur and the angel crowd can remain online, at some point a document outside the website has to be signed. This step is consistent with historical practices.

Crowdfunding is also possible for obtaining a loan (e.g., obtaining debt capital from a source other than a bank), so let us examine peer-to-peer lending. Have you ever asked a friend for a short-term loan? Did you establish a contract and spell out the terms in detail (e.g., duration, interest rate, and what to do in case of a default or missed payment)? Did your friend check your credit score? Your credit score is a number on a scale of ~300 to 850 that is calculated by credit reporting services such as Experian, TransUnion, and Equifax and reflects your ability to repay all your personal debts (mortgage, credit cards, auto loans, and so on). A higher score represents a higher likelihood that you will repay your debt, which is a good thing. Most people with "good credit" have scores above 700. Today, a person's credit score is a big factor in a lender's decision to lend to that person or her entrepreneurial venture. Since the banking system "shock" in 2008, bankers are increasingly tying an entrepreneur's personal credit to her business credit. Up to an estimated revenue of $15 million, your personal credit matters when it comes to what terms are extended for your business credit card application or revolving loan, if you are accepted at all. It is likely that your friend did not look up your credit score, nor did he think that such an effort was necessary at the time when the loan agreement was made and his money was put into your account.

Peer-to-peer lending, which is a practice that goes back centuries and was mentioned in Chapter 7, has evolved to become an efficient process through websites such as Prosper.com, in which the legal language in the contract and the terms, such as interest rate, duration, and principal amount, have all become more transparent and efficient. The Prosper Marketplace boasts a current membership base of 1.92 million people, who have collectively lent $606 million to each other. *Wow*, that is an effective marketplace for capital. For entrepreneurs with reasonable credit scores, a first-time borrower can obtain a 5-year term loan at 11.6% APR for an amount between $2,000 and $35,000. Applications and repayments all occur online. I suggest that, as with any other fund-raising activity, it is better to apply for a loan before you desperately need it. One successful strategy is to take out a small initial loan, pay it back early, then apply for a second loan at a better rate. It's also plausible to earn income as an entrepreneur by taking the role of investor on a peer-to-peer lending marketplace. The marketplace handles all the terms and helps to provide risk management and portfolio diversification. Maybe all this interpersonal "relationship" banking is getting obsolete? It may be too early to answer that question; however, experimenting with such a system makes a lot of sense to entrepreneurs.

A NOTE ON CROWDFUNDING VERSUS CROWDSOURCING

Crowdfunding differs from the broader umbrella term *crowdsourcing* in that the first is a subset of the latter. Obtaining money (through payments or similar online transactions) from the crowd (unrelated strangers in widespread geographies) is distinct from obtaining ideas, feedback, and services. Crowdsourcing requires making requests for tasks and generating information and feedback; crowdfunding indicates making appeals for sales or donations to support an early initiative; and crowdfund investing, as we have discussed earlier, indicates making offers of investment capital through an authorized funding portal.

Accepting money requires that you provide the promised goods or services in return; ideas have no such tether to payments.

Entrepreneurs can crowdsource for several reasons. Let's briefly look at how to get the crowd to perform tasks and generate information.

The entrepreneur may choose to enlist the crowd to perform tasks to support his new venture using the Internet in several ways. At the time of its launch eight years ago, Amazon's Mechanical Turk service was an experimental service in which entrepreneurs or companies posted jobs that needed to be completed, and workers logged on to complete the work. Radically, though, the work is parsed into such small increments that the cost per task completed can be as low as $0.01. That's not a typo—we are talking 1 cent! Each task is called an "HIT," or "human intelligence task," pointing to the fact that many of these tasks require people to complete them, rather than algorithms or machines. "Turks," or workers, receive pay for completing HITs in the time and manner dictated by the entrepreneur. For example, an entrepreneur based in London, England, who is engaged with website users from locations in both the Commonwealth of Nations (where British English dominates) and the United States (where American English dominates) may need human intelligence to check the spelling of the word *labor* versus *labour*. When his Commonwealth customers add the *u* in *labor* to make *labour*, it is not a mistake that is easily found by a spell checker. Rather than investing valuable time sorting in this out himself, the entrepreneur can enlist the Turks with a $0.01 payment per HIT to "find all words unique to British English and convert to American English." They can input either of those words, being fully concerned with saying what they mean while spelling the word correctly. The amount of time it takes to set up the work on Amazon's service and pay for all the HITs should be less than the entrepreneur's cost of her time to do the HITs herself.

CrowdSPRING.com provides entrepreneurs with the largest pool of designers in the world. This is one of a few specialized marketplaces where entrepreneurs can complete several design services: choose a name for the venture, have a logo designed, have a website designed, and even have a mobile app designed. What makes this marketplace of design talent so useful for entrepreneurs, however, is not what can be seen—it is the detailed and fair legal agreement set by crowdSPRING for all designers. This seems like an unimportant point; however, the time and expertise that it takes for an entrepreneur to negotiate the legal rights between a logo designer and himself carries a high cost and low value—no one wants a dispute over the rights to a logo. The cofounders of crowdSPRING .com include one graduate of the Law School at Northwestern University and one graduate of the Kellogg School of Management at Northwestern University. Jointly, they articulated the fair set of legal statements for both the designers and the buyers of the designs. This is an important piece of infrastructure that allows entrepreneurs to trust the results of the work, both in design and in terms of who owns it.

As for the actual designs, crowdSPRING brings to the entrepreneur a pool of more than 100,000 designers from more than 100 countries in the world. Compare this to asking friends or asking the entrepreneur next to you at your coworking space, "Who have you used to design your logo? I need one." Not only is that method of getting your logo done expensive and time-consuming, but one, two, or even three great referrals give you a much smaller set of choices. In a recent example, a U.S. entrepreneur received 203 logo design ideas within 7 days from 39 designers using a similar site called 99designs.com. He ultimately selected a design by a man who works from a small town in Italy. The total cost of the logo was $449.00. Some people might think that that was expensive, but it could also be seen as costing just over $2 per logo idea if you divide the total cost by the number of design concepts that were made available for review. Furthermore, the convenience of arranging submissions through this the marketplace was considerable, compared to the inconvenience of making personal arrangements to meet and see concepts through an individual designer. Coincidentally, the entrepreneur had been born and raised in a nearby small town in Italy before moving to the United States 30 years earlier.

Gathering information is another useful feature of crowdsourcing. It is so useful that an entrepreneur created a service offering in which he enlists a crowd of PhDs to read research papers, make summaries of them, and publish what the reviewer feels are the relevant findings of the research. Dinesh Ganesarajah ("Dino") founded PreScouter to provide his clients with several benefits from aggregating research papers, hiring more than 200 skilled reviewers (the PhDs) to assess research for the clients. His clients are vice presidents of research from 28 Fortune 500 companies who are interested in the flow of research in technical fields, such as biochemistry, solar energy, or quantum mechanics. In this example, the crowd is a set of PhDs in whom such technical skills can be reliably found (not always the case with a Mechanical Turk, of course), who are needed for a much smaller amount of time (compared to a large company's army of full-time R&D professionals) and at a precisely targeted cost. Dino's team of PhDs "scouts" research from 400 universities and 60,000 small businesses and private institutions to find what might be valuable to his clients. PreScouter earns profit from pricing his crowdsourced services higher than their cost, while providing his clients a service at a lower cost than the obvious alternative of hiring one or two of their own "scouts."

Conclusion

My alma mater, the Harvard Business School, once asked me to sit on a panel to discuss entrepreneurship. All the other panelists were current entrepreneurs, and the questions eventually focused on the future of entrepreneurship: Given the tough economic times, was this really the right time to consider starting a business? Everyone else on the panel shook his head no. By now, I think you can guess my answer: of course this is the right time to start a business!

In every recession, depression, and downturn that this country has ever seen, entrepreneurship has been the engine of growth. After September 11, 2001, the airline industry laid off more than 100,000 workers; in 2008, 162,000 automotive manufacturing jobs were eliminated; during the year 2012, local, state, and federal governments shed 101,000 positions. Which Fortune 500 company do you think will hire all those pink-slip recipients? If anyone is waiting for the big companies with thousands of employees to fill a cloudy day with sun and turn around these tough times, she is in for a long and disappointing wait.

Entrepreneurs hold the keys to the next generation of Fortune 500 companies. Of course capital is constrained, and investors are more scarce and skeptical than ever. In many ways, that's good news. It means that only the best companies—those with the best ideas and the best managers—will get financial backing. I'm a firm believer that good managers make better decisions when times are tough, and tough times make better managers. Expenditures are scrutinized more carefully, cash flow gets a closer look, innovative partnerships are born, and managers learn once again that execution is everything.

Is now the right time for you? Only you can answer that question. Volkswagen once had a catchy marketing campaign that told prospective buyers, "On the road of life, there are drivers and passengers. Drivers wanted." For future entrepreneurs, the worst thing you can do to yourself is to spend your life kicking the tires and wondering whether you should have taken a risk, cut the safety net, and taken the plunge. Entrepreneurship is about passion, vision, focus, and sweat, and no swing of the stock market will ever change that. Around every corner is the next idea, the next dream, and the next business opportunity. I wish you well on your adventure.

Notes

Chapter 1

1. John Greenwald, "Master of the Mainframe: Thomas Watson Jr.," *Time*, December 7, 1998.
2. International Franchise Association/IHS Global Insight, "Franchise Business Economic Outlook for 2013," December 12, 2012, http://www.franchise.org/uploadedFiles/Franchise_Business_Outlook_12-17-2012.pdf; accessed August 26, 2013.
3. Dunkin' Donuts, "Company Snapshot," http://www.dunkindonuts.com/content/dunkindonuts/en/company.html; accessed August 26, 2013.
4. Ibid.
5. Kerry Pipes, "History of Franchising: This Business Model Is an Original—and a Winner," Franchising.com website, posted on March 25, 2007.
6. "Answers to the 21 Most Commonly Asked Questions About Franchising," International Franchise Association home page, October 22, 2001, http://www.franchise.org/resourcectr/faq/ faq.asp.
7. International Franchise Association/IHS Global Insight, "Franchise Business Economic Outlook, p. 1, http://www.franchise.org/uploadedFiles/Franchise_Business_Outlook_12-17-2012.pdf; accessed August 26, 2013.
8. International Franchise Association, "Frequently Asked Questions About Franchising, Question 14," http://www.franchise.org/faq.aspx; accessed August 26, 2013.
9. International Franchise Association/IHS Global Insight, "Franchise Business Economic Outlook, p. 1, http://www.franchise.org/uploadedFiles/Franchise_Business_Outlook_12-17-2012.pdf, p. 1; accessed August 26, 2013.
10. International Franchise Association, "Frequently Asked Questions," Question 14, http://www.franchise.org/faq.aspx; accessed August 26, 2013.
11. Kristen Dunlop Godsey, "Market like Mad: How One Man Built a McDonald's Franchise Empire," *Success*, February 1997.
12. Hoovers online, Starbucks Company history, http://subscriber.hoovers.com/H/company360/history.html?companyId=15745000000000; accessed August 26, 2013.
13. 1–800-Flowers.com Inc., 2006 Annual Report, 1–800-Flowers.com Inc. home page, www.1800flowers.com.
14. Hoovers online, 1-800-Flowers.com, Inc., http://subscriber.hoovers.com/H/company360/overview.html?companyId=43451000000000, accessed August 26, 2013.
15. Radio One, Inc., 2005 Annual Report, Radio One home page, www.radio-one.com.
16. Duncan Maxwell Andersen and Michael Warshaw, with Mari-Alyssa Mulvihill, "The #1 Entrepreneur in America: Blockbuster Video's Wayne Huizenga," *Success*, March 1995, p. 36.
17. Ibid.

18. "Wayne Huizenga," video, University of Southern California.
19. David Gelernter, "Software Strongman: Bill Gates," *Time*, December 7, 1998, p. 131.
20. "The World's Billionaires," *Forbes*, http://www.forbes.com/billionaires/list/, accessed August 26, 2013. Note: net worth calculated March 2013.
21. Microsoft Investor Relations, "Acquisition History," http://www.microsoft.com/investor/Stock/AcquisitonHistory/All/default.aspx, accessed August 26, 2013. Counted all of the companies on the list.
22. Microsoft News Center, "Microsoft to Acquire Yammer," June 25, 2012, http://www.microsoft.com/en-us/news/Press/2012/Jun12/06-25MSYammerPR.aspx, accessed August 26, 2013.
23. Microsoft Investor Relations, "Earnings Release FY 13 Q4," Balance Sheet, Total Cash, Cash Equivalents, and Short-Term Investments," http://www.microsoft.com/investor/EarningsAndFinancials/Earnings/PressReleaseAndWebcast/FY13/Q4/default.aspx, accessed August 26, 2013.
24. "Top Entrepreneurs of 1999," *BusinessWeek*, January 2000, http://www.businessweek.com/smallbiz/0001/ ep3663075.htm.
25. S&P Capital IQ, Kate Spade LLC & Globalluxe Kate Spade HK Limited https://www.capitaliq.com/CIQDotNet/company.aspx?companyId=1006763 & https://www.capitaliq.com/CIQDotNet/company.aspx?companyId=207243126, accessed January 11, 2014.
26. Terri Roberson, "The Partners Behind the Day Spa Explosion," *Today's Chicago Woman*, December 1998.

Chapter 2

1. Jamie Pratt, *Financial Accounting*, 2nd ed. (Cincinnati, OH: South-Western Publishing Co., 1994), pp. 396–397.
2. Kathleen Morris, "No Laughing Gas Matter—A Dental-Tech Startup May Have Hyped Its Numbers," *BusinessWeek*, June 9, 1998, p. 44.
3. Stanford Law School, Securities Class Action Clearinghouse, http://securities.stanford.edu/1012/PLSIA98/.
4. Martha Brannigan, "Sunbeam Concedes 1997 Statements May Be Off," *Wall Street Journal*, July 1, 1998, p. A4.
5. *U.S. Business Journal*, February 2001.
6. IRS, "Accounting Periods and Methods," http://www.irs.gov/publications/p334/ch02.html#en_US_2012_publink100025090.
7. Laurie Cohen and Andrew Martin, "Theater Plan Not Living Up to Billing," *Chicago Tribune*, January 15, 1999.

Chapter 3

1. Jamie Pratt, *Financial Accounting*, 2nd ed. (Cincinnati, OH: South-Western Publishing Co., 1994), p. 709.
2. *Chicago Tribune*, July 25, 2000, p. 12.

3. Ibid.
4. Ibid.
5. Ibid.
6. Hans Greimel, "Japan's plants hum, but hurdles remain" *Automotive News,* October 10, 2011, http://www.autonews.com/article/20111010/OEM01/310109970/japans-plants-hum-but-hurdles-remain, accessed February 4, 2014.
7. Hoovers Online, http://subscriber.hoovers.com/H/company360/financialSummary.html?companyId=11190000000000.
8. Hoovers Online, http://subscriber.hoovers.com/H/company360/financialSummary.html?companyId=41781000000000.
9. Amazon.com, Inc. 10-K Report, 2012, p. 38, http://hoovers.api.edgar-online.com/EFX_dll/EdgarPro.dll?FetchFilingHTML1?SessionID=T_Fm6e9OXbh-WnF&ID=9041695#D445434D10K_HTM_TX445434_28.
10. S&P Capital IQ, "Alaska Air," https://www.capitaliq.com/CIQDotNet/Financial/Ratios.aspx?CompanyId=248501&statekey=bc1560207b544d87802d2688ade35cbc.
11. "What's Wrong with This Picture? Nothing!" *Inc.*, June 2007.
12. U.S. Inflation Calculator, http://www.usinflationcalculator.com/inflation/historical-inflation-rates/.
13. Team Marketing Report, "Fan Cost Experience," http://fancostexperience.com/pages/fcx/blog_entry.php?e=29.
14. Lauren Setar and Matthew MacFarland, "Top 10 Fastest-Growing Industries," IBISWorld, April 2012, http://www.ibisworld.com/Common/MediaCenter/Fastest%20Growing%20Industries.pdf.
15. "A Profit Gusher of Epic Proportions," *Fortune*, April 15, 2007.
16. Eric Nee, "Defending the Desktop," *Forbes*, December 28, 1998, pp. 53–54.
17. Richard Murphy, "Michael Dell," *Success*.
18. John Anderson, "The Company That Grew Too Fast," Inc.com from *Inc.* magazine, November 2005.
19. Howard Schultz, e-mail to senior Starbucks management, February 14, 2007.
20. CIT Commercial Services and *Home Furnishing News*, 2002 Customer Concentration Survey.
21. *Boston Business Journal*, June 18, 2004.
22. *Boston Herald*, June 12, 2007.
23. Motor Trend, http://wot.motortrend.com/toyota-regains-worldwide-sales-crown-in-2012-beats-gm-vw-321039. html, Accessed January 12, 2014.
24. Hoovers Online (Toyota, GM), http://subscriber.hoovers.com/H/company360/financialSummary.html?companyId=10640000000000.
25. "In Praise of Third Place," *New Yorker*, December 4, 2006.
26. Nintendo Co., Ltd., Hoovers Online, http://subscriber.hoovers.com/H/company360/incomeStatements.html?companyId=41877000000000, accessed February 4, 2014.
27. Hermann Simon, Frank F. Bilstein, and Frank Luby, *Manage for Profit, Not for Market Share: A Guide to Greater Profits in Highly Contested Markets* (Harvard Business Press, 1996).

28. Hoovers Online, http://subscriber.hoovers.com/H/industry360/financials.html?industryId=1262; accessed August 25, 2013.
29. Bruce Horovitz, "Big Markups Drive Starbucks' Growth," *USA Today*, April 30, 1998, p. 1B.
30. Scott Woolley, "Greedy Bosses," *Forbes*, August 24, 1998, p. 53.
31. Mid-Atlantic Venture Partners, 1997.
32. Shawn Rea, "Buy the Book," *Black Enterprise*, February 1999, p. 176.
33. Rosemary Batt, Virginia Doellgast, Hyunji Kwon, "U.S. Call Center Industry Report 2004, National Benchmarking Report, Strategy, HR Practices & Performance," School of Industrial and Labor Relations, Cornell University, http://digitalcommons.ilr.cornell.edu/cgi/viewcontent.cgi?article=1005&context=cahrswp, p. iv, column 2.
34. Bruce Phillips, "Small Business Problems and Priorities," National Federation of Independent Business, June 2004.
35. Hoovers Online, Company Reports [MSFT: http://subscriber.hoovers.com/H/company360/incomeStatements.html?companyId=14120000000000&period=annual¤cyType=USD] [GOOG: http://subscriber.hoovers.com/H/company360/incomeStatements.html?companyId=59101000000000].
36. Alex Gove, "Margin of Error," *Red Herring*, February 1999, p. 140.
37. S&P Capital IQ, S&P 500 Index (^SPX) Key Stats & Ratios, https://www.capitaliq.com/CIQDotNet/Securities/indexRatio.aspx?CompanyId=2668699.
38. Thor Valdmanis, "Cooking the Books, a Common Trick of the Trade," *USA Today*, August 11, 1998.
39. "The Fall of Enron," NPR.org, February 12, 2002, http://www.npr.org/templates/story/story.php?storyId=1137940.
40. "From Collapse to Convictions: A Timeline," CBS News Online, October 23, 2006.
41. "The Fear of All Sums," *CFO*, August 1, 2002.

Chapter 4

1. Jill Andresky Fraser, "Riding the Economic Rollercoaster," *Inc.*, December 1998, p. 126.
2. Michael Fernandez, "My Big Mistake," *Inc.*, December 1998, p. 123.
3. "Running on Empty," *Inc.*, August 1, 1994.
4. Ibid.
5. Fraser, "Riding the Economic Rollercoaster."
6. Gini Graham Scott and John J. Harrison, *Collection Techniques for a Small Business* (Grants Pass, OR: Oasis Press, 1994).
7. U.K. Survey of Small Businesses, 2005.
8. Dr. Craig R. Everett, Pepperdine Private Capital Markets Project: Capital Markets Report: 2014 http://bschool.pepperdine.edu/appliedresearch/research/pcmsurvey/content/ppcmp_2014_report.pdf, p. 73, Accessed January 21, 2014.

9. Holly Wade, "Small Business Problems and Priorities," National Federation of Independent Business, August 2012, http://www.nfib.com/Portals/0/PDF/AllUsers/research/studies/small-business-problems-priorities-2012-nfib.pdf.
10. Jill Andresky Fraser, "Getting Paid," *Inc.*, June 1990.
11. Ibid.
12. *Wall Street Journal*, October 25, 1999, p. 9.
13. *Chicago Sun-Times*, May 25, 1999, p. 48.
14. Ibid.
15. Jill Andresky Fraser, "Collection: Days Saved, Thousands Earned," *Inc.*, November 1995.
16. Jay Goltz, *The Street Smart Entrepreneur* (Addicus Books, February 1, 1998), ISBN-13: 978-1886039339
17. Amazon.com 2012 10K, p. 38. http://hoovers.api.edgar-online.com/EFX_dll/EdgarPro.dll?FetchFilingHTML1?SessionID=T_Fm6e9OXbh-WnF&ID=9041695#D445434D10K_HTM_TX445434_13.
18. Dell company financials as compiled by Hoovers, July 2007.
19. Skip Grandt, interview with author.

Chapter 5

1. Julie Schmidt, "Apple: To Be or Not to Be Operating System Is the Question," *USA Today*, September 24, 1996.
2. Thomas G. Stemberg, *Staples for Success: From Business Plan to Billion-Dollar Business in Just a Decade* (Santa Monica, CA: Knowledge Exchange, 1996).
3. Ibid.
4. Ibid.
5. *Chicago Tribune*, April 7, 2007.
6. Stemberg, "Staples for Success."
7. Ibid.
8. Ibid.
9. Udayan Gupta, "Companies Enjoy Privacy as Need for Public Deals Ebbs," *Wall Street Journal*, December 17, 1995.
10. PitchBook Decade Reports 2001–2010, Vol. 2, Investments, p. 5.
11. "Sperling Says Debt Crunch Could Tighten PE Purse Strings," Deal Journal, *Wall Street Journal*, July 25, 2007.
12. Bill Haynes, "Industry Risk—Merger Professionals Bullish About Continued Availability of Debt," Global Association of Risk Professionals, July 19, 2007.
13. John K. Paglia, "2013 Economic Forecast: Insights from Small and Mid-Sized Business Owners," Dun & Bradstreet Credibility Corp. and Pepperdine University, http://bschool.pepperdine.edu/appliedresearch/research/pcmsurvey/content/Pepperdine-SMB-Economic-Forecast-2013-Dataset.pdf,
14. *Forbes*, July 27, 1998, p. 112.

15. Stephanie Gruner, "The Trouble with Angels," *Inc.*, February 1, 1998, p. 47.
16. Bill Sutter, classroom presentation at Kellogg School of Management, March 10, 1999.
17. *Crain's Chicago Business*, May 5, 2008, p. 2.
18. Jeanne Dugan, "Will Triarc Make Snapple Crackle?" *BusinessWeek*, April 28, 1997.
19. *Chicago Sun-Times*, July 7, 2008.
20. "Tracking Bond Benchmarks," *Wall Street Journal*, wsj.com, October 28, 2013.
21. Dow Jones Industrial Average Fact Sheet, http://www.djindexes.com/mdsidx/downloads/fact_info/Dow_Jones_Industrial_Average_Fact_Sheet.pdf.
22. Current S&P 500 PE Ratio: 19.37 + 0.03 (0.13%), October 28, Mean: 15.50, http://www.multpl.com/.
23. Census Databases, NAICS 522298, http://censtats.census.gov/cgi-bin/cbpnaic/cbpdetl.pl.
24. *Newsletter of Corporate Renewal*, February 14, 2000.
25. Tim Jones, "Rich Harvests in Television's Killing Fields," *Chicago Tribune*, October 22, 1995.
26. Brian Edwards and Mary Ann Sabo, "A Grim Tale," *Chicago Tribune*, October 29, 1999, Section 6N.
27. Ibid.
28. *Barron's*, September 15, 1997.
29. *Crain's Chicago Business*, September 27, 1999, p. 57.
30. *Forbes*, July 27, 1998, p. 112.
31. "Jubak's Journal: Putting a Price on the Future," *Forbes*.
32. Ibid.
33. Robert McGough, "No Earnings? No Problem! Price-Sales Ratio Use Rises," *Wall Street Journal*, November 26, 1999, pp. C1–2.
34. S&P MidCap 400 Index - Total Return Historical - 1991 - USD Chart Builder" Market cap/Total Revenues, 1/1/1995-12/31/2013, accessed Feb 16, 2014.
35. Matt Krantz, "Web Site Revenue May Not Be Cash," *USA Today*, September 9, 1999, p. 1B.
36. Matt Krantz, "Vague Rules Let Net Firms Inflate Revenue," *USA Today*, November 22, 1999, p. 1B.

Chapter 6

1. *Chicago Sun-Times*, April 4, 1996, p. 44.
2. *Business Philadelphia* magazine, November 1996.
3. Global Entrepreneurship Monitor, "2006 Financing Report," p. 14.
4. Statistic Brain, "Startup Business Failure Rate by Industry, http://www.statisticbrain.com/startup-failure-by-industry/; accessed September 2, 2013.
5. Starbucks Company history, http://subscriber.hoovers.com/H/company360/history.html?companyId=15745000000000; accessed August 26, 2013.
6. *New Yorker*, August 11, 1997.
7. Pepperdine University, Center for Applied Research, Private Capital Markets Project, 2014, p. 69.

8. Global Entrepreneurship Monitor, "2012 United States Report," p. 23, http://www.babson.edu/Academics/centers/blank-center/global-research/gem/Documents/GEM%20US%202012%20Report%20FINAL.pdf.
9. NVCA Yearbook 2013, p. 27.
10. Pepperdine University, Center for Applied Research, Private Capital Markets Project, 2014, p. 70.

Chapter 7

1. *Time*, January 13, 1997, p. 49.
2. Microsoft Cash and ST Investments, http://ycharts.com/companies/MSFT/cash_on_hand; accessed September 2, 2013.
3. SBA Office of Advocacy, "Small Business Lending in the United States, 2012," July 2013, p. 5.
4. "Pepperdine Private Capital Markets Survey 2012," p. 24
5. Global Entrepreneurship Monitor, "2012 United States Report," p. 23.
6. Hoovers, http://subscriber.hoovers.com/H/company360/overview.html?companyId=40140000000000; accessed September 2, 2013.
7. Andrew J. Sherman, "Raising Money in Tough Times: An Entrepreneur's Guide to Bootstrapping," www.eventuring.org, January 1, 2003.
8. James Geshwiler, Marianne Hudson, and John May, "State of Angel Groups: A Report on ACA and ACEF," April 27, 2006.
9. Jeffrey Sohl, "The Angel Investor Market in 2012: A Moderating Recovery Continues," Center for Venture Research, April 25, 2013.
10. Ewing Marion Kauffman Foundation, "Business Angel Investing Groups Growing in North America," October 2002.
11. Angel Resource Institute, "Angel Capital Association," http://www.angelresourceinstitute.org/about-us/partnership.aspx?p=kF_HUKQ2GEeOfm5U3KovHg; accessed September 2, 2013.
12. *Crain's Chicago Business*, November 6, 1996.
13. Steven Lawrence, "Doing Good with Foundation Assets," Foundation Center, http://foundationcenter.org/gainknowledge/research/pdf/pri_2010.pdf, p. xiii.
14. Ibid., p. xv.
15. *Inc.*, February 1998, p. 80.
16. Milken Institute, Los Angeles Economy Project, Section 6, October 2005.
17. Ibid.
18. Small Business Administration, "SBA Lending Statistics for Major Programs," http://www.sba.gov/content/sba-7a-and-504-gross-loan-approval-volume-09-30-13; accessed October 22, 2013.
19. Ibid.

20. National Association of Government Guaranteed Lenders, "SBA Statistics," http://www.naggl.org/am/Template.cfm?Section=SBA_Statistics, http://www.naggl.org/AM/Template.cfm?Section=Right_Column&Template=/CM/ContentDisplay.cfm&ContentID=16152.
21. Small Business Administration, "General Small Business Loans: 7(a)."
22. Small Business Administration, "The Budget for Fiscal Year 2013," http://www.whitehouse.gov/sites/default/files/omb/budget/fy2013/assets/sba.pdf, Accessed January 22, 2014.
23. Small Business Administration, "SBA Loan Programs: Microloan Program," http://www.sba.gov/content/microloan-program. Accessed January 22, 2014.
24. Small Business Administration, "Business Loan Approval," September 30, 2013, http://www.sba.gov/sites/default/files/SBA%207a%20and%20504%20Gross%20Loan%20Approval%20Volume%20as%2009-30-13.pdf.
25. *Crain's Chicago Business*, August 13, 2001.
26. Small Business Administration, "Banking and SME Financing in the United States," June 2006.
27. Federal Reserve Bank of New York, "The Credit Process: A Guide for Small Business Owners."
28. Entrepreneur.com, "Bank-Term Loans."
29. "The State of Small-Business Funding," *Entrepreneur*, July 2006.
30. "How Small Firms Can Weather a Credit Crunch," *Wall Street Journal*, August 7, 2007, p. B9.
31. Department of the Treasury, "CDFI Fund FY2012 Report," http://www.cdfifund.gov/impact_we_make/research/FY%202012%20CDFI%20Fund%20Year%20in%20Review.pdp, pp. 13–14.
32. *Nation's Business*, July 1996, p. 45R.
33. *Inc.*, June 1987, p. 150.
34. *Crain's Chicago Business*, December 1996, p. 22.
35. Maureen Farrell, "Banking 2.0: New Capital Connections for Entrepreneurs," Forbes.com, February 2008.
36. Knowledge @ Wharton, "Peer-to-Peer Lending: Ready to Grow, Despite a Few Red Flags," January 8, 2014, accessed January 22, 2014 http://knowledge.wharton.upenn.edu/article/peer-peer-lending-ready-grow-despite-red-flags/.
37. Ibid.
38. BCR Publishing, "The World Factoring Yearbook."
39. "Fast Money," *Wall Street Journal*, August 20, 2007, p. R7.
40. *Nation's Business*, September 1996, p. 21.
41. *Black Enterprise*, July 1999, p. 40.
42. *Forbes*, December 28, 1998, p. 91.
43. *Black Enterprise*, March 1998, p. 84.
44. *Chicago Sun-Times*, July 17, 2001, p. 47.
45. *Crain's Chicago Business*, March 13, 2000.

46. Federal Reserve Board, "Consumer Credit—G.19, End of 2Q 2013," report dated August 2013.
47. Jesse Bricker, Arthur B. Kennickell, Kevin B. Moore, and John Sabelhaus, "Changes in U.S. Family Finances from 2007 to 2010: Evidence from the Survey of Consumer Finances," *Federal Reserve Bulletin*, 98, no. 2 (June 2012), p. 57, http://www.federalreserve.gov/pubs/bulletin/2012/pdf/scf12.pdf.
48. BCSalliance.com, "Credit Card Industry Profits," http://www.bcsalliance.com/creditcard_profits.html.
49. Eva Norlyk Smith, "Mailed Credit Card Offers Jump 36 Percent," Credit Card Guide, http://www.creditcardguide.com/creditcards/credit-cards-general/mailed-credit-card-offers-jump-36-percent-297/.
50. Donna Borak, "Fed Files Appeal on Court's Interchange Ruling," *American Banker*, October 21, 2013, http://www.americanbanker.com/issues/178_203/fed-files-appeal-on-courts-interchange-ruling-1063031-1.html.

Chapter 8

1. The Top 25 Managers—The Top Entrepreneurs, *BusinessWeek*, January 7, 2001, p. 55, http://www.businessweek.com/stories/2001-01-07/dan-lauer-haystack-toys.
2. Pepperdine University, Center for Applied Research, Private Capital Markets Project, 2013, p. 52.
3. Ibid., p. 46.
4. Will Schmidt, "9 of the Hottest AngelList and Silicon Valley Angel Investors," *Tech Cocktail San Francisco*, August 22, 2013, http://tech.co/top-angel-investors-2013-08.
5. *Forbes ASAP*, June 1, 1998, p. 24.
6. Edward N. Wolff, "The Asset Price Meltdown and the Wealth of the Middle Class," August 26, 2012, p. 59, http://kenhoma.files.wordpress.com/2012/12/net-worth-study.pdf.
7. *Forbes*, January 10, 2000, p. F.
8. PricewaterhouseCoopers MoneyTree Report, Q2 2013, https://www.pwcmoneytree.com/MTPublic/ns/moneytree/filesource/moneytree/filesource/exhibits/NatlAggSpreadsheet_Q2_2013_Final.xlsx, cell AJ18.
9. "The Angel Investor Market in 2012: A Moderating Recovery Continues," Center for Venture Research, University of New Hampshire, http://paulcollege.unh.edu/sites/paulcollege.unh.edu/files/2012_analysis_report.pdf.
10. *Inc.*, July 1997, p. 48.
11. *Crain's Chicago Business*, March 9, 1999, p. SB4.
12. *Buyouts*, February 8, 1999, p. 23.
13. *Private Equity Analyst*, August 1999, p. 36.
14. Ibid., p. 34.
15. Ibid.

16. "Corporate Venture Capital Activity on Three-Year Upward Trend," *Venture Capital Report*, February 21, 2012, http://venturecapitalreport.blogspot.it/2012_02_01_archive.html.
17. *Fast Company*, February 1998, p. 86.
18. NVCA Yearbook 2013, p. 24.
19. European Private Equity and Venture Capital Association, "Private Equity and Venture Capital Investing in Europe," http://www.evca.eu/knoledgecenter/statisticsdetail.aspx?id=414.
20. *Asian Venture Capital Journal*, http://www.avcj.com/static/research.
21. Emerging Markets Private Equity Association Special Report, p. 1, http://www.empea.org/_files/listing_pages/13676_EY_Latin_Study_v2_USLETTER_Singles_5pm.pdf.pdf.
22. Small Business Administration, "SBIC Program Annual Report," http://www.sba.gov/inv/annualreport.
23. Small Business Administration, "Early Stage 2013 FAQs," http://www.sba.gov/content/early-stage-2013-faqs.
24. Small Business Administration, www.sba.gov.
25. National Association of Small Business Investment Companies, February 2006.
26. *Directorship* magazine, Fall 1998, p. 1.
27. *The Economist*, May 3, 2001.
28. *Fast Company*, January 2000, p. 50.
29. Edward Chancellor, *Devil Take the Hindmost: A History of Financial Speculation* (New York: Farrar, Straus, Giroux, 1999).
30. *Boston Globe*, February 21, 2001.
31. *USA Today*, June 22, 2000.
32. *USA Today*, December 23, 1999.
33. *Time*, September 27, 1999.
34. NYSE Euronext, "U.S. Listing Standards," http://usequities.nyx.com/regulation/listed-companies-compliance/listings-standards/us.
35. NYSE Euronext, "NYSE Composite Index," http://www.nyse.com/about/listed/nya_characteristics.shtml; accessed September 12, 2013.
36. Nasdaq OMX, "Equities Market Share Statistics," December 2013, http://www.nasdaqtrader.com/trader.aspx?id=marketshare; accessed September 12, 2013.
37. *Chicago Sun-Times*, September 3, 2000, p. 47A.
38. Dow Jones Industrial Average Fact Sheet, http://www.djindexes.com/mdsidx/downloads/fact_info/Dow_Jones_Industrial_Average_Fact_Sheet.pdf; accessed September 12, 2013.
39. Prime Interest Rate History, http://www.fedprimerate.com/wall_street_journal_prime_rate_history.htm, accessed February 4, 2014.
40. *Wall Street Journal*, April 6, 2001, p. C1.
41. James Arkebauer and Ron Schultz, *The Entrepreneur's Guide to Going Public* (Dover, NH: Upstart, 1994), p. 297.
42. "Bill Ford Nearly Doubles Stake in Ford Supervoting Shares," *Automotive News*, June 26, 2013, http://www.autonews.com/article/20130626/OEM02/130629906/bill-ford

-nearly-doubles-stake-in-fords-supervoting-shares#ixzz2ejXUrV49; accessed September 12, 2013.

43. Arkebauer, *Entrepreneur's Guide*, p. 202.
44. *Inc.*, February 1998, p. 57.
45. *Success*, January 1999, p. 20.
46. *Inc.*, December 1996, p. 70.
47. *Essence*, May 1998, p. 64.
48. USA Today, April 29, 1997, p. 4B.

Chapter 9

1. "Census Bureau Reports Minority Business Ownership Increasing at More than Twice the National Rate," U.S. Census Bureau, July 13, 2010, based on 2010 census data, http://www.census.gov/newsroom/releases/archives/economic_census/cb10-107.html; accessed September 10, 2013.
2. The next Survey of Business Owners (SBO) by the U.S. Census Bureau is expected to be published in 2015 based on 2012 reported data, collected in 2013–2014.
3. "National Women's Business Council Releases Provocative Piece on Women-Led Businesses," National Women's Business Council, August 12, 2013, http://www.nwbc.gov/research/national-womens-business-council-releases-provocative-piece-women-led-businesses; accessed September 10, 2013.
4. "State of Women-Owned Businesses Report: A Summary of Important Trends, 1997–2012," commissioned by American Express OPEN, p. 25, openforum.com/womensbusinessreport, accessed September 13, 2013.
5. Ibid., pp. 25–26
6. "African American Women-Owned Businesses," National Women's Business Council, http://www.nwbc.gov/facts/african-american-women-owned-businesses.
7. U.S. Census Bureau, 2012 American Community Survey, ACS Demographic and Housing Estimates, (section of rows titled, "Hispanic or Latino and Race") http://factfinder2.census.gov/faces/tableservices/jsf/pages/productview.xhtml?pid=ACS_12_1YR_DP05&prodType=table, accessed February 6, 2014. Rows correspond to: Non-Hispanic White, Black or African-American, Hispanic-all, Asian-Native Hawaiian and Other Pacific Islander, American Indian and Alaskan Native and Other.
8. U.S. Census Bureau, 2007 Survey of Business Owners (most recent), Statistics for All U.S. Firms by Industry, Gender, Ethnicity, and Race for the U.S., States, Metro Areas, Counties, and Places: 2007, Report number SB0700CSA01, http://factfinder2.census.gov/faces/tableservices/jsf/pages/productview.xhtml?pid=SBO_2007_00CSA01&prodType=table
9. Ibid.
10. Alicia Robb, "Access to Capital among Young Firms, Minority-owned Firms, Women-owned Firms, and High-tech Firms," SBA Office of Advocacy, contract no. SBAHQ-11-M-0203, April 2013, http://www.sba.gov/sites/default/files/files/rs403tot(2).pdf, p. 13, Table 3: 2010, accessed February 11, 2014.

11. U.S. Department of the Treasury, Small Business Lending Fund, Report with Respect to Women-, Veteran-, and Minority-Owned Businesses, November 2011, http://www.treasury.gov/resource-center/sb-programs/DocumentsSBLFTransactions/SBLF%20 4112%20-%20Women%20Veteran%20Minority%20Impact%20Report.pdf, pp. 44–57.
12. Business Consortium Fund, Inc., http://www.bcfcapital.com/, accessed February 11, 2014.
13. Ibid., http://www.bcfcapital.com/lenders_list.htm, accessed February 11, 2014.
14. "Year to Date SBA Business Loan Approval Activity, Fiscal Years 2010, 2011, and 2012," period ending September 30, 2012, http://www.sba.gov/sites/default/files/SBA%20 7a%20and%20504%20Gross%20Loan%20Approval%20Volume%20as%20of%209-30 -2012.pdf.
15. See Intuit Quickbooks Financing at https://quickbooksfinancing.intuit.com/ Marketing, accessed February 11, 2014.
16. See Biz2Credit at http://www.biz2credit.com/business-loans, accessed February 11, 2014.
17. Actual details of the lending results are private to Intuit and Hinkle. Given information is based on an interview with Hinkle in October, 2013.
18. "Diverse and Minority Private Equity Firms Outperform General Industry," National Association of Investment Companies, October 1, 2012, http://www.naicpe.com/pdfs/ RecognizingTheResults-PressRelease.pdf.
19. Clarence V. Reynolds, "Communication Is Everything," *Journal of EDM Finance*, Fall 2011, p. 8, http://mydigimag.rrd.com/publication/?i=88591.
20. Biz2Credit, "Biz2Credit Analysis of Women-Owned Businesses Identifies Challenges for Female Entrepreneurs Seeking Small Business Loans," http://www.biz2credit.com/ research-reports/analysis-of-women-owned-businesses.html, accessed February 11, 2014.
21. Alicia Robb, "Access to Capital among Young Firms, Minority-owned Firms, Women-owned Firms, and High-tech Firms," SBA Office of Advocacy, contract no. SBAHQ-11-M-0203, April 2013, http://www.sba.gov/sites/default/files/files/rs403tot(2).pdf, p. 13, Table 3: 2010, accessed February 11, 2014 (same table as in Note 11, above).
22. Ibid.
23. Ibid., Table 4, calculated as sum of "Outsider Debt" years 2007–2010, p. 17.
24. Ibid., Table 4, calculated as average annual difference between females and males of "Owner Debt" in years 2007–2010, p. 17.
25. Ibid., Table 4, calculated as sum of differences between females and males in amount of "Insider Debt" in years 2007–2010, p. 17.
26. Wells Fargo, press release, May 2, 2006.
27. National Foundation for Women Business Owners, October 17, 1996.
28. *Atlanta Journal-Constitution*, July 4, 2007.
29. "Year to Date SBA Business Loan Approval Activity, Fiscal Years 2011, 2012, and 2013," period ending September 16, 2013, http://www.sba.gov/sites/default/files/SBA_7a_ and_504_Gross_Loan_Approval_Amount_as_of_8-16-2013.pdf.
30. *USA Today.com*, August 14, 2001, http://www.usatoday.com.
31. Alicia Robb, "Access to Capital among Young Firms, Minority-owned Firms, Women-owned Firms, and High-tech Firms," SBA Office of Advocacy, contract no. SBAHQ-11-M-0203, April 2013, http://www.sba.gov/sites/default/files/files/rs403tot(2).pdf, p. 17, Table 4,

calculated as sum of differences between females and males in amount of "Outsider Equity" in years 2007–2010 , accessed February 11, 2014 (same table as in Note 11, above).

32. "Women Entrepreneurs in the Equity Capital Markets: The New Frontier," National Foundation for Women Business Owners, 2000.
33. *Chicago Sun-Times*, March 24, 1999, p. 69.
34. Danielle Beavers, "Maria Contreras Sweet: A Big Win for Diversity at the Small Business Administration," January 16, 2014, http://greenlining.org/blog/2014/maria-contreras-sweet-big-win-diversity-small-business-administration/, accessed February 11, 2014.

Chapter 11

1. Gary Emmon, "Up from the Ashes: The Life and Thought of Joseph Schumpeter," *Harvard Business School Alumni Bulletin*, June 2007, p. 25.
2. Robert C. Wolcott and Michael J. Lippitz, "The Four Models of Corporate Entrepreneurship," *MIT Sloan Management Review*, Fall 2007, p. 77.
3. Adam Lashinsky, "Chaos by Design," *Fortune*, October 2, 2006, p. 88.

Chapter 12

1. "Let's Fix David Henneberry's Boat (That Got Ruined in the Boston Bomber's Standoff)!," Crowdtilt, https://www.crowdtilt.com/campaigns/lets-fix-david-henneberrys-boat-that-got-ruined-in-the-boston-bombers-standoff; accessed September 8, 2013.
2. Spike Lee, "The Newest Hottest Spike Lee Joint," Kickstarter, http://www.kickstarter.com/projects/spikelee/the-newest-hottest-spike-lee-joint?ref=live; accessed September 8, 2013.
3. "CrowdFunding Conference and Seminars," http://www.crowdfundingconferenceseminar.com/media-libarary-crowdfunding_planning-Conference-cloud_based_business_planning-crowdfunding_softwarecrowdfunding-crowdfunding_exchange/List-of-crowd-founding-sitess; accessed September 8, 2013.
4. "Kickstarter Stats," Kickstarter, http://www.kickstarter.com/help/stats?ref=footer; accessed September 8, 2013.
5. Student campaign: "Revelo LIFEbike: The Compact Ebike That Can Make a BIG Difference," Indiegogo, http://www.indiegogo.com/projects/revelo-lifebike-the-compact-ebike-that-can-make-a-big-difference (compact electric bike from OCAD); academic researcher campaign: "Kite Patch," Indiegogo, http://www.indiegogo.com/projects/kite-patch (patch that makes people invisible to mosquitoes as a way of fighting malaria).
6. "Kickstarter Stats"; accessed September 9, 2013.
7. Brian Allen, "Interview: Hunter Hillenmeyer Talks OverDog, Kickstarter and Gaming with Pro Athletes," *Technology Tell*, http://www.technologytell.com/gaming/109272/interview-hunter-hillenmeyer-talks-overdog-kickstarter-and-gaming-with-pro-athletes/; accessed September 8, 2013.
8. http://thomas.loc.gov/cgi-bin/bdquery/z?d112:h.r.03606:, accessed September 8, 2013.

Index

Note: Page numbers followed by *f* denote figures; page numbers followed by *t* denote tables.

About the Author

Steven Rogers is senior lecturer at Harvard Business School, his alma mater, where he teaches finance, annually, to hundreds of worldwide high-growth entrepreneurs. He was previously the Gordon and Llura Gund Family Distinguished Professor at the Kellogg School of Management, where he was the most decorated professor in the school's history. He was selected Professor of the Year a record two times in the MBA program and 26 times in the Executive MBA program. He was selected by Ernst and Young as "Entrepreneur of the Year."